Richard McGregor was born and
educated in Sydney. He has extensive
reporting experience throughout Asia
and is now China correspondent for the
Australian, based in Hong Kong.
Previously he was Tokyo correspondent
for the *Australian* and the ABC.

JAPAN SWINGS

Politics, culture and sex
in the new Japan

Richard McGregor

ALLEN & UNWIN

First published in 1996 by
Allen & Unwin Pty Ltd
9 Atchison Street, St Leonards, NSW 2065 Australia
Phone: (61 2) 9901 4088
Fax: (61 2) 9906 2218
E-mail: 100252.103@compuserve.com

National Library of Australia
Cataloguing-in-Publication entry:

McGregor, Richard, 1958– .
 Japan swings : politics, culture and sex in the new Japan.

ISBN 1 86448 077 7.

1. Japan — Politics and government — 1945– . 2. Japan –
Civilization — 1945– . 3. Japan — Social conditions — 1945– .
I. Title.

952.049

Set in 11.5/15 pt Casablanca by DOCUPRO, Sydney
Printed by Southwood Press Pty Limited

10 9 8 7 6 5 4 3 2 1

CONTENTS

ACKNOWLEDGEMENTS

There are many friends and colleagues who helped me over the five and half years I lived in Japan—too many to list here. Gingerly, I'd like to single out a few who were helpful, particularly in the process of writing the book. First and greatest thanks are due to Hiroshi Osedo, the news assistant in the Tokyo office of News Ltd. He has informed, guided, cajoled, scolded, argued with, and held the hands of countless Australian correspondents in Japan for nigh on two decades, and all owe a great debt to him, as I do. Thanks also to Gwen Robinson, who encouraged me to write the book, quickly, and offered a number of valuable suggestions. Murray Sayle, Gavan McCormack, Mayumi Yamada, Jake Schlesinger, Greg Dodds, Peter Hartcher, Andrew Butcher and Peter Robinson also provided helpful advice, ideas, information, translations, friendship, chatter, criticism and corrections. Thanks to Sebastian Malleby and Jeff Carr at the *Economist* for clarity of conversation, and the use of a printer; to Paul Kelly, the editor-in-chief of the *Australian*, Ean Higgins and the foreign desk, and Shelley Gare for their support; to Sophie Cunningham at Allen & Unwin for dealing with me with a minimum of fuss; and also to my mother, for putting up with me in the book's final stages, and all sorts of other help way beyond th call of duty.

Hong Kong, February 1996

NOTE: Exchange rates are set at the rate on September 11 1995: $A1.00/US75.26; $A1.00/Yen75.28.

CHAPTER 1

THE MISTS OF CONCEALMENT

'Subhuman, inhuman, lesser human, superhuman—all that was lacking in the perception of the Japanese (wartime) enemy was a human like oneself.'

John Dower, historian

Before I first came to Japan to work as a journalist, an older and wiser colleague pulled me aside to proffer some friendly advice about how best to deal with the locals. 'Don't try and understand them, mate, just report them', he said, worried that I would go the way of a predecessor who he felt had done too much of the former, and not enough of the latter, until his sense of the world had disappeared into a sinkhole of cultural relativism. At first blush, this was a charmingly 'Orientalist' piece of advice. My colleague had never been in Japan for any length of time, and his vision of the country was blurred by a mixture of awe, admiration, angst and, because of the war, anger. For an Australian of his generation, the near north would always remain

1

the Far East, and aside from his favourite Asian restaurants he was happy to leave it that way. But my colleague had a point. Everything about the way the Japanese present themselves to the world condemns foreigners, especially professional observers like journalists, to try to 'understand' Japan and then to explain it. Merely reporting Japan is never enough, a fact which propels observers to constantly interpret all happenings, rather than simply let them speak for themselves. When Freud famously remarked that 'sometimes a cigar is just a cigar', he clearly did not have Japan in mind.

Some people look at Japan these days and see a pluralistic, thoroughly Westernising society, full of jostling individuals with differing opinions and democratic impulses. But mostly Japan still starts life as a monolithic entity, with individuals only hazily visible through their thickly-coated Japaneseness. So descriptions of Japan and the Japanese are peppered with phrases like 'in a country which', or 'for a people whom', or 'in a typical reaction to', as if there were no need to differentiate the individuals from the masses. The main reason that few avoid the cultural traps in Japan is that the Japanese are so adept at setting them. The Japanese so joyously stereotype themselves that it is hard not to do so in return.

The first trap is the myth of Japanese uniqueness. The pseudo-science of *nihonjinron*—the art of 'talking about the Japanese'—is a thriving cottage industry in Japan. Scores of scholars and personalities produce everything from highbrow academic books to popular television programmes perpetuating the myth of a Japan that is socially and racially homogeneous, and virtually unchanged from prehistoric times down to the present day.[1] The Japanese speak about themselves as if they, and the rules of their society, are culturally and racially programmed—like a single organism, with 120 million hearts beating as one. Many foreigners take this largely undifferentiated Japanese message on board, and unwittingly turn themselves into a sterile echo chamber for what are truly the most conservative views of the Japanese power elite. The foreigners' own prognostications complete a self-fulfilling and self-perpetuating circle. 'Control your gestures. Keep your hands at your sides. The Japanese find big arm movements threatening. Speak slowly. Keep your voice calm and even', says John Connor, the Japan-wise detective in Michael Crichton's techno-thriller about Japan's insidious business practices, *Rising Sun*. In this world, no Japanese truly deviates from the norm.

The result of the all-pervasive stereotyping is that the behaviour of individual Japanese is explained, even now, on the edge of the 21st century, not by any reference to any ordinary Western norms of rationality. Rather, it is constantly illuminated by some throwback to history and culture. In 1992, when Japan's then political kingmaker, a grizzly 78-year-old called Shin Kanemaru, was wanted for questioning in a corruption scandal, he locked himself inside his Tokyo residence, playing mah-jong with his supporters and refusing to come out. According to prominent commentators, both foreign and Japanese, Kanemaru's defiance wasn't simply an arrogant display of personal power aimed at getting the best deal out of the authorities, which he eventually did. No, they said, Kanemaru was following the practice of isolating oneself after personal disgrace in line with a tradition going back to samurai days. Likewise, when American trade negotiators rail against the *keiretsu*, the corporate families which bind large companies like Toyota to their small suppliers, or conglomerates like Mitsubishi to their numerous affiliated companies, they are told not to disturb the 'harmony' of Japan's 'all in the family' economic system. The same went for the few Japanese managers who openly tried to sack staff during the recession. They were denounced by the press for their coldly rationalist application of Western management principles. 'In such a society, it is difficult to say and do something which may disturb harmony. Such moves [as sacking workers], viewed as mere business decisions elsewhere, in Japan take on cultural and social overtones', says Richard Koo, of the Nomura Research Institute in Tokyo.[2]

Journalists and scholars alike are transformed into amateur anthropologists, stumbling over stereotypes in the search for the truth dwelling 'behind the mask', and inside 'the Japanese mind'. But observers settle on very different slots when pigeon-holing the Japanese. The necessity to interpret Japan breeds incessant reinterpretation, constant disagreement and, because of the force of the stereotyping, violent reactions. Japan's rise as a global economic power, and the relative decline of the United States and Europe, has increased the stakes in the competition to explain Japan, returning it as a subject to the level it occupied during wartime. The study of Japan is no longer an academic parlour game, but a politically charged minefield for governments and scholars around the world. Respectable people everywhere have vehemently different opinions about events in America, Europe or Australia, but in no other country is the nature of reality subject to such harsh manipulation, bitter competition and extreme interpretations as it is in Japan.

Take the economy, which has dominated perceptions of Japan in the half a century since the war. In the decade from the mid-1980s, Japan lurched between two polar opposites. It was frequently characterised as an invincible economic foe, and then a few years later as an economy on the verge of a calamitous collapse. Japanese businessmen, unscrupulously and insensitively, bought up the precious assets of other countries using money that had been lent to them by their banks at virtually no cost. A few years later they were scurrying home through a maze of bankrupting firesales and embarrassing scandals, and their banks were imploding under the weight of bad debts. But for every expert who dismissed Japan and its economy as a spent, irrelevant force, there was another who asserted, with all

4

the figures at hand to prove it, that it was an unsinkable aircraft carrier, so cleverly constructed that it was still humming smoothly and silently through the deepest recession of the postwar period.

Like all countries, Japan has its own particular ways of organising life and work. Companies extract lengthy, even slavish, service from their employees, but for the most part, even in the latest economic downturn, reward them in good times and hang onto them in bad. The police presence throughout society is pervasive, but the streets are safe. Strict rules govern behaviour on some occasions, and allow a free-for-all on others. Likewise, the economy has its strengths and weaknesses. In the 1990s, for example, property prices collapsed and the yen soared, dragging the economy into the lengthy slowdown. But right through this bleak period, Japan's world-beating manufacturing industries continued to hang onto their virtual global monopolies for a range of strategic products. In any other country, observers—local and foreign alike—learn to sort the good from the bad, or at least separate one from the other, and balance them. But in Japan that is rarely the case, because inevitably culture gets in the way.

All behaviour, of course, must be seen in its 'cultural' context. Culture, broadly defined, is passed down through families, communities and countries over generations, and influences all aspects of the way people live their lives and perform their jobs. But in Japan, power and politics often masquerade in the guise of culture—and separating the two is not easy. The debate about opening Japan's rice market in the early 1990s was a classic case. Foreigners offering to sell good rice which was about eight times cheaper than the homegrown product were scolded for wanting 'to change Japanese culture!'. This was a potent argument. Negotiating over the hard facts and figures of trade can get tricky if the ground shifts to warm and wet notions of culture. The real issue, however, was the protection of valuable and entrenched interests, which, in the case of rice, revolve around wealthy farmers' associations. The small-time, struggling Japanese farmer does exist, and rice does occupy a special place in the society. One of my Japanese language teachers, a sophisticated and internationally-minded young woman not given to parroting sloppy theories about Japanese 'uniqueness', remembers her father telling her as a child that 'every grain of rice contained seven gods'. The Emperor plays his part by donning long plastic boots every year to wade into his own rice paddy to plant a seedling. Rice also plays an intimate role in the Emperor's sacred and mostly secret enthronement ceremony.

But behind this facade of folk culture and Emperor worship stands a massively wealthy agricultural collective, Nokyo, which has long bankrolled well-behaved politicians. Nokyo's bank, Norinchukin, has assets of $694 billion, making it one of the largest banks in the world. The bloated bureaucracy which administers Japan's strict controls on the import and sale of rice, the Food Agency in the Agriculture Ministry, has 10 000 staff, thousands more than are employed in the whole of the Foreign Ministry, both in Japan and overseas. Every single one of Norinchukin's depositors, and the Food Agency's staff, has a valuable interest in perpetuating Japan's rice myths, and they have exercised enough raw power to ensure that others did as well.

Through this politico-cultural mist, the Japanese complain often of being misunderstood, but they only have themselves to blame. For all their laborious efforts to 'explain' themselves to the world, the Japanese have long revelled in their opaqueness, a trait noted by perceptive Japan-watchers from way back. 'No people could be less entitled to complain of being misunderstood, unknown or neglected than the Japanese, whose first and last urge is to lead a life unseen by others. The Japanese can be called a "walled island hidden by clouds",'[3] wrote Kurt

Singer, who lived in Japan in the 1930s, in his classic text, *Mirror, Sword and Jewel*. Singer dubbed this purposeful cultural fog 'the mists of concealment'. Hundreds of years earlier, the head of the Jesuit mission in Japan from 1570 to 1581, Francisco Cabal, reached the same conclusion. 'Among the Japanese, it is considered a matter of honour and wisdom not to disclose the inner self, to prevent anyone reading therein', he wrote. 'They are trained to this from childhood. They are educated to be inscrutable and false.' French writer Jean Raspail depicted Japanese life as a kind of elaborate comedy.

> Inflexible customs, concern with saving face, hypertrophied pride, insincerity exalted into virtue, an obsolete conception of honour, the desperate quest for perfection, an arrogant self-consciousness, a frantic fear of being misunderstood combined with a longing for no one to understand—all these factors, plus innumerable contradictions, make up this many-sided comedy.

More prosaic expressions of a similar sentiment can be found regularly now in daily newspapers, in which columnists remind their readers of how the Japanese (don't) express themselves. US president Bill Clinton's private advice in a 1993 meeting with Russian leader, Boris Yeltsin—that when the Japanese say 'yes', they often mean 'no'—prompted lots of tut-tutting about his cultural brutishness from Japanese diplomats, and their well-trained foreign Japan-boosters, after it was leaked to the media. But amongst ordinary Japanese the statement provoked little surprise. Columnist Genichiro Takahashi wrote that the average Japanese saw virtue in vagueness. 'What's so great about telling the truth, knowing well it would hurt others' feelings? Even children can do that. Even stupid people can do that if all they have to do is say what they really think. What is education for?' he wrote in his regular newspaper column. Takahashi concluded that it went without saying that no Japanese would verbalise even this sentiment in public![4]

7

In all societies, there is a distance between the formal, polite facade and real intentions. No politicians in any country tell the unadorned truth all the time—none would be re-elected if they did. But in Japan, the discrepancy between appearances and reality is presented as a ritualised part of everyday dialogue. Sensitivity to the different levels of meaning is considered crucial to cracking the code of any public or private statement. Likewise, authority has been traditionally separated from power in Japan. The Japanese language is full of terms which distinguish between the formal exercise of power and the genuine wielding of it. The terms include *tatemae* (pretence) and *honne* (reality), *soto* (external) and *uchi* (in the family), *omote* (formal) and *ura* (hidden), *kagemusha* (shadow warrior) and *kuromaku* (behind-the-scenes stringpuller), and *ningyo* (puppet) and *kuroku* (puppeteer).[5] Japan has had many powerful prime ministers, for example, but most, especially in recent years, have been mere figureheads or symbols of a lowest-common-denominator compromise. For that reason, prime ministers are often derided as 'portable shrines', who are carried from ceremony to ceremony to perform their duties while others exercise the real power behind the scenes. No Japanese leader has the authority of an American or French president, or a British or Australian prime minister. Political leaders like Margaret Thatcher and Ronald Reagan, whose singular leadership transformed many institutions in their countries, could not exist in Japan.[6]

There is another reason why perceptions about Japan swing violently between so many different poles—the visceral moodiness of the political culture itself. Writer Tetsuya Kataoka once attempted to list all the contradictions and paradoxes that swamp Japanese political behaviour and foreign policy. It is a very long list. Japan, he said, is a strange combination of strength and weakness, resilience and fragility, expansiveness and subservience, aggressiveness and self-effacement, keen competitiveness and placid stupor, cohesion and apparent headlessness, and cynicism and innocence. Japan is also constantly strung up—emotionally and politically—between East and West, and allows itself to swing constantly between them. 'Those who mind only one side of the coin and ignore the other, do so at peril to themselves', says Kataoka.

It is important to be aware of codes of communication and behaviour in Japan, but it is just as easy to stray too far down this path into a nether world where you completely suspend belief in the contents of any debate, and in official information. The most recent person to fall headlong into this trap is author Eamonn Fingleton. In an iconoclastic book released in 1995, just as the Japanese economy was sinking back into a double-dip recession, Fingleton asserted that all Japan's strong points—its high-tech monopolies, massive savings pool and cumulative trade surpluses—left it perfectly positioned to maintain the strategic high ground of the global economy.[7] Far from being down and out, as the doomsayers contended, the crafty Japanese were still on top. It is a compelling theme, and one which was wildly applauded by some of the new 'revisionist' school of Japan-watchers, who had been thrown onto the back foot by Japan's prolonged economic slowdown.

The revisionists emerged in force in the late 1980s with arguments that powerfully reshaped international debate about Japan. A disparate group, they earned their collective tag because they powerfully 'revised' the dominant analysis of Japan, and the West's response to it. The Clinton administration's periodic ditching of market forces in favour of demands for clear numerical targets in trade negotiations with Japan followed a prescription dictated by the revisionists. Unlike the opposing 'chrysanthemum club', whose members have long held that if Japan was not already a co-operative Western-style democracy then it would inevitably become one, the revisionists asserted that Japan was different, often in dangerous ways, from the rest of the world. They portrayed it as a mercantilist state which had tied its national security to a merciless pursuit of economic power, while lacking any true centre of authority which could be held to account for these policies. Foreigners, or indeed Japanese, who wanted to discover who was making the real decisions, had to bypass ostensible powerholders, like the Prime Minister and the cabinet, and plunge into a maze of competing and complementary networks in politics, business and the bureaucracy, operating through a raft of unofficial controls not regulated by law, nor subject to open discussion. Many revisionists were also motivated by more than the need to explain Japan. Mostly they were Americans who used the example of Japan's business successes to galvanise the lost cause of industrial policy in their home country.

For some (but by no means all) of the revisionists, the 'misreading' of Japan's downturn by others merely reinforced the historical tendency of foreigners, particularly Americans, to underestimate Japan. One reason they cited was cultural hubris, and a dogged, almost conspiratorial, refusal by Western free-marketeers to accept the existence of an economic system which diverged from the textbook tenets of neo-classical capitalism. The other reasons stemmed from the inability of outsiders to crack the codes of Japanese culture. Fingleton writes that foreigners are fooled by the polite Japanese habit of ritualised understatement. It is true that the Japanese are habitually modest. When someone hands over even the most extravagant of presents, for example, they customarily say, 'Please accept my trifling gift'. The same applies in international relations, where the Japanese are rarely boastful in public about their power in the way that the more outgoing, explicitly aggressive Westerners are. That's not only because, as the revisionists correctly point out, power is exercised in a piecemeal, often unarticulated fashion by corporations and bureaucrats, rather than by a central government. As a result, there is none of the grand imperial theatre so beloved by Western powers, no prime-time visions of new world orders or democratic nirvanas. Nor is this studied modesty only a reflection of what Takahashi was referring to as the Japanese habit of shying away from direct statements. Japan's modesty is also borne of necessity, because the world does not trust Tokyo to exercise its power in a responsible and transparent manner. More to the point, nor do the Japanese themselves, an issue we will return to later.

Often, when the Japanese do speak their minds—as the then Speaker of the lower house, Yoshio Sakurauchi did in 1993 when he said that America was becoming Japan's 'sub-contractor'—they quickly withdraw and apologise, usually by explaining that their comments were not meant for overseas consumption. By 1995, Japanese business leaders had changed their tune, and were warily eyeing off resurgent US computer and high-tech firms. 'If the current situation is left unattended, then Japanese companies will end up becoming sub-contractors of US firms', said the president of Toshiba Corp., Fumio Sato. Conspiracy theorists would place these two statements firmly into a cultural context. Sakurauchi was saying what he really meant—showing his *honne*, the Japanese say—whereas Sato's statement was a polite *tatemae* expression designed to flatter and placate America, and galvanise Japan. Authors like Fingleton see this as part of a deliberate pattern. They say that Japanese leaders go well beyond their habit of polite understatement and engage consistently in a policy of conscientious Oriental duplicity to trick outsiders. 'Japanese officials and business leaders have found it is good strategy to play down Japan's economic strengths. They are practised hands at acting out pantomimes of exaggerated anxiety that serve not only to spur Japanese workers to ever greater efforts but to foster complacency amongst foreign rivals', Fingleton writes. No wonder 'foolish' foreigners have always exaggerated Japan's weaknesses and belittled its strengths! The same school maintains that Japan's economic boom of the late 1980s was a managed attempt to project Japanese power into the world, and that the slowdown in the mid-1990s was a clever, strategic retreat by the same forces to disarm Tokyo's formidable international critics, before the Japanese economic machine headed back out into the world.

Like any government or corporation, the Japanese will put a spin on events for their own PR purposes. This is no big deal. But by elevating this effort to the Machiavellian heights that they do, these Japan-watchers overlook all the times that foreigners have overestimated the Japanese. Foreigners (and Japanese) aren't so much guilty of consistently underestimating Japan, so much as misjudging its strengths and weaknesses altogether. This happened most disastrously in the lead-up to the Pacific War, but also in assessing the economy in the late 1980s and early 1990s. Before the outbreak of hostilities in the war, American and British military officers—much more than Australians—smugly and ignorantly belittled the fighting skills of the Japanese. Historian John Dower records the assistant naval attaché at the US Embassy in Tokyo in the fateful year of 1941 telling members of the American Club: 'We can lick the Japs in 24 hours'. When told that Japanese troops had landed on the Malay Peninsula, the British civilian governor in Singapore coolly replied: 'Well, I suppose you'll shove the little men off!'. After the audacious attack on Pearl Harbor and Japan's stunning early successes in the war, the subhuman little man was transformed into a mythic Goliath, who in the end could only be tamed by the devastation wrought by two atomic bombs. 'Subhuman, inhuman, lesser human, superhuman—all that was lacking in the perception of the Japanese enemy was a human like oneself', says Dower.

The same pattern can be found in commentaries on the rise and fall of the Japanese economy from the mid-1980s onwards. When Sony bought Columbia Pictures in late 1989, *Newsweek* magazine said that an invincible Japan was doing more than buying 'America's soul'. 'America is slowly ceding its economic destiny to Japan', *Newsweek* reported. 'It has allowed the Japanese to take the lead in vital technologies, from microchips to high-definition television.' Only four years later, after the meltdown of Tokyo share prices, the same magazine announced on its front cover that 'The [Japanese] System Has Crashed'. 'A funny thing happened on the way to Japan's economic takeover of the world. What once seemed to be an unstoppable juggernaut has run off the rails.' And high-definition television? *Newsweek* reported that this had become a 'significant—but by no means solitary—example, not of irresistible dominance, but of Japan's lag in a wide range of high-tech industries'.

Japan's prolonged economic slowdown was badly timed for many revisionists. The Japan Inc. that they had built up into an economic version of the evil empire began disintegrating before their eyes. Many of the real life myths and cultural certitudes built up in modern Japan by the Japanese and foreigners collapsed along with it. The myth that land prices couldn't fall; that the bureaucrats could micro-manage the economy; that Japan was immune to the sorts of market forces that affected Western economies; and that Japanese people were cautious and congenitally frugal, to name just a few. But the most destabilising and bewildering development of all for the country and its postwar institutions has been a loss of purpose. Since the Pacific war, the Japanese state had marshalled its resources, and people, in a singular effort to build the economy, and catch up with the West. Ideology, politics and foreign and defence policy were all subjugated to the god of economic growth. Only a few years after declaring victory, however, the country found itself mired in a drawn-out, confidence-sapping slump, with no ideas about how to replace the hot pursuit of Western economies that has possessed it since the war.

Japan in the 1990s faced a hydra-headed set of challenges. The economic crisis either triggered, or coincided with, the collapse of Japan's postwar political system, and the end of the

Cold War, which had provided the rationale for the presence of American troops in Japan. At first blush, Japan appeared to have responded by launching itself on a path of irrevocable and radical reform. The end of the Liberal Democratic Party's one-party rule in 1993 paved the way for a new Western-style, democratic political system. Political leaders began a concerted effort to anchor Japan's interests in Asia as bulwark against an increasingly hostile West. People power was transforming the economy, as consumers flocked to a proliferation of new discount shops, undermining the cosy cartels and retail networks which had dominated Japanese business. The social contract which bound workers to their companies was unravelling, and young people were rejecting their parents' values in favour of more leisure, foreign travel and freer sex. In short, the Japanese people were making an historic and liberal transition from subjects to citizens, with all the chaos and destruction of institutions that such a change implied.

But to recall Kataoka's phrase, this was only one side of the coin. The social contract was stressed and strained, but not broken. Far from wanting to quit their jobs, in the recession most people hung on to them for dear life. The high-pressure school system, which regimented its rote-learning pupils and fed them into rigidly hierarchical workplaces, remained untouched. Also mostly unscathed was the nationalist ethos which underpinned education. The bureaucracy continued firmly to oppose efforts to strip it of powers that, in other democracies, are the responsibility of elected politicians. A new generation of political leaders emerged, but they were rarely more frank, and certainly barely more enlightened about Japan's wartime history. Japanese leaders do talk incessantly about Asia, but in their hearts, they remain profoundly Japanese. Their resolute, nationalistic insularity made it impossible for Japan to provide any political leadership to match their country's economic prowess. The bright new political system which was meant to rise out of the ashes of one-party rule floundered at its first hurdle.

Japan is a restless and hyperactive country, in a constant state of 'mental hunger', in the words of one writer. With no consensus about a new rationale to replace economic growth, the nation's institutions have either turned themselves upside down, or found themselves frozen in the grip of old habits. Foreigners would be wise to be wary of excessive hand-wringing by the Japanese. Few countries are as practised at reinventing themselves. Few countries, faced with such a reckoning as Japan faces, have been as adept, flexible and practical at turning it to their own advantage. But the wrenching process of sorting out what is worth keeping from the old system and what needs to be ditched is forcing the Japanese to confront many of their own myths, and dispose of them. Politician Ichiro Ozawa says he wants Japan to become a 'normal nation', one which stands side by side with the United States as an independently armed ally, with a transparent political system. Leading revisionist writer Karel van Wolferen has a different idea of what Japan would look like as a 'normal nation'. 'Among other things, every fourth or fifth car on the road would be non-Japanese', he says. 'Most medicines in Japan would be American or European imports because almost all Western pharmaceuticals are better and cheaper. Sony television sets and Nissan cars would be full of American, German and Korean parts. Owners of a number of companies in strategic Japanese industries would live in places like Hong Kong, San Jose and Amsterdam.'[8]

Such prescriptions, which would be fairly mundane in most advanced countries, remain radical for Japan, and on any analysis the country's politicians have so far proved themselves ill-equipped to manage such a transition. The politicians, as a whole, have failed to persuade the Japanese people that their country should play a more active role in international politics, and they are tied too closely to business lobbies to force them to radically change their economic behaviour. Although they like to flatter themselves about their prescience and vision, as they do anywhere in the world, the politicians are not in the vanguard re-making Japan. They are following, not leading; and reacting to, rather than creating, pressures for changes that they cannot control.

The most dynamic force for reform in Japan is the global political economy, in two of its manifestations—foreigners, who complain that Japan is dangerously out of step with the industrialised world, and individual Japanese, in their expanding role as foot soldiers of a new consumer class. Foreigners have long occupied an honourable position as a catalyst for change inside Japan. They will demand more of Japan in a range of areas—in political leadership, in opening its markets, in military spending—and Japan will be forced to respond. That these demands will often be contradictory—the United States and China, for example, have very different views on Japanese defence policy—will only make Tokyo's dilemma more exqui-site. The Japanese people, usually portrayed as having about as much individual will as sheep, will also make their presence felt, and not only at the ballot box. The Japanese people now are richer, more mobile and better travelled than at any time in the country's history, and have the power as consumers to transform large sections of their society. The politicians and bureaucrats who want to preserve the status quo can slow change, but they can no longer prevent it.

Japan will not shed its distinctiveness. Its protective cultural crust will crumble, but never disappear altogether. But the 1990s have been a profoundly sobering and humanising period for Japan from which it has yet to recover. That Japan will continue to evolve—although not converge—with the West and its own region is proved most conclusively by what had distinguished it most from other nations since the war—the performance of the economy. The world witnessed a whole new breed of Japanese during the late 1980s—real-estate spivs and sharemarket speculators, many of them with organised crime connections. The Japanese call them 'grey people'—literally, 'of doubtful colour'. They dazzled many of their equally 'grey' counterparts overseas in places like the Gold Coast in Australia, and in Hawaii, with their wads of cash. Unlike their dour, blue-suited compatriots, with their exacting long-term manufacturing plans and workplace requirements, here, at last, were Japanese businessmen who wanted to make nothing except deals! Mostly, the deals imploded one after the other. Never was the ruthless genius of Japanese capitalism more tellingly contrasted with its irrational, greedy groupism than during the late 1980s. The madness of crowds had nothing on Japan in full flight. 'Japan is a country of paradoxes and extremes, of great wisdom and great stupidity', wrote US Ambassador Joseph Grew in the 1930s, as he watched the rise of fascism, and he might have said the same about the last decade.[9]

The doomsayers who now contend that the Japanese economy is a spent, irrelevant force are wrong. But the alarmists who screamed only a few years before that it was going to take over the world have been proved even worse judges. Far from being mythically superhuman, the Japanese have been shown to be all too human after all. If one ever needed reminding of this, the story of the 'Bubble Woman', Nui Onoue, provided all the proof in the world.

CHAPTER 2

BEYOND THE BUBBLE

'Traditionally, the American currency was linked to gold and the Arabs had oil. They could exchange that for money. Whereas in Japan, we have nothing. Land prices are Japan's strength.'

Kichinosuke Sasaki, a (bankrupt) Tokyo property developer

'In the wake of the Great Hanshin [Kobe] Earthquake, it has become clear that Japan is a closed, confused country entering its terminal phase.'

Yasuhiko Shibata, Yomiuri Research Institute

For the Japanese who know her, Nui Onoue is the Dark Lady of Osaka, but some like to call her the Bubble Woman, after the era of feverish land and share speculation in which she thrived, and which she came to symbolise. She cut a sad figure on the few occasions I sat in at Osaka District Court for hearings of the massive fraud charges against her. Looking like a distressed widow at her husband's funeral, she sobbed quietly and lightly dabbed her eyes, occasionally stiffening to sternly shake her head in disagreement with the evidence against her. Onoue, who is in her late sixties, had much to be upset about. Before the bubble economy burst, she was—on paper at least—one of the 25 richest people in the world, which was no small achievement for the daughter of a local hoodlum in rural Japan who knew nothing about high finance. 'When she bought warrants, she thought "warrants" was the name of a company', one of the reporters covering her case told me.[1] Onoue based her share purchases on tips she proclaimed came from 'the gods', and in the process became the biggest individual shareholder in several of Japan's, and the world's, largest companies. By the time her fortune unravelled, she'd left a trail of fraud leading right to the top of a number of Japan's most august financial institutions.

The time of the 'Bubble Economy' was an extraordinary period in Japan, giving rise to 'the greatest speculative fever seen this century'.[2] The land and sharemarket boom was triggered by the decision of the world's big economies in the 1985 Plaza Accord to allow the yen to strengthen. The theory, which was as shaky in 1985 as it was a decade later, was that a stronger yen and a weaker dollar would naturally balance trade between Japan and the industrialised world. The Japanese authorities responded by cutting interest rates to record lows, allowing exporters squeezed by the strong yen to feed on a diet of ultra-cheap credit to see them through the hard times. The hard-pressed exporters took advantage of the low interest rates to marshal their defences against foreign competitors. But thousands of others, from large corporations to medium-size gangsters and small-time investors, got in on the act, borrowing money to plough into the spiralling land and sharemarkets. At its height on 31 December 1990, the Tokyo sharemarket was worth more than 40 per cent of the value of all world stockmarkets, and one and a half times the value of the Japanese economy. Rationally minded critics were warned to suspend judgement. Japan was not like other countries—share prices could not, and would not fall. Likewise, land and property values surged to the point where the aggregate value equalled five times the annual output of the economy, and four times the value of all real estate in the United States.[3] The land enclosing the Imperial Palace in central Tokyo alone was worth more than the state of California. Once again, sceptics were told that ordinary rules did not apply. Everyone from respectable analysts to notorious land sharks like Kichinosuke Sasaki, who invited foreign correspondents up into his marble-domed penthouse to deliver his pronouncements about real estate, spoke authoritatively about the special place land occupied in Japan's economic culture. 'Traditionally, the American currency was linked to gold and the Arabs had oil. They could exchange that for money', said Sasaki. 'Whereas in Japan, we have nothing. Land prices are Japan's strength.'

A new Central Bank chief, an austere, prudent career bureaucrat, Yasushi Mieno, whose interests were watching sumo and drinking sake, pricked the bubble as soon as he took office. He lifted interest rates immediately after his appointment at the tail of 1989, and kept raising them to let the hot air out of the bubble until there was very little left. Share prices more than halved, and land prices dropped by as much as 60 per cent. Japan's land and share boom turned out to be a giant conjuring trick. Like many people in Japan, Sasaki, the owner of 92 buildings in central Tokyo, had all his illusions stripped away by the collapse of the land market. He formed a debtors' association to fight against high interest rates, and complained darkly to his visitors about the machinations of 'Jewish and North Korean' investors against Japan. But the bureaucrats shunned Sasaki and his ilk because of their connections with right-wing and gangster groups. They wanted 'grey people' like him to fall, but they hadn't counted on the collateral damage the bursting of the bubble would have on wide sections of the economy for years to come.[4] As the mists of concealment gradually cleared, wreckage was discovered strewn through all sectors of society. The heads of the country's largest security firms resigned for promising to make under-the-table payments to clients who had lost money. Gangsters were caught with large wads of increasingly worthless shares. Senior bankers who tried to call in their loans were assassinated. Political scandals followed one after the other with numbing regularity, and even the bureaucracy, the institution which commands the most respect in Japan, was caught with its hand in the till. At the bottom of the pile, thousands of small investors lured into buying shares saw their hard-earned savings disappear down the drain, and resolved to shy away from the sharemarket for life.

And, in a parable of the madness of the times, Nui Onoue went bankrupt.

Onoue's first big break had come about 25 years before, when she became the mistress of the head of a large Osaka construction company. The businessman rewarded her with money to open two restaurants. One of them, Egawa, which opened in 1965, became the headquarters of her sharetrading empire. It was only by visiting the restaurant that you could appreciate how astounding Onoue's story was. To find Egawa, you had to wind your way through the back streets of Osaka's sleazy red-light district, past the peep shows and love hotels, and the 'Pink Salons' and 'Soaplands', various kinds of brothels cutely categorised by the services they offer. Unlit and empty when I visited it in late 1992, Egawa stood between a flashing neon sign, which offered 'Women and All You Can Drink', and a strip club. This seedy setting became a mecca for the members of Osaka's financial community. Brokers from Japan's big four securities companies based themselves in her restaurant all day to manage her trades, and then settled in for the night, when the real action took place.

It was then, in midnight-to-dawn seances held around two Buddhist statues, one representing the Goddess of Mercy and the other a metre-high toad, that Onoue would seek financial

21

advice from the gods. 'Although I am an amateur stock trader, I am successful because I listen to the divinities', she told all comers. Once she appeared on television fingering beads, waving a wad of share certificates and praying trance-like for guidance from above. 'All the people who were called in to listen to the gods said it was a load of rubbish, but if you didn't do it, she'd get upset and you'd lose business', said Naoji Shibata of the *Asahi Shimbun* in Osaka, who covered her trial. No sharetrader could afford that. The sheer size of Onoue's transactions turned the small branch offices of securities firms in the red-light district into some of the most profitable in the country. It was the equivalent of moving the parts of the Sydney Stock Exchange to a small betting shop in Kings Cross, or Wall Street in New York to 42nd Street's red-light district.

The original source of the money which launched Onoue's career in the market remains a mystery, and a long-standing rumour that it came from a criminal syndicate has never been proven. She first raised a large amount of cash from what was to become her main source of credit, the most respectable pillar of Japanese capitalism, the Industrial Bank of Japan (IBJ). She used this capital to invest in shares, which in turn provided her with more collateral to borrow money elsewhere, which she put back into the stockmarket as well. Everyone was happy—as long as share prices continued to rise. The bank was really being paid to lend Onoue her own money. And she got money to invest in a stockmarket which was then only moving in one direction, as well as gilt-edged collateral to boost her borrowings elsewhere. By the start of 1990, Onoue was worth Y1.13 trillion ($15 billion), and was the biggest single individual shareholder in IBJ itself, Dai-Ichi Kangyo Bank (then the world's biggest bank) and a host of other blue-chip companies, including Toshiba, Sumitomo Bank and Fuji Heavy Industries. One local businessman ruefully noted that her fortune was about equal to the cost of building a massive new airport near Osaka, a project which had been the dream of the business community for half a century.

But the start of 1990 was also when the bubble began to lose air. A desperate Onoue scrambled to cover her losses by heavying the president of a small credit union to issue her with fake deposit certificates. She used these to borrow more money to cover her loan repayments so she could stay afloat, but eventually the game was up. Onoue went bankrupt and was subsequently charged with fraud. How a woman with little education and no family connections or financial skills could become the glamour girl of some of Japan's most powerful and prestigious financiers is a question that has never been answered.

Onoue's case is one of the most colourful tales of financial debauchery from the period, but there were scores more companies and individuals who lost comparably vast sums.

It wasn't only at home that Japanese investors lost a fortune. Overseas—in real estate in England, the United States and Australia; in a headlong rush to buy Hollywood film studios; in massive purchases of foreign bonds, often just before the currency they were bought in collapsed, leaving the holder sitting on massive foreign exchange losses—Japanese investors lost billions of dollars into thin air. 'No other people are as bad at spending money as the Japanese. The Japanese may go down in world history as the worst spenders', Hiroshi Takeuchi, chairman of the Long-Term Credit Bank's Institute of Research and Consulting ruefully told the *Yomiuri Shimbun* later. Takeuchi had learnt this himself the hard way. The Long-Term Credit Bank bankrolled one of the most notorious high-flyers of the bubble era— Harunori Takahashi of EIE International. Takahashi had married the daughter of an infamous share manipulator and political bagman, Yasushi Iwasawa, and used this connection to turn EIE, a computer services company, into a global real-estate empire stretching from Australia through the Pacific and Hong Kong and on to London and the United States. His slick American-educated sidekick, Bungo Ishizaki, hailed Takahashi as a 'genius' at the time, but was less flattering when the entrepreneur and his bankers were finally snared in a major scandal in 1995, which tarnished not only EIE but also the august central Bank of Japan, and the Finance Ministry. Ishizaki described one EIE fund-raising technique in which its executives chose a famous European painting they wanted to buy, and then engaged 'the services of a retired French prostitute' for a meeting with the bankers. 'I'd ask her to draw up a valuation certificate, for say, $10 million, and then the bankers would come and look at this painting', said Ishizaki. 'The bankers didn't know a Cézanne from a Monet, but they'd nod and say, "Yes, this is worth $10 million and we'll lend you $8 million against it". Then my French friend would sell us the painting, probably under a different name, and take a commission on the deal.'[5]

Throughout this craziness, and even after the bubble burst, many commentators confidently predicted that the hyper-inflated Japanese economy was unstoppable, and on its way to overtaking the mighty United States. Deutsche Bank economist in Tokyo, Dr Kenneth Courtis, said Japan could be outproducing the US by a factor of three by the year 2050. In other words, the present generation of Japanese high-school students would be responsible for nearly half the world's production. Eamonn Fingleton saw the moment of truth coming even earlier, in the year 2000, when, he said, the Japanese economy would become the largest in the world. But Fingleton was wrong. Japan over-took the United States much earlier, but not in the triumphant way that he, or others, had predicted.[6]

FEET OF CLAY

For a fleeting moment on 10 April 1995—in as brief a time as it takes for the latest value of a country's currency to flash up on the screens of global currency traders—the Japanese economy did become the largest in the world. This might ordinarily have been a cause, if not for celebration, then a modest commemoration of some kind. Here was a series of islands with half the population of the world's sole economic and military superpower, the United States, a fraction of its resources and none of its nuclear firepower, matching the nation that had humiliatingly reduced it to smouldering ashes and vanquished poverty exactly 50 years before. Just five years beforehand, in 1990, at the end of the go-go bubble era, the size of the Japanese economy had measured only slightly over half that of the United States. But in the next half a decade, while Japan was blearily recovering from the excesses of the 1980s, international currency markets were prescribing steroids for the yen, buying and building it up in waves, and dumping what had been until then the world's reserve currency, the US dollar.

Once a critical mass of traders had decided the yen would rise, everyone in the markets had no choice but to go along for the ride, even if he or she doubted the wisdom of the decision. The central Bank of Japan was helpless. The muscular yen's 40 per cent advance in the early months of 1995, by one measurement, swelled the value of the country's economy in dollar terms to match that of America.[7] There were many reasons given for the yen's surge. One was America's semi-permanent trade and budget deficits. But the key was in Japan, where companies were bringing home money earned and invested overseas to shore up their finances during the lengthy downturn. They sold dollars onto the world market to do so, and ended up with a yen so hard that it threatened to choke them. The Japanese had indeed toiled selflessly and ruthlessly for 50 years in an effort to catch and then surpass the West, but they knew they had been propelled over the final hurdles by forces that had spun out of their control. The moment when Japan matched America economically produced none of the self-congratulation and overweening hubris that the Japanese had displayed when they went on their cocky and swaggering global shopping spree in the late 1980s, using their new wealth to buy everything from Hollywood Studios to whole islands in the Pacific. The strong yen set off panic and alarm about the fate of the economy. Anguished exporters screamed that the soaring currency was sending their businesses broke. Companies which relied on cosy domestic markets yelled for protection against everything from cheaper imports of textiles from China to noodles from the United States, and a wave of no-brand products from any place where the new breed of discount retailers could find them.

Japanese politicians stood by helplessly, paralysed by their inherent powerlessness and internal bickering, and preoccupied by a desperation to survive the upheavals taking place in their own world. The supposedly all-powerful mandarins in the mighty Ministries of Finance and International Trade and Industry (MITI) tried to cushion the successive blows, but could do nothing to prevent them landing. Suddenly, all the things that the Japanese had seen as their postwar strengths—from a uniform education system to lifetime employment and an elite bureaucracy—were being reviled in the media as rigidities that were bringing the country to ruin. There was no point, either, in looking to 'big brother' in the United States for help to ease the pain. In fact, Washington—in league with other foreign forces—was blamed for maliciously engineering the yen's rise in an impatient, last-ditch effort to cut the massive Japanese trade surpluses that it had failed to check in two decades of acrimonious negotiations. One senior cabinet minister complained that America was treating the Japanese 'like black slaves brought from Africa to produce wealth'.[8] After being left for 50 years to nurture its economy under the shelter of America's nuclear umbrella, Japan was on its own.

The spooky, fin-de-siècle feeling spread by the alarm over the yen's rise was exacerbated by two other dramatic events at the time. The first was the pre-dawn earthquake which shattered the port city of Kobe in western Japan in January 1995, and the second was the lethal nerve gas attack on peak-hour commuters in Tokyo in April. The quake killed more than 5000 people, injured thousands more and reduced large swathes of one of Japan's most attractive and cosmopolitan cities to ruins. In the eyes of the Japanese, the quake was not simply a natural disaster but a reminder of the country's acute, almost mythological, vulnerability to nature's catastrophes. It is no accident that the rituals of the country's native Shinto religion aim to placate the natural gods and encourage harmony between man and nature. Japan is built on a chain of volcanoes; violent storms batter the coast during 'typhoon season', and steep landslides triggered by torrential rains often engulf and kill scores of people whose homes are built on the sides of steep hills. Anyone who lives in Tokyo either quickly adjusts to the small earth tremors which shake the ground underfoot on average every 7.7 days[9] or moves to another city, or country.

Japan was meant to be well prepared for natural disasters, but Kobe proved that it wasn't. 'It is as if we are sitting on a piece of land that is perpetually quivering like a huge pile of Jell-O, or on a firecracker that is ready to burst at any time. So we are resigned to natural catastrophes, hoping to do our best when the time comes', said novelist Reiko Hatsumi. '[But in this case] highways and buildings that we were told were impregnable toppled like clumsily built Lego sets, railways hung in the air. When fires broke out, they spread unchecked. Citizens were left without food, water or bedding in near-freezing temperatures, while the rest of Japan stood back, seemingly unable to help.'[10] The quake exposed the inner workings of the Japanese political and bureaucratic system 'like an X-ray', said Professor Takeshi Sasaki of Tokyo University.

The government's response was a textbook example of revisionist theory. At the top was a hapless, powerless prime

minister, Tomiichi Murayama, passive even by Japanese standards, who received less information, and at a later time, than
US president Bill Clinton in the immediate aftermath, and even
then was powerless to shift the bureaucratic roadblocks in the
way of sending emergency aid. The first cabinet meeting, at 10
am, after the quake at 5.46 am, barely discussed the issue.
Japan's military, the Self-Defence Forces, weren't called in to
help until after midday, more than six hours later, because of
the anti-army allergy of the left-wing local governor, whose
permission was needed for them to help in a crisis. Later, the
local SDF commander broke down and cried when apologising
publicly for the unnecessary loss of life. Numerous offers of
foreign help, from Swiss sniffer dogs to foreign doctors and
painkilling drugs, were initially rebuffed by the bureaucracy
because they had not passed the necessary red tape. Even the
country's biggest and most notorious *yakuza* gangster group, the
Yamaguchi-gumi, headquartered in Kobe, shamed the authorities by mounting a swift and efficient relief effort.[11] At a cabinet
meeting the day after the quake, an outspoken minister, Makiko
Tanaka, interrupted a 'flowery report' on the situation to suggest
that energy food supplements like bananas or cheese be sent to
survivors. Her suggestion reportedly prompted chuckles. 'Isn't
it just like a woman to be thinking only in these terms', said
one minister. 'What about sending them some rice?'[12] The
public and press reaction to the government's bungling was
bitter. 'In the wake of the Great Hanshin Earthquake, it has
become clear that Japan is a closed, confused country entering
its terminal phase', wrote Yasuhiko Shibata of the *Yomiuri
Shimbun* Research Institute.[13]

If the strong yen was punishment from beyond Japan's
borders, and the earthquake the wrath of the gods, then the
next calamity came from the enemy within—a fringe religious
sect called *Aum Shinrikyo* (Aum Supreme Truth). The stereotypical picture of Japan as a stifling conformist society is a

half-truth. Japan is enormously tolerant of all manner of tribes, cults, sexual adventurers, wayward eccentrics and outspoken critics, so long as they don't intervene in mass society. By 1995, the Aum sect was just one of 183 000 officially registered religious groups in the country. Total membership of all religions was 220 million, almost double the population. Japan is nothing if not flexible in such matters. A majority of these registered religions were small family temples, but about one in ten were classified as 'new religions'—in other words, groups which were neither Shinto nor Buddhist. Most of these were fronts for small-time demagogues keen to find a business with a tax-exempt status. Few, however, were as sophisticated as Aum in tapping into the kind of post-modern spiritual ennui that has sent people flocking into pseudo-mystical sects throughout the world.

With long hair, a bushy, unkempt beard and flowing purple Indian robes, Aum's leader, His Holiness Master Shoko Asahara, looked every bit like the Oriental guru from central casting. He borrowed bits of teachings from Hinduism and Buddhism, and even claimed to have discovered that he had been Jesus Christ in a previous life on his first reading of the Bible in 1981. He enticed new followers by promising them he could make them special, an attractive alternative to many Japanese facing life on a pitiless corporate conveyor belt. Otherwise, Asahara preached a grim message of Armageddon, while his followers executed their numerous critics and kidnapped believers they suspected of wanting to quit the religion. Horror stories emerged about the cult's practices—they drank the guru's blood, injected their children with drugs and fitted out their followers with electronically wired 'hats of happiness' that sent small shocks through their bodies. Sect leaders tested the loyalty of a number of believers by demanding that they strangle dissenters in front of the guru himself. Aum was believed to have killed nearly 200 wayward followers, many of them in acid baths and ovens built in their compounds. The sect stymied the authorities' investigations by warning them against religious persecution, a pitch with great power in Japan, where the postwar state has been willing to cut would-be gurus a bit of slack rather than revive the spectre of prewar religious suppression. But on 20 April 1995, Aum went too far.

On that morning, sarin, a nerve gas, was spread through the world's busiest subway system in Tokyo during rush-hour in a horrifying attack, killing twelve people and injuring more than 5000 others. The authorities, which had been restrained from pursuing previous allegations about the sect, were let off the leash, and mounted the largest police raids in recent history. Hundreds of sect members were arrested and detained, initially on mostly trivial charges, ranging from making noodles without a licence, to parking a car in the wrong spot (police can hold and question suspects for up to 23 days without charging them in Japan). When this period lapsed, police simply re-arrested many sect members, and continued to interrogate them relentlessly.

One man they had wanted to detain, the head of the sect's 'Science and Technology Ministry' was stabbed to death outside the sect's headquarters in Tokyo in front of scores of television cameramen and newspaper photographers. In film replayed ceaselessly on television the next day and night, the assassin, a 29-year-old ethnic Korean gangster, plunged a 21-centimetre sushi knife into the sect leader. He stood back after the job was complete, chewing on gum, and calmly and disdainfully threw the bloodied knife onto the ground in front of a group of journalists frozen in a circle around him, transfixed by a mixture of fear and fascination. The government's chief spokesman later complained not so much about the sect official's brutal murder, as about the damage to the investigation, because the police could no longer interrogate the dead man. The authorities intensified their campaign when the country's police chief, who had been heading the investigation, was gunned down outside his apartment—the first killing of a senior government official in more than a quarter of a century. Police began dismantling, piece by piece, the sect's properties and entire infrastructure. Unnerved by the violence, 'public opinion', which had apparently restrained police from acting before the sarin attack on the subway, swung behind the authorities and noisily applauded their efforts to wipe the sect out.

The triple whammy of these apparently unrelated events— the strong yen, the Kobe earthquake and the sarin attack—induced a mood of overwhelming pessimism in Japan. It became fashionable to compare Japan in the 1990s to Japan in the 1920s, when a brief flowering of liberalism and democracy was overwhelmed by financial panic and a military takeover of the government that eventually led to the Pacific War. Similarly, according to Iwao Nakatani of Hitotsubashi University, the collusive 'iron triangle' of bureaucrats, businessmen and politicians which had run postwar Japan was overcome with systemic fatigue. Japan faced a new crisis of leadership. 'In the 1920s, the politicians were unable to control the military. Today, they are unable to exercise leadership, hamstrung by collusion between bureaucrats and business groups. The "iron triangle" is ruining Japan, just as the military once ruined it', said Nakatani.[14]

Other commentators—most of them mainstream liberals like Nakatani—were painting the same dark scenarios. (Ms) Ayako Doi, the editor of the Washington-based *Japan Digest*, recalled that the great Tokyo earthquake of 1923 was followed two years later by the formation of the military's notorious secret police, and then the entire military apparatus which drove Japan into fascism and war. 'Coming at a time when frustrations are still high over the Government's inept response to the Kobe earthquake, the subway gassing may become one of those pivotal incidents that make a people, after 50 years of unfettered freedom, long once again to give the state more power.'[15] The magazine *Business Intelligence* compared Japan's coming collapse to the calamity of liquefaction, when ostensibly solid foundations turn to mush during an earthquake.[16] Publishers hurriedly reissued the best-seller, *Japan Sinks*, written during the hysterical period of the first oil shock in the early 1970s. In this novel, the whole nation has to be evacuated, including millions to northern Australia, when the entire Japanese archipelago sinks into the sea after an earthquake.

Those Japanese who had at least felt some pride about the new economic and social model Japan had built and bequeathed to its fellow Asians now despaired. 'The "Japanese Way" . . . is now viewed chiefly as an interesting example of how not to go about developing one's economy . . . and is studied chiefly as means to avoid making similar mistakes', said prominent economist, Naoki Tanaka, bemoaning the protracted business slump. 'Though [Asians] admire the Japanese for their hard work, quality products and relatively crime-free society, they do not wish to be like them. They see a crowded expensive country, with cluttered streets and ugly buildings. They also see tight government control over business and political corruption.'[17]

Even allowing for the usual level of hyperbole employed by commentators to attract attention in the punditry marketplace, these appraisals were astoundingly black. The gloom was partly a product of the professional pessimism that grips many Japanese, a people instructed from a young age that they live in 'a small island nation with no natural resources'. Insecurity and vulnerability are inbred in Japan, and work as powerful motivating forces. But typically, the tidal wave of despair gave nothing like a true picture of Japan's strengths and weaknesses as it moved towards the 21st century.

POOR LITTLE RICH COUNTRY

Most countries would be overjoyed to be the sort of irrelevant, spent force that Naoki Tanaka describes. In the middle of its longest economic slowdown since the war, Japan had a 3.4 per cent official unemployment rate, half the savings on the globe tucked away in its own banks and post offices, a sound budget and massive trade surpluses with the United States, Asia and most European countries except for Italy and Denmark. The few remaining countries which were lucky enough to sell more to Japan than they bought—like Australia, New Zealand and the oil-producing Gulf States—only did so because they were resource-rich and population-poor. In all areas of high value-added manufacturing, there was no contest—Japan was winning hands down. Japan's high-tech manufacturing monopolies made sure of that.

Japanese companies dominate the global production of cameras, laser jet printers, small copy and fax machines, the latest model video cameras, flat panel or liquid crystal display screens used in computers and a range of other devices. They have a stranglehold on a host of crucial components used in manufacturing—high-tech batteries for cellular phones and computers; precision machines for making semi-conductors, or computer chips, and the ceramic packaging which encloses them. Most pieces of optical scanning equipment—the machines used for everything from automatically sorting letters to reading subway tickets and prices at supermarket checkouts—rely on hardware from Japan. Japanese manufacturers also hold virtual franchises for many sophisticated machine tools and car-making equipment, which are no less important for being obscure. These monopolies allowed many companies to avoid being savaged by the strong yen. In 1994, when the currency was soaring, Japan's 26 largest electrical component-makers increased profits by nearly 70 per cent.[18] Japan even held its position as the world's

33

largest shipbuilder and exporter, an enterprise cheerfully abandoned as an expendable 'smokestack' industry in places like England, the United States and Australia decades ago. South Korea overtook Japan in 1994—courtesy of the strong yen—but Japan regained its position the following year.[19]

Japan's dominance is a logical result of national policy which continues to regard manufacturing as the commanding heights of a modern economy. As a result, its trade with the United States and with resource producers like Australia retains strong elements of a classic colonial relationship—Japan exports manufactured goods, and imports food and raw materials. Japanese companies also made sure they maintained control of their high-tech franchises when they fled overseas to escape the increasingly forbidding cost of manufacturing in Japan. Professor Hajime Karatsu of Tokai University calculates that 75 per cent of Japanese companies which had shifted production overseas by the mid-1990s still supplied the most valuable parts from their factories at home. US companies, by contrast, had abandoned suppliers in their own country, and had become hostage to foreign suppliers—most notably, Japanese ones. 'The US is depending on other countries for virtually all the key components used to produce machine tools. As a result, the busier the American manufacturing industry becomes, the more imports increase. US manufacturing industries would collapse if this external support disappeared', he said.[20]

Japan's trade surplus—one of the primary sources of political, economic and financial discord amongst global powers—will drift down in the final years of this century for two reasons. The strong yen has resulted in double-digit increases in import volumes from 1994 onwards. Japanese companies are also shifting more and more production overseas, thus shifting exports off Japan's own national accounts and onto that of the countries in which they have invested. But the surplus will remain high, because the US and many other countries depend on goods that only Japanese companies make. The US was quick to claim victory after the acrimonious negotiations between the two countries over the trade in cars and car parts which concluded in 1995, for example. The car trade is worth more than half of the bilateral trade imbalance, but the negotiations only affected a small part of it—15 per cent of $88 billion. Japan's lead negotiator, the Ministry for International Trade and Industry (MITI) vice-minister, Yoshihiro Sakamoto, openly admitted that little would change as a result of the agreement. 'There are no signs that the US trade deficit will significantly decrease, and no signs that Japan's surplus will shrink substantially', he said when he returned home, with the claims of 'victory' from America's lead negotiator, Mickey Kantor, ringing in his ears. The car industry is just one of many industries in which Japan had established a strategic beachhead. A report issued in 1995 by Japan's overseas trade body, the JETRO organisation, found that 13 per cent of Japan's exports to the United States in 1993 were in sectors where there was no American competitor. Another 50 per cent were in 'market segments in which Japanese firms accounted for 75 per cent or more of US imports', calculated Merril Lynch's economist in Tokyo, Ronald Bevaqua. As the US is Japan's chief global rival, the advantage Japan enjoys over it is magnified in its trade with Asia.

Through the sharp economic contraction of the first half of the decade, Japanese companies have resolutely resisted giving up another of the country's symbolic pillars of postwar success—the lifetime employment system.[21] Companies have used all sorts of underhand tactics, such as removing workers' desks, or sending clerks to work in factories, to force people to leave their jobs, but because of peer pressure, their own rational calculations and the 'culture' of lifetime employment, most have shied away from large-scale sackings. But where some Japanese see harmony in their co-operative capitalism, others now increasingly worry about atrophy and disaster. The proud boast of capitalism,

Japan-style, is that it has avoided the ravages of the invisible hand, Adam Smith's proverbial guiding force for an efficient market economy. Japanologist Ronald Dore wrote in the early 1980s that the Japanese had refused to unleash the invisible hand in their economy, because they simply didn't believe in it. 'They believe—like Mao unleashing the Cultural Revolution and all other good Confucionists—that you cannot get a decent moral society, not even an efficient society, simply out of the mechanisms of the market powered by the motivational fuel of self-interest, however clever, or even divinely inspired, those mechanisms might be,' writes Dore.[22]

Left to their own devices, the Japanese power elite would have been happy to continue with their distinctive brand of 'victimless capitalism'. But in the 1990s, Adam Smith snuck in the back door of the Japanese economy, courtesy of the strong yen and American demands for open markets, and also turned up at the front, with flowers in his hand, dressed as a cut-price retailer, so charmingly that the father of the house could no longer prevent his daughters from being wooed by him. The 'price destruction' unleashed by the new breed of discounters, and embraced by consumers, threatens more than anything else to transform Japan, by busting the cosy networks that have dominated Japanese business for decades.

The whole premise of Japan's postwar industrial strategy— its single-minded belief in manufacturing—also looks shaky. The explosion in the global workforce following the end of the Cold War means there is now a limitless supply of cheap labour to perform quite complex manufacturing tasks. Thus, the prices of many of the products that Japan has specialised in, like television sets, compact disc players and VCRs, are falling, along with the profits of the companies that make them. At the same time, a host of new opportunities is opening up for software suppliers—an area where Japan is relatively much weaker. 'While Mitsubishi and Matsushita struggle to restructure their operations to cope with intense new cost pressures, Microsoft and Madonna see a world of new opportunities', says Peter Tasker, a leading Tokyo securities analyst.[23] Tasker says that in the new information age, manufacturing may become as peripheral an economic activity as farming. In 1993, just under a third of Japan's workforce was employed in manufacturing, down from 40 per cent in 1970. More than half of the employees in large manufacturing companies are white-collar workers, who, says Tasker, 'only get their hands dirty with newsprint and copy toner'.

The Japanese have always complimented themselves on their love of nature in all its simplicity. The passing of the four distinct seasons, and the annual celebration of cherry-blossoms, with their intimations of sadness and beauty, all bespeak a nation with deep romantic rural roots.[24] But sentimental feelings about nature are more and more out of sync with the dense urban habitats of the new Japan. Real farmers are an endangered species in Japan, as they are around the world. About 60 per cent of the country's 4.4 million full-time farmers are over 60 years old, and nearly 80 per cent are over 50. Only 2000 young men take up farming as a career each year. In 1993, Japan's food self-sufficiency reached an all-time low; its farmers provided only 37 per cent of food on Japanese tables, compared to 47 per cent in 1990. The idealised rural life which supposedly formed the backdrop to rapid industrial growth barely exists any more.

Modernisation, and by extension, Westernisation, has always been equated by many Japanese with a loss of core values. 'Japan will disappear', wrote the nationalist novelist Yukio Mishima. 'It will become inorganic, empty, neutral-tinted; it will be wealthy and astute.'[25] The passage from economic miracle to mid-life depression has done more than accentuate this fear of hollowness. It has plunged Japan into a fully-fledged identity crisis as well.

CHAPTER 3

ASIA'S SIREN SONG

'Asia should thoroughly absorb what the West has offered, and develop a new set of universal values that it can transmit to the world. The solution [to the problems of modernisation] is not necessarily to be found in Western civilisation.'

Kazuo Ogura, bureaucrat

'Asia is just an illusion that the Japanese have. From an economic point of view, creating a sense of unity is important. But without economics, we have nothing to share.'

Naohiro Amaya, former bureaucrat

'We . . . we . . . we're not Asians. We Japanese—we're WHITE!'

Yakuza gangster in the film *World Apartment Horror*

You might call the movie *World Apartment Horror* a period piece. In this low-budget film made at the peak of the bubble economy, a small-time *yakuza* gangster is hired to evict a group of Asian workers out of a rickety dormitory in the Tokyo suburbs.

Real estate prices remained so high that it was worth employing thugs to clear property before redevelopment. And foreign workers were still being lured into Japan at the time to do all the dirty work that the free-spending locals spurned. The Japanese dubbed the jobs, like cleaning and construction, 'three-k' work—*kitanai* (dirty), *kitsui* (difficult) and *kiken* (dangerous). The gangster tries every trick in the trade to move the 'three-k' workers on. He even has sex with his girlfriend at the end of the corridor near the workers' quarters, so raucously that the sound of their groans and orgasms pierces the building's paper-thin walls, and travels through all the rooms. But the workers are unmoved. The Asians in the movieland dormitory—from the Philippines, Thailand, Pakistan and elsewhere—naively believe they can befriend their landlord. They ignore his antics, smile at him in the corridor, and try to get on with their lives. Gradually, their funny cooking smells, noisy 'ethnic' parties with extended family and friends, and their plain niceness get to the gangster. Finally he turns on his tenants, screaming at them in one of those violent, guttural voices that you think are a parody of Japanese male macho-speak when you hear them in films, until you experience them for real. Even after this outburst, the lodgers are puzzled, and gently approach the gangster to appeal to what they think are his best humanitarian instincts. 'We're all Asians, aren't we?' they say. 'Asians?' the slow-thinking gangster ponders for a moment, before blurting out roughly. 'We . . . we . . . we're not Asians. We Japanese—we're WHITE!' The workers are stunned. They withdraw to their rooms with looks of astonishment on their faces. And the gangster, as one critic wrote, is 'left on the landing, aghast, humbled, and deeply perplexed by the palpable idiocy of what he has just uttered'.

Like the gangster, Japan has always been notoriously ambivalent about its place in the world. Confused might be a better word, except that Japan's confusion on this issue has usually either been too comforting, or convenient and deliberate, for the dilemma to be damaging. Ever since the black ships of Commodore Matthew Perry of the United States forced the shogunate to end the country's three centuries of self-imposed isolation from the world in 1853, Japan has swung, almost schizophrenically, between 'insisting on not being Asian at all, and declaring itself the epitome of Asianness'.[1] This schizophrenia is a product of the principles that have guided its foreign policy over the past century. The Japanese are imbued with an intense sense of race, coupled with deep feelings of inferiority; they have an emotional commitment to Asia, but also a desire to conform to world trends to avoid isolation; and above all, a deep-seated concern to lift Japan's standing in the globe.[2]

By the mid-1990s, Japan found itself walking a tightrope in straddling the East–West divide. Its political, economic and military policies since the war had all been intimately tied to, and in many respects controlled by, Washington. Half a century later, however, the contradictions in the relationship had sparked a harsh reassessment on both sides of the Pacific of the partners' long-term interests. Japan's awesome economic power, massive trade surpluses and increasing business presence in Asia were more and more at odds with its military dependence on the United States. Japanese political leaders like Ichiro Ozawa, often with the encouragement of the United States, began debating the country's military role, and by extension the worth of the US alliance. Politicians and trade bureaucrats courted popularity by talking tough to the United States and saying 'No' to Washington's demands that it buy more American goods. The pin-up boy of conservative politics, Ryutaro Hashimoto, launched his successful campaign to become LDP leader in late 1995, and then Prime Minister in 1996, by standing up to the Americans as MITI minister in negotiations over the trade in cars and car parts.

The feeling of dissatisfaction was mutual. The Congress in Washington grumbled about providing for the security of Japan and its surrogate economies in South-east Asia, while simultaneously going into massive debt to them. Although it pulled back from the brink of direct retaliation, the Clinton administration, more than previous American governments, explicitly linked America's defence of Japan with a new deal on trade. Some revisionist thinkers even advocated doing away with the US–Japan security alliance and withdrawing American troops from Japan altogether. They said that a troop withdrawal would provide the necessary shock therapy to force Japan to grow up and develop a political system mature enough to look after its own security. Even as Japanese leaders chafed at the demands of their 'big brother', the United States, they usually sulkily concurred that they were, for the foreseeable future, stuck with them. Japan, said one commentator, had turned into 'a resentful and mercantilist power locked into a state of infantile dependence on US security'.[3] The Americans also usually backed away from any showdown, but on both sides of the relationship confrontation was in.

At its crudest and most extreme, this confrontation was racial, fuelled by cries in Japan for the country to join other 'Asians' to unite against the 'white' Westerners. This conjured up the worst-case scenario for Japan's mainstream rulers, but one they were increasingly forced to confront. More than anything, they wanted to avoid choosing sides and declaring whether Japan stood with the West, or with Asia.

THE BLACK SHIPS

At the time when Commodore Perry forced Japan to open its ports for business, Japan was a xenophobic and isolated feudal state, ill equipped to deal with the powerful and technologically sophisticated West. The practical Japanese were quick to spot this, and their historical and emotional attachment to Asia and

and China, as tenuous as it was by then, was swept aside in an effort to learn from Europe. The prominent nineteenth-century intellectual, and founder of Tokyo's Keio University, Yukichi Fukuzawa, coined the phrase '*datsu-a, nyu-o*'—'Out of Asia and into the West'—as the rallying cry which spurred Japan's breath-taking leap, from a poor, isolated and basically rural country to a global industrial power in the space of decades. Modernisation was, first of all, Westernisation, and the fruits of this copycatting and co-opting policy are still visible all over Japan today. The political, legal, education and transport systems were all system-atically borrowed in whole or part from the West, mainly Europe, and so were many of the trappings that went with them.[4] Schoolboys in Japan still dress in dark, gold-buttoned jackets taken from Prussia last century (although to younger eyes the uniforms look more like well-tailored Mao suits), and schoolgirls wear replicas of sailor uniforms. The Imperial Family and mem-bers of their court wear clothes modelled on Victorian royalty's at many official ceremonies. Cars are driven on the left-hand side of the road, a result of the transport system being borrowed from England. The red-brick Tokyo Station in the centre of the capital was modelled in 1914 on the central station in Amster-dam. Even the state guesthouse, the Akasaka Palace, where foreign dignitaries stay on official state visits to Japan, is mod-elled on the Versailles Palace.

But the embrace of Western ways and technology always ran in parallel with, and in tension with, a movement calling for the maintenance of Japan's Eastern spirit, under the banner of *wakon yosei*—'Japanese Spirit, Western Learning'. Japan's brilliant vic-tory, with the use of naval ships from Britain, over Russia in 1905—the first by a 'yellow' nation over a 'white' one—was as much proof of the Japanese spirit, so the argument went, as the military firepower acquired from the West. The militarists in the 1930s grotesquely exploited similar ideas to launch their sacred mission to banish the white colonialists from Asia and build a

42

Greater East Asian Co-Prosperity Sphere under the leadership of Japan, and left their country defeated and in smouldering ruins. Japan was then made to put its Asian ambitions back in a box. It gave up an independent foreign and defence policy as penance for its wartime sins, to act as America's 'unsinkable aircraft carrier' in the frontline of the Cold War in the Pacific. Japan had an energy policy to secure resources from Indonesia, Australia and the oil-producing states, and built its own bridges with China after the shock of US president Nixon's secret rapprochement with Beijing. Otherwise, Japan toed the American line and concentrated on building its economy, until a series of events in the early 1990s brought Japan's Asian identity crisis out of the closet with a thud.

The end of the Cold War did more than start unravelling an intricate tangle of interests which split the ruling Liberal Democratic Party and ended the compact on which Japan's postwar political order had been built. It also fundamentally affected the way that Japan related to the United States. The Soviet Union's dismemberment, Japan's emergence as the regional economic superpower, with the dragons of Asia speeding in its wake, and growing resentment in Tokyo at constant criticism from the United States, brought all the old sentiments and debates about Asia welling to the surface. Politicians, bureaucrats and business leaders in the 'pro-Asia' camp turned Fukuzawa's catchcry on its head, and called on Japan to 'leave the West and return to Asia'. Politically, the region became both a sword and shield for Japan—a place to which it could retreat to protect itself from the increasingly belligerent Americans and Europeans, and from which it could launch itself anew into the fastest-growing economies in the world. The 'Asia boom' spread quickly through the popular media. Yuppie magazines for both men and women began featuring glossy spreads on Asia. Sanyo, the giant electronics company, launched a generic national advertising campaign, 'Asian Age'. Both the magazine spreads and the advertisements showcased Asia as an exotic locale featuring young and innocent-looking beauties loitering in traditional vegetable markets and in rice paddies in the countryside, with not a single Sanyo in sight. In many ways, the media image matched the idealised Western view of the exotic Orient, but for Japan, the 'restoration of Asia' involved much deeper and fundamental choices.

Most Japanese leaders were happy to leave the rhetorical running in this debate to demagogic neo-Asianists like Malaysian prime minister Mahathir Mohamed. They deftly sidestepped—in public at least—committing themselves to Mahathir's anti-American crusade, not only in deference to US sensitivities but also because ordinary Japanese weren't prepared for an immediate showdown with Washington. But Mahathir's determined diplomacy from 1991 to establish an Asians-only trade grouping—dubbed the caucus without Caucasians—struck a deep chord in Japanese business and political circles. Japanese resentment redoubled when Washington exercised its power of veto and ordered Japan not to join Mahathir's planned group. Mahathir's aggressive 'Asianism' became the perfect vehicle for Japanese nationalists wishing to revive the prewar concept of the region as a sort of spiritual self-defence against the corrupting and overbearing West, and the destruction of the Japanese 'soul'. One of the most outspokenly nationalistic of Japan's politicians, Shintaro Ishihara, penned a book with Mahathir— *The Asia That Can Say No: A Policy to Combat Europe and America*—about the superiority of Asian values over the West's. Ishihara's previous book co-authored with Sony founder Akio Morita, *The Japan That Can Say No*, which suggested that Tokyo could gain leverage over Washington by withholding vital military technology, had sold 1.3 million copies. In the tome written with Mahathir, the familiar litany of contrasting values was trotted out. Asians were culturally relative and tolerant, whereas the Christian-based Westerners insisted on moral absolutes.

Asians were peaceful and co-operative, while Westerners were contentious and militaristic. Asians respected authority and valued the family, whereas selfish Westerners cared only about themselves, and so on.[5] Naturally, this sweeping set of values was assumed to fit all Asians, and the Japanese as well.

The Asia boom emboldened a new breed of nationalists in the Japanese bureaucracy, also weary of constant niggling from Washington on trade. 'Japanese history since World War II is a history of Americanisation', said the Finance Ministry's Eisuke Sakakibara, one of the most aggressive defenders of Japanese economic policy. 'It's time to think about post-Western civilisation. We have to stop being afraid of the United States. I will not avoid some kind of breakdown with the United States.'[6] Sakakibara was well known for bringing his aggressive style to the negotiating table. During bilateral talks initiated by the United States in a bid to open Japan's insurance market, Sakakibara read a paper presented by the Americans outlining their demands, and then disdainfully remarked across the table that he wouldn't bother to mark it if it had been presented to him by one of his students at university.[7]

Sakakibara, and others like him who promoted Japanese capitalism as an alternative to American laissez-faire, have won a wide audience in Asia. Sakakibara himself saw the Japanese style as pragmatic, and dismissed attempts to promote it as an exclusively Asian model. 'There are no Asian values as such. Chinese civilisation is different, Indian civilisation is different. South-east Asia is different, and in between, there are countries like Vietnam and Thailand', he said. '[Mahathir and Lee Kwan Yew] are not philosophers, they're politicians and politicians can talk in all different sorts of ways.'[8] But for all Sakakibara's protestations about diversity, the Japanese model of economic growth and political stability set an example that inspired a new generation of bureaucrats and managers throughout the region. Some countries, like South Korea, copied the Japanese system almost completely. A confident Japan began to push its own development model more assertively in international forums. A World Bank study of Asia's tiger economies, cooked up and paid for by the Finance Ministry in Tokyo, directly challenged the dominant US view that free markets and democracy were the best recipe for development. Finance Ministry officials in Tokyo were particularly critical of the ideological shock treatment prescribed by the West to the creaky economies of the former Soviet Union. 'If there are successful cases in economic development on the one hand, and unsuccessful on the other, it would be quite natural that one would be tempted to draw lessons from the former with a view to applying them to the latter', one of the Japanese officials who promoted the study, Isao Kubota, acidly remarked.

But as Asians knew all too well, scratch a Japanese promoter of Asia, and you might soon find an ultra-nationalist underneath. One wondered how Shintaro Ishihara's sugar-coated pan-Asianism went down in Beijing. The Chinese remembered Ishihara best of all, not for his tolerance of cultural diversity and professed predilection for peace, but for the time he called the Nanjing Massacre a 'fabrication', and the war in China one of 'liberation'. Many other Japanese who were thoroughly anchored in the West found the anti-Western diatribes of the Malaysians and their ilk absurd. Around the time the Mahathir/Ishihara book was published in 1994, one senior Japanese bureaucrat visiting a Malaysian counterpart for talks on trade policy told me he had been surprised to find himself receiving a long lecture about the perversion of family values in the West by homosexual marriages. The Malaysian thought that his Japanese visitor, being a fellow-Asian, would warmly agree, and was taken aback when his guest from Tokyo bluntly asked him: 'What's homosexuality got to do with trade liberalisation?'. One of Tokyo's most famous bureaucrats, and a veteran of years of tense trade talks with Washington, the late Naohiro Amaya, was gloomily cynical when he was asked whether Japan would turn away from the United States to return to its Asian roots. Amaya saw the movement to 'return' to Asia as something that the Japanese defensively and somewhat sulkily pursued when things got a bit rough with the United States and Europe. 'Asia is just an illusion that the Japanese have', he said. 'From an economic point of view, creating a sense of unity is important. But without economics, we have nothing to share.'[9]

CO-PROSPERITY RIDES AGAIN

If Japan had a personality, a psychiatrist might diagnose it as passive/aggressive. In defence and foreign policy, for example, Japan has passively endured its status as America's 'little brother' in the Pacific since the renewal of the security treaty between them in 1960. Violent mass protests against the treaty's renewal brought down the government at the time, but since then the policy of pacifism has not been seriously challenged. In fact, just the opposite has occurred, as politicians across the spectrum have elevated it rhetorically to the status of a near-religion. To be sure, parties and factions have interpreted the policy different-ly—with the long-time permanent opposition, the Socialists, plumping until 1995 for 'one-country pacifism', and the majority of ruling LDP factions backing the US alliance. Any politician with an interest in maintaining his or her career would not campaign for Japan to develop nuclear weapons. That has always been Washington's preserve. In Japan, defence hawks do well to hold their fire. Many Japanese leaders may believe Japan should have an independent defence policy, but few dare to say it.

In the day-to-day management of its economic relationship with the United States too, Japan has, until recently, also appar-ently been subservient and self-effacing, ostensibly giving ground whenever seriously threatened by the United States on trade issues. In the early 1980s, Japan decided to 'voluntarily restrain' its exports of cars to the United States to head off trade sanctions. In 1985, as described in Chapter 2, Japan caved in to pressure from America and Europe to allow a massive appreciation of the yen, thereby making its exports more expensive, and imports cheaper. A few years later, MITI agreed to ensure that foreign manufacturers of computer chips gained 20 per cent of the Japanese market after more threats from the United States. In agricultural trade, Japan gave in one by one on allowing imports of beef, oranges, rice and apples, all of which had all been either banned or subject to quotas for years.

But a glance at the other side of the ledger makes Japan look anything but subservient and self-effacing. By 1995, the yen had more than doubled in value from the point at which it started to rise in 1985, but Japan's trade surplus with the United States, after dipping briefly, was bigger than ever—US$66 billion in 1994. More than half of the value of the surplus was a result of the imbalance from the trade in cars and car parts, the commodity that Japan had agreed to 'voluntarily' restrict exporting fifteen years beforehand. Even more significant was what Japan had managed to achieve in South-east Asia and China during the same period. In 1991, Asia surpassed the United States as Japan's largest export destination. The following year, Japan's trade surplus with Asia swelled to overtake the politically problematic surplus with the United States. In 1994, Japan invested more in Asia than in the United States for the first time in the postwar period. (By the 1990s America's investment in Asia was running almost equal to Japan's, but half of it was sunk into oil. Japanese firms put their money into manufacturing and distribution that allowed them to mainline their consumer goods into all the markets in the region.)[10] Japan's economic advance, of course, took place in a region secured by the US military and its nuclear arsenal.[11]

'What you are seeing', said C.H. Kwan, of the Nomura Research Institute in Tokyo, 'is the Asianisation of Asian economies'.[12] What you were also seeing was the Asianisation—and thus, de-politicisation—of Japan's contentious trade surplus with the United States. Take the journey of the humble videocassette recorder made by Sanyo Electric Co. Until 1991, all Sanyo VCRs exported to the United States were made in Japan. According to the *Asian Wall Street Journal*, Sanyo then decided to concentrate on making the high-end technology-intensive VCRs in Japan, and shifted production of the low-end VCRs to a new factory in Indonesia. The 700 000 VCRs Sanyo exported that year to North America were recorded as 'Indonesian' exports. Tokyo-based economist Kenneth Courtis estimated that at least US$15 billion of Japan's surplus with the United States of the early 1980s had been shifted to Asia a decade later.

The decision by Japanese companies to manufacture off-shore was entirely pragmatic, as a response to the strong yen, cheaper labour, and political pressure to invest in countries to which Japan wanted to export. The task of economic integration, however, was carried out with the methodical sophistication for which Japan's business and bureaucracy are justifiably famous. With the guidance of the visible hand of MITI, investment followed clear patterns. The first stage was low-wage assembly lines, using parts imported from Japan, and resource projects. The strong yen and the increasing skills of Asia's workforces gradually allowed more advanced manufacturing, and local production of parts in regional countries. But Japan has a bottom line here—the sophisticated manufacturing jobs which add the most value are kept at home in Japan, and only allowed out when companies are ready to discard the technology and move up another level.

Japan's secret weapon in its penetration of Asian economies has been its massive aid budget—known as Official Development ment Assistance, or ODA. The Japanese very well understand the benefits of foreign aid. Few of the visitors to Tokyo who marvel at the rapid *shinkansen* (bullet trains) and cower under the large overhead freeways which criss-cross the capital are aware that both were funded in part by loans from the World Bank in the 1950s and 1960s when Japan was still a poor country. Japan, a model of development for the World Bank, paid back the last of its loans in 1990 to take itself off the debtors' list—by which time it was the largest creditor nation on the globe. For four straight years since 1990, Japan was the world's biggest foreign aid donor, doling out a record $17.3 billion in 1994.

The bulk of Japan's aid has always been deliberately directed at Asia—from a high of 98 per cent in 1971, to about 65 per cent of the total budget in the 1990s. Aside from its role as 'guilt' money for wartime aggression, Japan's aid has always been directed strategically—to secure natural resources, and to promote economic growth and political stability. If America is the region's policeman, then Japan has styled itself as its banker and management consultant. Japanese aid, mostly in the form of yen loans rather than grants, goes predominantly into large infrastructure projects, like roads, bridges and electricity generation. Whether Japan's big aid budgets translate into raw political power is an issue that we will return to later in this chapter, but certainly the potential is there. In 1990, Japan provided Indonesia—the largest supplier of energy to Japan and a growing consumer market of nearly 200 million people—with 70 per cent of its foreign aid, which was equal to more than 10 per cent of Jakarta's entire budget outlays. The biggest beneficiary of Japanese aid now is fast-growing China. The budget of the world's second biggest aid donor, the United States, by contrast, is divided up according to the fruits of its 'great power' diplomacy in a way that gives it almost no economic spinoffs at all. More than half of American aid goes to the Middle East, and the bulk to Israel and Egypt, as reward for their peace accord in the late 1970s. Only about 15 per cent goes to Asia, where American business is struggling to compete head-to-head with Japan.

As good an indicator as any of the value of Japanese aid is the way cash-hungry politicians in Tokyo have muscled in for a cut over the last decade. Factional leaders compete to head the parliamentary 'friendship leagues' for countries receiving Japanese aid and, in true Japanese style, have organised the division of spoils between them. Ichiro Ozawa reportedly gained control over Burma, while former prime ministers Yasuhiro Nakasone and Noboru Takeshita got Bangladesh and China respectively. The kingpin was former foreign minister Michio Watanabe, who looked after Indonesia and Vietnam until he died in late 1995. A Japanese magazine reported that the normal kickback for a politician shepherding a project from a foreign country through the Tokyo bureaucracy ranged from 10 to 30 per cent. '"Dietman's Friendship Leagues" are money-collecting agencies', said one politician.[13] The other great advantage of aid was that it allowed not just the politicians, but Japanese business as well, to be in on the development of the booming Asian economies on the ground floor.

Metaphors abounded for Japan's harnessing of Asia's booming economies. Japan as the Asian brain was one favourite. Japan leading a V-shaped flock of flying geese was another. (It was usually overlooked by the Japanese who eagerly used this metaphor that flying geese generally take turns to lead the V-shaped flock.) No one, except the most impolite observers, dared call it an Asian Co-Prosperity Sphere, although the pattern of hierarchical integration of the region's economies, with Japan at the top, was uncomfortably close to the prewar model.

MITI unconsciously encouraged these notions by assiduously exaggerating its role as an all-powerful co-ordinator of which industry would go where in the region. The ministry produced papers of astonishing detail for each country, outlining its plans to make Malaysia, for example, the world's biggest producer/assembler of word processors and fax and answering machines. 'We deeply hope that these will be the most important industries in Malaysia', the MITI section told one foreign reporter 'with a smile', presumably a devious one. The same official said that MITI's regional division of labour had allocated textiles, forest products and plastics for Indonesia, and furniture, toys and die-cast models for Thailand. The journalist concluded his story with a hardy perennial about Japan in Asia: 'Herein lies a remarkable twist: What Japan was unable to achieve with military force 50 years ago, it is achieving today through its money, diplomacy and technical skill'.[14]

Business leaders also tended to describe their visions of the region in clinically vertical terms. Toshihiko Sekimoto, Asian general manager for the large trading house, Itochu, worked out his own productivity scale for Asian workers, and freely publicised it in conversations with foreign reporters. He put Indonesia and Malaysia at the bottom, with a score of 1. India and Sri Lanka got 1.5, Thailand 2, Japan and China 3, Korea 3.5 and Vietnam 4. Sekimoto complained that workers in Bangkok would quit his enterprise after a year and then boast that they had been trained by 'a genuine Japanese company'. 'But it is important that workers want to go on learning. If you go to Vietnam there are lots of bookshops. They are always wanting to learn', he said. 'A monthly salary in Thailand is between $93 and $106, but in Vietnam, it is $26. The Vietnamese are twice as productive, which makes them eight times cheaper than Thai workers.'[15]

These tell-tale signs of hierarchy were galling to many of Japan's neighbours. When government officials in Tokyo said 'First of all, we are Asians', what they really meant, said one commentator, was first among the Asians. The vertical relationship was also reflected sharply in trade between Japan and Asia. The United States had the largest absolute trade deficit with

Japan, but when the comparison is based on proportion of total trade with Japan, the top five deficit countries—Singapore, Hong Kong, Thailand, South Korea and Malaysia—were all Asian. Singapore and Hong Kong's deficit with Japan was worth over 10 per cent of the value of their entire economies, compared to a paltry 0.7 per cent for America. But the shift to offshore manufacturing did not necessarily reduce the imbalance immediately. A Japanese government survey found that in 1992 only seventeen out of the 114 responding Japanese companies in Singapore bought parts from local suppliers. The remainder imported parts, mainly from Japan. Although the strong yen is rapidly forcing Japanese companies to buy more parts locally—Toyota, for example, expects to boost its Asian parts-making network to include 100 parts by 1998, up from twelve in 1995—Japan's closely guarded grip on the manufacture of high value-added goods means it will maintain its strategic trade surpluses throughout the region.

The irascible Mahathir, while stroking Japan in political forums, complained angrily about the refusal of Mitsubishi Motors—the company chosen by Malaysia to help it build a car industry—to transfer state-of-the-art technology to the national car, the Proton. 'Japan does not want to transfer technology, and it also does not want to import Malaysian products. Japan should change its attitude', he said.[16] Mahathir sought the co-operation of the Korean conglomerate, Hyundai, in 1994, to put pressure on the Japanese, but he was most likely barking up the wrong tree. A large percentage of the value of every South Korean car is made up of exports from Japan. As a Korean trade official, Lee Sang Kul, confessed to the *New York Times* in 1993, 'We're hooked on Japan, I'm afraid. When the Korean economy was just starting to develop, we had to rely on Japan for technology and parts. Once we had their system, we kept buying'. And as for the large trade deficits with Japan that these Asian countries were running in the meantime—that was just part of growing up and becoming adult nations. 'The trade deficits are the cost to be paid by recipient countries in the initial stage of substantial inflows of foreign investments', said Gorota Kume, of the Japan Institute for Overseas Investment.[17] Not all of Japan's neighbours were so sanguine. One report by the Association of South-east Asian Nations called the Japanese market 'difficult to fathom' and 'inscrutable'.[18] Of all the words to choose! 'Inscrutable' was the classic racial construct used by the politically incorrect West decades ago to describe crafty and scheming Asians, as in 'The Inscrutable Dr Fu Manchu—Evil Genius'.

Japan does not have Asia to itself, as some contend. Already, by 1995, its companies were being challenged by cash-rich adversaries in Hong Kong, Singapore, Taiwan and South Korea. A greater 'Chinese' co-prosperity sphere to rival Japan's is also emerging around mainland and overseas Chinese networks. But Japan's interests in Asia will continue to grow nonetheless. More and more companies are fleeing the strong yen to build their factories offshore, particularly in China, and they are making more money than they can anywhere else in the world. A MITI survey in the early 1990s found that manufacturing investments in Asia yielded a 5 per cent return, compared to 3.2 per cent in Europe and –0.9 per cent in North America. If Japan needed a further incentive to 'come home' to Asia, then these extra profits provided it.

Plainly, Japan's burgeoning economic interests in the region had far outstripped its political relationships. But Japan's renewed advance into Asia still bore the scars of history, and all the ill-will that went with it. Money alone was no longer enough. Its kinder, gentler co-prosperity sphere needed protection, something that a number of prominent politicians and bureaucrats set about providing as the turn of the century approached.

WE'RE ALL ASIANS NOW

Few Japanese bureaucrats reacted as strongly to the chill winds of trade wars and cultural hostility blowing in from the west as Kazuo Ogura, a senior official on the fast track in the Foreign Ministry. In a ministry notorious for its 'follow-the-leader' approach to relations with the US, Ogura angered Washington with an article in the influential magazine *Chuo Koron* in mid-1993 calling for a 'new concept of Asia'. Washington was acutely sensitive to his views, as he headed the bureau responsible for trade negotiations. Ogura's bold article opened a new front in the country's foreign policy debate with its demand that Japan should forget about aping the West and turn its attention to spreading 'universal Asian values' around the world. 'Asia' had been 'created artificially, used politically, exploited economically and plundered culturally' by the West, he wrote, but had now emerged for probably the first time in history with a substance that was both steadfast and real. 'Asia should thoroughly absorb what the West has offered, and develop a new set of universal values that it can transmit to the world. The solution [to the problems of modernisation] is not necessarily to be found in Western civilisation.'[19]

The first problem that Ogura ran into was the same that confronted many people who had traversed similar territory—that Asia, an area which covers 17 million square miles and thousands of ethnic and linguistic groups, doesn't exist as a single entity. The idea of Japan and Asia is also meaningless unless it is broken down into its parts. Japan's relations with China and South Korea, where the memories of the war and colonialism are strongest, are quite different to its ties with Thailand, Malaysia and Indonesia. Taiwan was also a colony of Japan's, but it admires Tokyo more than it resents it. On the same symbolic day in 1995—the 50th anniversary of the end of the war—that South Korea began pulling down the former

Japanese governor-general's residence, a hated building in the centre of Seoul, the Taiwanese president, Lee Teng Hui, went to work as usual in his office in Tokyo's old colonial head-quarters. Even on its own terms, Ogura's thesis was rather shaky. He confessed that the new 'Asian spirit' was 'visible only in outline and only vaguely at that'. Groping around for examples of the Asianisation of the globe, he came up with a hotch-potch of examples, like the proliferation of world-class Korean violinists, the popularity of Japanese management techniques and hoary old chestnuts like 'harmony' and the 'family'.

Ogura's aim was true on one major issue. If the new Asia stood for anything, it was as a testament to Japan's postwar economic miracle. The Japanese are proudly boastful about this. 'Half of the prosperity of south-east Asia is the achievement of Japan', said former senior diplomat Hisahiko Okazaki.[20] Where Ogura's assertiveness fell flat was on Japan's political agenda—a point sharply made by a senior colleague who penned a reply to Ogura's article. Tadashi Ikeda, then head of the ministry's Asian Affairs Bureau, a position from which you would normally expect an official to be a captive of the 'new Asianism', chastised Ogura for taking refuge in a 'simplified ideal' of 'Asia as One'. For Ikeda, the 'Asia as One' slogan sounded dangerously like wartime Japan's catch-cry of Tokyo bringing 'all the corners of the earth under one roof', and he warned that such notions could revive memories of Japan's darkest days. 'Narrow-minded Asianism runs the risk of being taken as attaching priority to the unity and interests of non-white people, something that is in no way desirable, as proven from the war-time relations between Japan and other countries in Asia', Ikeda wrote.[21] Here Ikeda was getting to the nub of the argument—that Japan was in no position to lead Asia at all. Standing between Japan and its neighbours and, until recently, the Soviet Union, was America's nuclear arsenal, and the US troops stationed on Japanese soil. As long as they stayed there, Japan's political power and ability to speak with an independent voice would be stifled. What was also clear was that most Japanese, and nearly all their neighbours, preferred it that way.

This single, fundamental fact undermined all pretensions of the Japanese to show political leadership in the region and elsewhere, but you often wouldn't have known it living in Japan. With a few notable exceptions, it is a rare foreign political leader visiting Japan these days who does not urge his or her hosts to show greater 'leadership' in the world. Japan is an economic giant, but a political pygmy, the script goes, and the natural order of things requires that the two roles somehow be balanced. 'You have nothing to be afraid of. Get a little confidence!' Margaret Thatcher told her audience in one of her many lecture tours to Japan extolling her brand of leadership. But those who wanted to harness Japan's political and economic clout had conflicting agendas. Leadership for former US Secretary of State James Baker meant buying more American products and making bigger military contributions to the Western alliance. Leadership for Malaysia's prime minister Mahathir meant signing on to his Asians-only trade group, the East Asian Economic Caucus (EAEC), and standing up to the pushy Americans. Leadership for most Japanese meant hedging their bets, keeping their heads down, and swinging between both camps.

These calls for Tokyo to show leadership put business and political leaders into a terrible stew, and invariably resulted in many of the most popular headlines in the Japanese press— about Japan being put in a 'difficult position'. In the week before the summit of Asia–Pacific leaders in Indonesia in late 1994, I counted at least four—Japan was simultaneously caught 'in a difficult position' between the competing demands of China and Taiwan; between developing and industrialised countries on free trade; between two groups on the details of an investment code; and strung between Asian and Western countries on the issue of human rights. Underlying the 'difficult position' in each case was the age-old dilemma—whether Japan was part of the East or West, a member of Asia or an instrument of the United States, which is how the debate between the likes of Baker and Mahathir was broadly structured.

Mahathir dangled the prospect of China joining his trade caucus in front of a reluctant Tokyo in an attempt to lure it into signing on. It was just one of the many ploys that Mahathir tried in his long-running campaign to win Japan over. He surprised Prime Minister Murayama during a trip to Malaysia in late 1994 by saying that Japan should stop apologising for the war. 'Joining the EAEC will be much more meaningful than a thousand apologies for events that took place more than half a century ago. If Japan really wants to make amends, the EAEC would do so much better than the Diet passing resolutions expressing regret', he said.[22] The response of China and South Korea to this cynical and rather ridiculous conscience-cleanser for Japan is not recorded.

Mahathir had announced the EAEC at a time when negotiations to liberalise international trade were stalled by a dispute over farm subsidies between Europe and the United States. He said it would provide a voice for Asia in global forums that were dominated by Westerners. But Mahathir's aggressive anti-American rhetoric, and Washington's virulent response, soon turned the EAEC into a sort of smelly litmus test of Japan's loyalty to Asia or the West. Mahathir wasn't solely to blame for upping the stakes. Secretary of State James Baker brutally went out of his way to derail the project. During a meeting with the South Korean Foreign Minister in Seoul in 1991, Baker reportedly thundered across the table at his prevaricating host to remind him where his loyalties lay. 'Malaysia didn't shed blood defending [South Korea]—America did!'.

Many Japanese got a kick out of Mahathir's anti-Western broadsides. 'Japanese people are finding in Mahathir a defiant voice which they themselves cannot raise out of fear of upsetting ties with the US', wrote Masahiko Ishizuka in the *Nikkei Weekly*. 'In a sense, the Malaysian leader is an alter ego for the Japanese.'[23] But faced with a choice between a small Asian nation of 17 million people and the world's sole superpower, and its security provider, Japan was always going to go Washington's way. By contrast, the rival body to the Asians-only caucus, the Asia Pacific Economic Co-operation (APEC) forum, demanded none of these choices. It was omni-directional, straddling the Pacific, embracing the three Chinas (mainland China, Taiwan, Hong Kong), and drawing in South-east Asia and Australia and New Zealand as well. The EAEC threatened to isolate Japan as an Asian power, and force it into a role of political leadership in the region that it neither wanted nor was prepared for. APEC, by contrast, oozed with that most Japanese and Asian quality, harmony, when it wasn't being dominated by Washington.

In the meantime, the Japanese well knew they would be attacked whatever they did—criticised if they did not substantially increase military spending, and denounced if they did. Japan was caught in a similar bind when trying to use its economic power to influence the policies of neighbouring countries.

CHINESE SHADOWS

When Prime Minister Tomiichi Murayama met the Chinese President, Jiang Zemin, during the 1994 APEC summit in Indonesia to formally seal Japan's latest aid package to its neighbour, he muttered a short protest about Beijing's recent nuclear test, and then moved quickly on to another less sensitive topic. Or to quote the precise phrase used by the Japanese press in reporting the meeting, Murayama uttered the protest with a 'heavy mouth', an expression which means he was reluctant to say anything at all. Japan had agreed to lend China a massive

Y580 billion ($7.7 billion) for three years from 1996 for 40 different projects, in the fourth and final round of a series of programs which had commenced in 1979. It wasn't as though Murayama was not well within his rights to raise the issue. China flunked all three tests set by Japan in 1991 as benchmarks to qualify for its lucrative yen loans. China tested nuclear weapons, was rapidly lifting arms spending, and made no secret of its disdain for Western notions of democracy and human rights—all big no-nos, according to the letter of Tokyo's aid program.

But Murayama's protest, as brief and ritualistic as it was, didn't calm Jiang, who launched into an aggressive reply about 'certain historical facts'—code for Japan's war against China. 'It's no good that militaristic views still emerge from time to time in Japan', Jiang steamed. Ryutaro Hashimoto, who was also present as MITI minister, reportedly glared away in anger and embarrassment at the Chinese leader's humiliation of his prime minister. Jiang showed remarkable gall in pocketing the money and lecturing the donor at the same time, but he got away with it easily. The Chinese leader's performance was more than just a reminder that Beijing regarded Japan's money not as aid, but as de facto war reparations, to which no strings could be attached. The incident was a textbook study of Japan's inability, and refusal, to use its aid money power for overtly political ends.

In most respects, the conditions laid down by Japan to receive its aid were classic *tatemae*—in other words, just a facade to encourage Westerners to believe that the democratically-minded Japanese would apply the same human rights standards that they did. In truth, the Japanese government repeatedly ignored human rights abuses in recipient countries. After the Thai military coup in 1991, the US suspended aid but Japan kept it flowing. A Thai diplomat told me how he had reacted in a meeting with Japanese government officials when there was a suggestion that Japanese aid would be cut. 'Do you want to act like that big bully, America?' he said, banging the table for emphasis.[24] Japan kept aid flowing to Indonesia after troops killed protesters in East Timor in 1991, without having to explain itself to noisy pressure groups, as the governments of Australia and the US had to, or publicly criticise President Suharto. Never once did Japan explicitly link human rights in East Timor to aid, and its diplomats carefully calibrated their criticisms to keep them a few notches below the condemnations issued by Western nations. A senior Japanese diplomat told me that the government had written a private letter outlining its views to President Suharto, who had circulated it at a cabinet meeting and ordered his ministers to take note of its contents, and essentially that was that. The US suspended aid when Peruvian president Alberto Fujimori staged a coup in 1992. Japan expressed concern and regret, but did nothing more. Japan was also the first country to resume a dialogue and aid to the governments of China and Myanmar after the crackdown on student protesters in both countries.

An American expert on Japanese aid, Robert Orr, said Tokyo's responses proved 'it was not yet ready to exercise leadership in the area of democracy'.[25] Tokyo officials sometimes like to reduce differences on such issues to conflicts over style rather than substance to mollify Western critics. But in truth, the Japanese see their approach unambiguously as a virtue—a low-key, consensual 'Asian' way of making one's objections known, without crudely attempting to interfere in the affairs of a friendly sovereign nation or threatening its stability. Japan practises the politics of economic growth, and has little interest in policing human rights in neighbouring countries. It possesses neither the missionary zeal, nor the ideological idealism of the West. In the case of its giant neighbour, Japan also lacked the credibility to give lectures, something that Beijing exploited ruthlessly.

China's cynical use of war guilt had long cowed all manner of Japanese institutions, including the media. Japan's major newspapers were given permission to station reporters in China in the mid-1960s only after they gave undertakings not to pursue 'a hostile policy' towards Beijing, nor plot to create 'two Chinas',[26] and they continue to pull their punches today. The one paper that refused to give these guarantees, the conservative *Sankei Shimbun*, has never been allowed to open a bureau in China. The *Sankei* has offices in the 'rebel capital' of Taipei, but every other major Japanese media newspaper and television organisation still refuses to station correspondents there, for fear of offending Beijing. Taiwan is covered discreetly out of Hong Kong. Japan's national broadcaster, NHK—its equivalent of the BBC—has what insiders call a 'three-T' policy to tread carefully whenever mentioning the touchy topics of Taiwan, Tibet and the Tiananmen Square massacre.[27] Not surprisingly, NHK journalists refer to the killing of hundreds of protesters in central Beijing as the Tiananmen Square 'incident', not 'massacre', which at least makes it perversely consistent with the way Japanese school textbooks long described the Nanking 'incident'.[28]

China's nuclear tests, however, posed an entirely different challenge. The tests were an aggressive projection of Chinese power, and a direct challenge to Japan. China's actions also opened the way for France, and possibly the United States, to resume testing as well. Murayama's mealy-mouthed protest and Jiang's sharp rejoinder were harshly criticised in Japan. So when China conducted another test in May 1995, Tokyo announced a cut in aid, and also delayed a loan granted through the Ex-Im Bank. The sanctions were announced with great fanfare, but they were not so momentous in the fine print. Tokyo stopped only a small amount of its humanitarian aid, and left the big-ticket economic assistance items intact. The sanctions' significance lay solely in their symbolism. For Japan, at least, they were strong and important signals of a more assertive approach to dealing with its neighbour. A third Chinese test in August 1995, provoked a similar Japanese response—and a traditional retort from the Chinese Ambassador in Tokyo suggesting that Japan reflect on the 'damage' it had caused other nations.

Japan's reluctance to confront China is understandable. In an ideal world, Japan desires neither a weaker China nor a stronger China. A weaker China raises visceral fears of chaos and instability, with the threat of hundreds of thousands of refugees, and greater demands for aid. A stronger China and its 1.2 billion market is a potential economic nirvana, but it could also be a launching pad for Beijing's unpredictable political ambitions as a regional rival and adversary. In Tokyo's most insecure moments, and they are not infrequent, China is presumed to have the ability to isolate Tokyo internationally. At the height of the Clinton administration's tensions with China in 1995, Tokyo government officials and scholars talked not so much of the regional instability that the clash might cause, rather, they looked fearfully into the future and worried about the new phenomenon of America 'by-passing' Japan, as the benefits to Washington of cosying up to China become so much greater. 'America will become interested in China, rather than endeavouring to continue its hard-bargaining with such a foreign country as Japan, which will not move unless America uses a crowbar', warned academic Iwao Nakatani.[29]

Japanese leaders often discuss cosying up to China and Asia themselves as an alternative to the West. But the prospect of an alliance with China is so daunting, and unreal, that it sends them scurrying back under the shelter of the US nuclear umbrella. In other words, after reams of rhetoric about Japan's Asian roots, the Japanese end up back where they started—in big brother's fold. Ichiro Ozawa encapsulated Japan's dilemma as bluntly and cynically as anyone in an astoundingly frank interview in 1994. Ozawa was not a politician to hide behind the much-touted notion of Japan as a unique 'peace-loving nation',[30] and his refreshing views are worth quoting at length.

> Can Japan survive without America? Absolutely not. Because if that happens, we will not be able to obtain resources anywhere. Asian partners would shun doing business with Japan, and that means we would lose our market in Asia . . . But more fundamentally, it is because Japan swings back and forth emotionally like a pendulum. For many Asian neighbours, Japan appears to be a country with its finger in the wind.
>
> Do you know why America is keeping up its alliance with Japan? That's because tying up with Japan is only rational in view of the international situation today, nothing more. America will not drive Europe into isolation, that's for sure. But toward Japan? Who knows? America is looking at Japan with a cool glance. America might come to deliver a note of divorce, declaring 'OK Japan. That's it. We have decided not to associate with you anymore.' That very moment, I'm afraid, Japan would lose its ground and become rootless. That's the end of Japanese diplomacy. So we must prove that Japan will always be an important ally and partner who is willing to shoulder the world leadership with America.

Japan's embarrassing impotence was brought home most sharply during the Gulf War. After a few years of airy commentary about how economic power was surpassing military might in the post-Cold War era, the Japanese only had to turn on their television sets at night to find out which country was the most powerful in the world. The video-game shots of the American jet fighters zapping the hapless Iraqis were invariably followed by shots of Japanese politicians wringing their hands and vacillating about how they could contribute to the allies. Saddam Hussein must have regretted it was the United States, and not Japan, that led the fight to make Kuwait's fiefdoms and oil wells safe for the world, because it took them months to make up their minds to pay money. To demands that it provide concrete backing to the anti-Iraq coalition—in other words, to do more to secure a world that it increasingly owned—Japan during the Gulf crisis reacted with a mixture of 'evasiveness, humility, resentment and arrogance'. After trying and failing to send a 'peace corps' of troops, Japan eventually contributed nothing but cash—$17.3 billion. And to America and Europe's anger, it did so only after an interminable debate and sustained external pressure. 'Japan learned that respect cannot be purchased', wrote Francis Fukuyama and Kongdan Oh.

> *Kinken gaiko* (money diplomacy), which comes naturally to a country in which politics is basically the practice of *kinken seiji* (money politics) is not a substitute for military force. Offering money only seemed to reinforce the impression abroad that Japan is exclusively a business enterprise (Japan, Inc.) interested only in making and spending money.[31]

The shock of the Gulf War did provide a circuit-breaker for politicians like Ozawa who wanted to loosen the straitjacket of the postwar constitution and lift Japan's global military role. But it still took two whole years after the invasion, and months of delicate political negotiations capped off by four excruciating all-night sessions of the Diet, before the parliament passed a bill allowing Japanese troops to join UN peacekeeping operations overseas. The Japanese troops were only allowed to carry light arms, and their commanders retained the power to withdraw them immediately should any fighting break out nearby. When the troops did go to Cambodia on their first overseas mission, they distinguished themselves not by their warrior-like deeds, but by the comfortable quarters and Japanese-style hot tubs that they took with them. And when a number of Japanese civilian police were killed, the samurai of old was nowhere to be seen—in fact, many of the troops meekly asked to be allowed to come home.

The major check on any Japanese military expansion

remains public opinion, both in Japan and in the Asia that Japan is said to now dominate. For a host of other reasons, ranging from a deep-seated allergy to projecting military power, to unresolved war guilt and Japan's longtime attachment to the West, the present consensus decrees that Japan's position in Asia is, and should be, anchored by the United States. The sole regional leader who consistently asserts that the American military is no longer needed or wanted in Asia is Mahathir. The Malaysian prime minister may one day prove to have been visionary on this point. He also makes the point that while America may be in the Pacific to protect Japan, it holds no brief to help Malaysia. But for the moment, Mahathir seems unable to recognise that the one way to shatter his pan-Asian ideal would be to conscript Japan to lead it. Likewise, the Japanese are not sure whether they want to be fully fledged Asians anyway. In public, Japan enthuses about its return to its regional roots, but in private, there is ambivalence and a deal of agony, a feeling that is generally reciprocated in Asian countries. 'The Japanese are Japanese', a friend, an advertising executive, once told me. 'We were never brought up to feel part of Asia, and I never categorise myself as Asian.'

The momentum in Japan intellectually, economically and politically may be away from the West and towards Asia. Emotionally, however, it is a different story.

HEART TO HEART

When film director Yojiro Takita was searching for a country in which to set a movie about Japanese businessmen abroad bribing corrupt Asian leaders—a common enough occurrence, he says—he didn't have to look far to find one. Carving out a bit of Bangladesh and Burma, he called the new country Talckistan. The people who live there are called 'Talcs', naturally, and like a lot of people in Asia and elsewhere, when they see the Japanese coming, they think of only one thing—money. 'It's true', the director said, when I met him in a small coffee shop in Tokyo. 'The Japanese are dominated by money-making ventures.'

In the film, *We Are All Still Alive*, two pairs of Japanese businessmen from rival Japanese construction companies compete to win a bridge-building contract to be financed by development aid from Tokyo. The businessmen match their wits and their gifts at every turn. But just as one has outbid and outbribed the other, and won the contract, the recipient of their generosity, the crafty Talc despot, is deposed in a coup. All four businessmen are then plunged into a *Lord of the Flies*-like trek through the jungle to safety. The journey also acts as a sort of personnel odyssey through the frustrations of the hapless Japanese salaryman (*sarariman*, or white-collar worker), thanklessly toiling abroad for his country and company. 'Of course, we are Japanese', says Takita. 'But in the eyes of foreigners, we have no face. We are just products—cars and electrical goods and the like. And when there are international crises, Japan just contributes money. We have no identity. I am not saying we are no good any more, but we have to work together to create our own identity. Self-criticism is important.'[32]

We Are All Still Alive is a witty movie about the serious issue of how a rich, insular country like Japan relates to developing countries in Asia that crave its technology and aid. The movie and its promotional material, however, unconsciously mimicked its own critique of Japan's 'vertical relations' with its Asian neighbours by stereotyping them as tightly as they pigeonholed the Japanese businessmen. Just as the businessmen are slick, insensitive and crooked, the locals are backward, naive and corrupt. Some of this was satire, but some of it was not. The publicity notes for the film's Japan release contained details of the prices paid to hire props to make the movie. A tank, with fuel and a driver, cost Y50 000 ($660) a day; an elephant Y25 000 ($330); and a cobra Y2500 ($33). But to hire an extra in Thailand, where the film was shot, set the film-makers back only Y200 ($2.60) a day. 'Why is hiring people cheaper than hiring a snake? And why are Asians cheaper than whites?' the publicity notes quipped. After the shooting was finished, the publicity notes said that the cast and crew returned to Japan to be 'rehabilitated' back into 'normal society'. Takita believes that the movie's *sararimen*, like most of his countrymen, can never truly cast off their Made-in-Japan straitjackets. 'Even if this character tries to deny it in himself, he is still Japanese.' Switching briefly into English, Takita smiled and confessed, 'Me too'.

Japan's love–hate relationship with Asia is still infused with memories of war and colonialism, but it has also developed another layer. The Japanese that Asians now see are business-men bent on a profit, *sararimen* on sexual sprees and young women flashing credit cards in shopping malls. More recently, young Japanese women have also been going on their own sex tours in the region, a topic we will cover in a later chapter. There are also, of course, well-behaved Japanese tourists and lots of companies wisely investing in Asia and providing jobs. But there are enough 'ugly Japanese' who flock to Asia solely for shopping, sun and sex to ensure that Tokyo's relations with its neighbours retain a cool, colonial flavour, and a visceral, emotional under-current.

No country exemplifies the deep and contradictory com-plexes that these Asian nations still harbour more than South Korea. For half a century, Seoul nurtured its grudge against Japan for its harsh colonial rule from 1910 to 1945. The Japanese stripped Koreans of their names, their language and their cul-ture. They conscripted their men to work as labourers, and their women to work as prostitutes. After the end of the war and liberation, the 'sentiment' of the Korean people dictated a ban on all Japanese magazines, films or books, and also encouraged a large industry dedicated to publishing any critical material about their neighbour. Seoul's first tentative efforts to ease the culture ban ended in disaster in early 1994 because it coincided with renewed bickering over compensation for the wartime sex slaves. Protesters barged into a museum in Seoul and smashed display cases containing priceless exhibits of some of Japan's officially designated national treasures. They said they were angry about Japan's 'insufficient war reparations program'. The next attempt was a qualified success, mainly because Tokyo's cultural denizens decided to put on a decidedly un-Japanese show for their country's sensitive and symbolic return to the Seoul stage. The organisers ditched plans to stage something traditional, like a Kabuki play, or a Noh drama. Instead, with scores of armed guards circling the theatre to prevent violent demonstrations, the Tokyo troupe staged a Japanese-language production of the musical *Jesus Christ Superstar*.

Far from criticising this pseudo-religious Western musical for masquerading as Japanese culture, most commentators commended it as a canny, politic and sensitive way to return to the stage, and not just because one-third of South Koreans are Christians. The musical was a smart choice because it did not present the face of Japan that elderly South Koreans remembered from their youth, and that young people now learn about at school. But even *Jesus Christ Superstar*, although it was packed most nights and very popular, managed to offend sections of the Korean media still struggling to cope with the breach of the taboo on all things Japanese. One paper likened it to a 'performance under martial law', while another dismissed it as a 'beachhead for the arrival of [Japanese] popular culture'. Despite the musical's success, the official cultural ban was quietly reimposed when the season finished.

Japan-bashing is still one of Korea's national sports and favourite pastimes, and remains a sure-fire formula for a best-selling book. One fantasy work of fiction, *The History of the*

Korean Empire's Invasion of Japan, reassuringly turned truth on its head, and had Seoul taking over and colonising Tokyo. A Korean television journalist, Chon Yo-ok, returned from a two-and-a-half-year stint in Tokyo in 1994 to write one of the most withering (and popular) books, called *Japan Isn't*. I had a personal dose of her views when we worked in neighbouring offices in NHK headquarters in Tokyo for a period. One day, after she asked a colleague what he really thought of the Japanese, and he gave a polite, politically correct reply—about their having 'good and bad points' and so on—he asked for her opinion. 'I really hate them', she replied flatly. A mild-mannered, gentle woman in person, she wrote a searing book which ascribed Japan's success not to its people's diligence and industrial ingenuity, but to its exploitation of the Korean and Vietnam wars, and the American consumer market. 'We have nothing to learn from them. Japan is not a model that South Korea should follow.' Chon's book sold nearly 700 000 copies, and turned her into an instant celebrity on the lecture circuit in South Korea.

But there is a flipside to this intense dislike of Japan that any casual visitor to Seoul cannot fail to notice, but that some, like Chon, choose to ignore. No country more resembles Japan than South Korea, all the way from the government's economic policies to youth fashions. Even Korean cars look Japanese—for good reason. Japanese cars are barred in South Korea, but the Korean cars built by big companies like Hyundai and Daewoo are built with Japanese designs and technology. The same goes for the book market. Chon's best-seller, *Japan Isn't*, was matched by a book by a former South Korean diplomat, *Japan Is*. He complained that Chon's book was a throwback to the attitudes reflected in ancient Chinese records, which referred to the Japanese as 'dwarf people'. 'Japan succeeded as a result of her practical values and open-minded study', he said.[33] His book sold a respectable number of copies, but his message was never going to be as popular as Chon's.

Such post-colonial contradictions and complexes are embedded in the psyche of young South Koreans. In one opinion poll, young Koreans said they disliked Japan more than any other country. The same students put Japan at the top of the countries they wanted to emulate. 'On an emotional level, most Koreans condemn anything Japanese', said the *Korea Herald*. 'But rationally and subconsciously, they are envious and fearful of the universally recognised credentials and exploits of Japan in economics, science and culture.' Another survey published in the weekly *AERA* magazine recorded 61.7 per cent of people polled in South Korea as hating Japan. Sixty-five per cent of the Koreans surveyed also said they thought the Japanese hated them. In the same poll, only 16 per cent of the Japanese surveyed said they disliked Koreans, but 76 per cent admitted they thought that Koreans hated them. 'The shameful legacy [of the colonial period] is so deeply rooted in the hearts of South Koreans that even today there is no sign that the deep chasm between the two peoples can easily be filled', the *Asahi Shimbun* reported.[34]

This kind of sentiment will take a long time to soften, but occasionally it eases, enough, for example, for Korea's national broadcaster, KBS, to broadcast a soap opera in 1995 with a plot unthinkable just a few years ago—a love story between a Korean man and Japanese woman. Despite the official culture ban, there is also a thriving underground trade in Japanese pop CDs and comics, and a new enthusiasm amongst young people for the study of Japanese language and history. South Korea is, in fact, very much like other Asian countries in this respect. Japan's cultural exports are not ikebana and the tea ceremony, but up-to-date consumer products, and pastimes like video games and karaoke singing. The youth subcultures in Taiwan and to some extent in Hong Kong are also identifiably Japanese, and in Thailand, there is even a special word—*Dek Tot*—to describe teenagers hooked on trends from Tokyo. Some ultra-nationalists like the politician Ishihara take these trends to indicate that there is a common cultural sensibility throughout Asia. In his book with Mahathir, Ishihara cites the regional success of the weepy Japanese soap opera *Oishin* as an example of merging pan-Asian sensibilities. But in truth, the box office receipts of these shows pale next to money earnt by Hollywood. The Asian youth sub-cultures are also only Japanese in the way they absorb, adapt and mimic the trappings of the dominant global youth culture coming out of the United States. The form is Japanese, but the content is Western.

Selling Asia back to Japan is just as problematic. One of the most successful of a small new breed of pan-Asian performers is Singaporean singer Dick Lee. In a typically schizoid cultural twist, one of the secrets of Dick Lee's success in Japan is that he sings in English. Other Asian entertainers who perform in their own languages, like Indonesian and Cantonese, are classified as 'ethnic'. 'For Asians, Japan is like a mecca in the entertainment business, but the trouble for a lot of them in Japan is that they don't sing in English', Lee told me. Lee's biggest hit in Japan was a pan-Asian 'oriental pop-opera' Nagra Land in which an Asian youth so Westernised that he had become a 'banana' (yellow on the outside, and white on the inside) is transported into a mystical world which transcends East and West. The musical was written by a Singaporean (Lee), directed by an Indonesian, choreographed by a Malaysian, produced by a Japanese and starred a Filipino. The sponsor, naturally, was Japanese—the Mitsubishi Corporation.

The relative success of the musical convinced Lee that his theme tapped a chord in Japan.

> The Japanese are Asians, and that's something they can never run away from. When they go overseas to the West, they are perceived as Asians. I find I get lots of letters from people [here] who say they only used to listen to Western music. I play all over Asia

with the same message and I get the same response from all of them. [But] I am trying to redeem the image of Asians—I'm saying we are not all the same—why look down on us. Here comes a guy from Singapore who is not a labourer. Take another look. One of my songs is called 'You don't know me at all'. You think you know me, but you don't. We share a history, except you don't know anything about it, except some vague idea of regret. You should get to know me, I tell them, but I think it will take another generation.

Lee has struggled to transcend Asia's static and out-of-date image inside Japan. Young Japanese still mostly bypass 'exotic' Asia to look for inspiration in Europe and America, and many people carry the same negative stereotypes about their neighbours that Westerners do. The first stereotype of Asians is as cheap labour, something, ironically, that Japanese authorities went out of their way to avoid. When employers started complaining they couldn't find workers at the start of the decade, the Labour Ministry initially eased regulations for people of Japanese origin from Brazil and Peru, while keeping Asians out 'to preserve racial harmony'. Their race, rather than their colour, was the determining factor. But the ugliest manifestation of the image of 'Asia' in Japan is the sex trade—both in Japanese men travelling to Asia on sex tours, and Asians being transported, sometimes knowingly, sometimes not, to work as prostitutes in Japan. Westerners are not so free of sin that they can cast the first stone on this issue, but the scale of Asian prostitution in Japan far outstrips that in any other country. So blatant are sex tours that a mainstream Tokyo publisher released a travel book in 1994 for men travelling to Thailand on sex tours. Written by four members of a group studying 'sex manners and customs in Asia', *Textbook for Prostitution in Thailand* gave details of clubs to buy sex, listed prices and Thai phrases for chatting with hostesses. The first print run of 15 000 quickly sold out. The book was retailed in ordinary bookshops for about six months before a campaign by support groups for Asian women forced its withdrawal.[35]

The same support groups made a cause célèbre of the case of three Thai women convicted of killing a bar worker who they said had forced them into prostitution. The facts of the case were depressingly familiar to anyone who had followed the boom in flesh trafficking into Japan in the early 1990s. Two of the women claimed they were recruited in Thailand with a promise they would be working in a restaurant, and the third said she was told she would get a job at a factory in Japan. But on arriving at the airport in Tokyo in January 1991, the three women were traded through a number of brokers before being handed over to a pimp, a compatriot by the name of Lek, whom they would later kill. In the process of being bought and sold, the women ran up tens of thousands of dollars in debts which they had to repay by selling themselves in a small bar in rural Japan. The three women were convicted of murdering Lek and were sentenced to ten years in jail. Two other groups of Thai prostitutes later killed their bosses in separate incidents while trying to escape, and were also convicted and jailed. But the first trio won a modicum of justice while they were behind bars. Their supporters successfully sued the bar owner for the women's back wages. The judge said 'unspeakable psychological damage' had been inflicted on the women, and awarded them Y12.2 million ($160 000) in wages in arrears. It was a somewhat weird, but well-rounded end to the case—the women had traded their lives for a small fortune in yen, fulfilling the deal that had been made for them when they arrived in Japan.

An investigation by the *Tokyo Journal* found that Lek had spent Y56 million ($760 000) to buy 28 Thai women in the nine months from January 1991 until her murder. There were many other traders like her—the numbers of Thais overstaying their visas rose from just over 2000 in 1987 to 53 383 in 1995, about half of whom are in the 'entertainment business', code for prostitution. The number of Filipinos was even higher— 42 000 of 76 000 who entered Japan in 1994 came on 'entertainment' visas. These women were soon exploited as a source of income by people other than their Japanese bosses. Officials from Manila's embassy in Tokyo began visiting bars to investigate 'complaints' from Filipino workers about labour conditions. In a number of cases, the officials' accommodation outside Tokyo was paid for by the bar owners, who also 'donated' equipment such as fax machines to the embassy when fault was found with the conditions.

As well as dealing with Japanese gangsters and corrupt compatriots, Asian women were also singularly identified with the AIDS virus. The large number of Asian women working as prostitutes has left Japan with one of the highest rate of women carrying the AIDS virus in the industrialised world (relative to total HIV-positive population). A Health Ministry survey in Tokyo reported that over 85 per cent of the 785 women in Japan who had been tested HIV-positive up until mid-1994, and more than half of the 55 women with full-blown AIDS, were foreigners, in other words, prostitutes from Asia.

For these Asians, Japan meant one thing—the yen, and all the opportunity and degradation that it entailed. One male Filipino labourer, Rey Ventura, wrote a book about the lives of Asian labourers, *Underground in Japan*. In one passage he captured perfectly the ambivalence that Asians felt towards their overpoweringly rich neighbour.

There is no Japanese dream, and yet Japan, for the Filipino, has become a second America. There is no Statue of Liberty in Yokohama—why should there be? A statue of Yen would be more appropriate. We do not dream of becoming Japanese citizens— even for the brides who achieve this, it is a secondary consideration. We do not imagine we will settle there for ever. We know that we will not be accepted and anyway we cannot imagine submitting to the extreme discipline of Japanese life.

Still, more and more, we see Japan as part of our future.

Japan embraced Asia with the same dismal enthusiasm that Asia felt in embracing Japan. But that did not lessen the political risks that such a move entailed. The return to Asia coincided with Japan's longest economic downturn since the war, and a collapse in confidence in the bureaucracy and the co-operative, state-guided capitalism that it espoused. So, in a crisis of leadership, with the ultimate certainties of the Cold War and the American alliance gone and Japan's Asian neighbours beckoning on the horizon, where did people turn? To the politicians? In Japan, this would be like gracing a billion-dollar airport with a ten-cent control tower. Politicians have long ruled Japan, but they have rarely run it. The day-to-day business of the government has been the preserve of bureaucrats. Out of the rubble of the bubble in the 1990s, a number of political leaders started a movement to build a new control tower to guide Japan, with themselves firmly behind the controls. But it has proved to be no easy task.

CHAPTER 4

MONEY POLITICS

'The closer the relationship between the politician and the industrial sector, the greater the political donations. Most of Japan's prime ministers have been implicated in questionable campaign-funding deals. They may not have liked being caught, but raising money is a pre-requisite for the office in the first place.'

Kazuo Aichi, politician

'The Japanese are a spiritual people, but also crassly pragmatic. This is perhaps their strength.'

Hideaki Kase, commentator

The most powerful man in Japan at the peak of the bubble economy was Shin Kanemaru, a grizzly political kingmaker with heavy-lidded eyes whose public utterances were delivered in a thick, barely discernible mumble. So inaudible were his muffled mutterings that when he was finally snared in a corruption scandal in late 1992 and called a press conference to announce his resignation from a top position in the ruling party, an aide had to re-read his official statement aloud to the assembled reporters, just to make sure they had understood what Kanemaru had said. Dubbed the 'don of the dons' by the Japanese media, Kanemaru could be clear and sharp if he wished, but mostly, he preferred to be more delphic than direct in public. His style matched his role—he was a *kuromaku* (a behind-the-scenes string-puller) in the classic tradition of Japanese politics, presiding over a vast political machine that operated as a kind of clearing house for government patronage. Business fed in enormous sums of money at the one end, and Kanemaru and his cronies doled it out at the other. With the money came power. As the leader of the largest and richest faction in the ruling Liberal Democratic Party (LDP), Kanemaru had been instrumental in choosing the previous four prime ministers, while remaining more powerful than them all.

Kanemaru arrived at the press conference unruffled, greeting reporters with a breezy '*Konnichi-wa*' ('Hello'), but his following announcement had an electrifying impact on the political world. The kingmaker confessed he had accepted a political donation of Y500 million ($6.6 million), and had breached the law by failing to declare it. 'I deeply regret accepting the money because it contradicts political ethics', Kanemaru said. But in his next breath, he thanked the businessman who had given him the cash, hand-delivered to his adviser in large parcels in the garage under his central Tokyo office, for his 'good will'.[1] The two successive statements were completely at odds, but entirely in character for Kanemaru. The first, the ritual apology, was to be the beginning of a 'purification' rite he thought would allow him to return to the frontlines of public life. With the second, Kanemaru was discharging, or at least acknowledging, his debt of obligation to the donor. It mattered little in his eyes that the businessman was at the centre of a massive influence-peddling investigation, and was himself under arrest. The traditional Japanese value of *giri-ninjo* (one's obligation to one's fellow man)—cited in equal parts by everyone from ordinary *yakuza* gangsters to powerful politicians to justify their behaviour—overrode any moral considerations.

After admitting to the offence, Kanemaru shut himself inside his large three-storey Tokyo apartment and flagrantly ignored demands by prosecutors that he submit himself for official questioning. For a full 35 days, Kanemaru remained at home, playing mah-jong, the Chinese game of chance, and receiving visits from loyal consorts bearing gifts of flowers and whisky. Scores of journalists maintained a 24-hour vigil outside. The press was joined by busloads of sightseers on weekends, who crowded into the narrow street in the up-market Azabu area to gaze up at the kingmaker's eyrie. Sympathetic tabloids compared Kanemaru to a 'besieged samurai' waiting patiently for the enemy to exhaust his energy.[2]

Kanemaru had an artful story to keep the prosecutors at bay. He claimed the Y500 million he received from the businessman was a 'seasonal gift' for himself, that he had distributed to his factional colleagues. Under Japanese law, prosecutors had to prove that Kanemaru granted the businessman a favour in exchange for the money to convict the politician of accepting a bribe. But if the money was simply a gift, he had only breached a relatively minor political funding law which says that all donations above Y1.5 million ($20 000) must be declared. Eventually, Kanemaru's loyal factional lieutenants negotiated a deal with the prosecutors—he would plead guilty to breaching this minor law, drafting his confession from the luxury of his home, in return for avoiding the humiliation of a public trial and paying the maximum fine of Y200 000 ($2600), roughly equivalent to the amount levied for repeated parking offences!

The deal done, Kanemaru emerged from isolation—ironically on Respect for the Law Day—and brazenly prepared to resume his role as the most powerful man in Japanese politics. But Kanemaru and his cronies had badly misjudged the mood of the times. His high-handed behaviour had not only sown the seeds of his own destruction. It also triggered bitter infighting in the ruling party, which ultimately left Japan's postwar political order in ruins.

SEASONAL GIFTS

To understand Kanemaru, you have to first understand the cult of gift-giving in Japan. Conservative commentator Hideaki Kase thinks that one important reason why politicians like Kanemaru were able to get away with being so corrupt for so long was because the Japanese people were all 'little Kanemarus' themselves, giving and receiving cash gifts on many different occasions throughout their lives. Take, for example, the Japanese wedding. 'Japanese couples, when they reach a certain level of maturity, are asked at least once or twice in their lives to play the role of go-betweens at the wedding ceremonies of their employees and subordinates', Kase wrote. The go-betweens praise the virtue of the bride and the families in their speeches, and a few days later, are called upon by the parents of the happy couple. The parents bring cash in a ceremonial envelope with special symbolic motifs—usually about Y200 000–300 000 ($2600–4000). They hand it to the go-between, mumbling discreetly, '*Kimochi desu*', meaning: 'This is just the expression of our feelings'.[3]

The Japanese logic runs as follows, says Kase. People who talk too much are undignified, so cash is a better means of expressing sincerity. Giving money is the Japanese way of saying 'We mean business'. Cash is a means of communication, and the magical word *kimochi* renders the money spiritual and sacred. 'It is no longer money, but a symbolic offering', Kase says. For the recipient, one million yen becomes much the same as 50 yen (66 cents). The sum isn't the point, because the money is just an expression of pure heart from the donor. To refuse it would cause a severe loss of face.

I learnt about *kimochi* money the hard way, when a water accident in my fourth-floor apartment in Tokyo flooded the units of the two families living immediately beneath me. After much haggling, the insurance company paid for the damage to my neighbours' apartments, but was unable to cover the cost of the hurt to their 'feelings'. My Japanese friends insisted that I had to give my neighbours some *kimochi* money as a sign of my 'sincerity' to finally settle the issue. The insurance man advised me to pay it as well, even though he admitted he could never insure me for it. The money was really a form of informal legal settlement, without lawyers or any laws. If I had pulled in a lawyer at any stage, I would have committed an unpardonable sin.

In Japan, lawyers are seen as a Western disease—cold-hearted, troublesome, adversarial and expensive—and the bureaucrats quarantine them like some necessary but dangerous bacteria. The Justice Ministry limits the supply of lawyers by allowing a quota of only about two out of every 100 law graduates who sit for the Bar exam to pass. So Japan has lots of law graduates, but only a few practising lawyers. In the absence of formal legal avenues for redress, vague concepts such as 'sincerity' and 'feelings' are easily manipulated and exploited. This is often done by *yakuza* gangsters, who have traditionally filled the legal vacuum left behind by cases of bad debts and traffic accidents. A similar ambiguity surrounds the cash that flows in dark subterranean channels through a myriad of transactions in the political world and leaves ample opportunity for all manner of camouflage for what in any other country would be out-and-out bribes. 'Between what the Japanese call *tatemae*, the beautiful facade, or ideals, and *honne*, the reality and the true business of life, there is an unbridgeable chasm', says Kase. 'Therefore, all criticism of politicians for money politics, however hysterical, remains strangely ineffectual. (Only words, no cash!) The Japanese are a spiritual people, but also crassly pragmatic. This is perhaps their strength.'

Nobody understood this psychology as well, and exploited it more ruthlessly, than the man who made Kanemaru and the money-addicted political system he thrived in, Kakuei Tanaka.

THE TANAKA FACTOR

When he first stood for election in 1947, Tanaka ran on the conservative ticket, but wooed Socialist-leaning farmers by promising to send them 'highways, schools, reclamation projects, tunnels, railroads and snow removal services in return for their votes'.[4] And that's exactly what he did—then and for the rest of his political career for the next four decades. To ensure that these prizes of public works were constructed where he decided they were deserved, Tanaka built the wealthiest and most powerful political machine in the history of Japan. His credo was simple: 'Politics comes from power, power is in numbers, and numbers depend on money'.[5] Naturally, Tanaka attempted to drape his big-time money-politics in a homely coat of grass-roots 'culture'. In his memoirs, he recalled an episode in his childhood in which he stole some money from his mother's purse. She scolded him, but he retorted that he had used the money to look after his friends.[6] In his political life, he was doing nothing more than he did for his friends as a child. It was a tale that Shin Kanemaru would have been proud to tell himself.

Born in 1918 in the snow country of Niigata in western Japan, Tanaka was the son of 'a cattle broker and dissolute gambler'. He never finished high school and was the first modern Japanese prime minister not to have graduated from university. He was charged with bribery for the first time in

1948, and ran most of his campaign for re-election to parliament from his prison cell. But Tanaka had remarkable qualities which allowed him to steamroll all obstacles in his path—a raw, endearing and at times raunchy earthiness which captivated many ordinary Japanese, combined with superior intelligence and an extraordinary memory. His skills gave him the rare ability amongst Japanese politicians to take on and match the powerful bureaucrats on their own turf. 'He cultivated them, worked with them, outsmarted them and used them', says Japan scholar Chalmers Johnson. Bureaucrats were flattered that years after meeting them, Tanaka could remember not only their names, but the tiniest detail of the advice they had given him. Tanaka advised his protégés to learn to do the same. 'Study the bureaucrats' personnel structure so hard that you can remember it ten years later', he told them.[7]

But Tanaka did more than charm bureaucrats. He confronted them with all the force of the ruling LDP's biggest and wealthiest faction behind him. Tanaka knew better than anyone else that Japanese politics didn't run on fresh air, and built his power base by mastering the substance that did power it—money, the mother's milk of political life in Japan. Tanaka regularly gave out cash under the guise of customary gift-giving. Tanaka's victory in a nasty contest to become prime minister in 1972 was widely reported to have cost so much money—distributed in the form of gifts to individual politicians—that the country's inflation rate was nudged up by a few points. On one occasion in 1974, Tanaka gave out *o-chugen* (summer gifts) of Y3–5 million ($40 000–66 000) to *every* MP, and numerous bureau chiefs in the bureaucracy.[8] Tanaka's influence was so deeply entrenched that even when he was forced to resign as prime minister in 1974 after the Lockheed bribery case, he remained the most powerful man in politics. For more than a decade after he was charged with bribery, Tanaka ruled Japanese politics as the 'Shadow Shogun' from behind the scenes. He maintained control of his faction, which became popularly known as the *Tanaka gundan* ('Tanaka army corps'), and boosted its number to ensure it maintained its dominance of the ruling party. Changing prime ministers, he boasted to colleagues, was 'as easy as changing hats'.

Tanaka's sources of funds were multifarious, but the most important was the construction industry. Construction is both the biggest business in Japan, and one of the largest employers. In 1993, Japan had an astounding 530 665 construction companies, which employed 6.4 million people. This was an increase of 210 000 people on the previous year, despite the economic slump then prevailing. Massive public works programmes overseen by the Construction Ministry in Tokyo have always ensured there is ample work to go around. About 10 per cent of Japan's national budget in 1993 was earmarked for public works, an amount much greater than in the United States, a country with 25 times the land mass. Chalmers Johnson calculates that Japan spends *more* on public works than the Pentagon's military-industrial complex in the United States did on defence, even at the height of the Cold War.[9]

Tanaka codified the construction companies' political donations by plugging himself permanently into the cosy industry practice known as *dango*, or bid-rigging. Tanaka, and later Kanemaru, organised political protection for this system under which the companies rigged bids on public works to divide the jobs between themselves 'to keep the industry running smoothly'. 'Without adjustments, contractors are bound to come to blows amongst themselves', one construction company official told the *Yomiuri Shimbun*. 'Excessive competition will follow, forcing companies to undertake work at a loss.'[10] Japan's pro-competition body, the Fair Trade Commission, has long been powerless to stop the practice. Between 1990 and 1995, a time when prosecutors launched numerous high-profile raids against construction companies over *dango*, and the press raged against its practitioners, the commission prosecuted only two minor industries for what was in reality an everyday offence in large sections of the economy. The cost of *dango* is ultimately carried by the hapless Japanese taxpayer. A 1993 survey of the Federation of Road Constructors, the members of which receive the bulk of their work from public agencies, found that they averaged a profit of 11.9 per cent per job, compared with the government's guidelines of just 2 per cent. The taxpayer makes up the difference by paying exorbitant road tolls. The short three-hour drive from Tokyo to the resort area of Nikko, for example, is peppered with toll-collecting booths which extract Y8000 ($106) in tolls from each motorist by the end of the journey. The construction industry's power also explains why one of the first things you notice when you arrive in Japan, and the last thing you see when you leave, are gangs of men—and now women and foreigners, because of labour shortages—digging up the roads day and night.

Any doubts about Tanaka's deep involvement in bid-rigging were dispelled in an interview given by former Construction Minister Kosei Amano in 1994. He recalled how Tanaka, just after he had become prime minister, had shown him a list of 48 dam projects worth Y800 billion ($1.06 billion) with Tanaka's own bid-rigging scheme attached. In return, 'contractors were supposed to offer three per cent of the contract value for dam, road and railway construction projects' to Tanaka.[11] 'I'm all for bid-rigging', said Amano. 'What's wrong with bid-rigging if it helps the construction industry operate smoothly and secure jobs?'. The 3 per cent rake-off was delivered in cash to Tanaka personally at his wooded estate in Tokyo, even when he was Prime Minister. Amano complained that if the companies had not set aside exactly 3 per cent, then he had to make up the difference. Three per cent of water control projects alone in the years that Tanaka collected money equalled Y24 billion ($320 million).[12]

The Construction Ministry became the 'citadel' of the Tanaka faction and its cronies, and the font of institutionalised corruption in the political and business world. Academic Gavan McCormack described it as an arena where 'political bosses and gangsters, bankers and bureaucrats, rubbed shoulders and exchanged bundles of cash . . . and prime ministers (bought) office and then fed their troops'.[13] The same cast of characters and the collusive links between them were at the heart of the political upheaval which snared, and finally toppled, Shin Kanemaru.

KANEMARU FALLS

The night that Kanemaru and his cronies plotted to take control of the Tanaka faction in January 1986, the 'godfather' gathered secretly with 25 politicians in an exclusive *ryotei* restaurant in Tokyo, and announced: 'We are here to take a blood oath!'.[14] One commentator compared the ceremony to a *yakuza* ritual—'You kill the Boss, and declare: "I am the new Boss" '. Tanaka already had an inkling of his underlings' imminent treachery. He had recently sent Kanemaru's close ally, Noboru Takeshita, on the usual cash-collecting rounds, and had been livid to discover that the younger MP had been putting some of the money into his own accounts. Tanaka summoned Takeshita to a closed-door meeting, and disciplined him in the way a feudal lord might scold a disloyal vassal. Taking off his slipper, he slapped Takeshita's face with it, and yelled: 'You've still got another ten years to go! Go back to scrubbing floors!'.[15] But it was too late. A breakaway group was formed in February 1986, and 20 days after the audacious coup, Tanaka suffered a massive stroke which left him physically and politically paralysed.[16]

The three people behind the coup were Kanemaru, Takeshita and Ichiro Ozawa, another ambitious Tanaka acolyte who had been persuaded to jump ship as well. The ties that bound the three ran deep. Kanemaru's first son was married to Takeshita's daughter. Ozawa was also related by marriage to Takeshita through the sister of his wife.[17] The Tanaka faction was renamed the Takeshita faction, and Kanemaru was anointed as its behind-the-scenes leader. Together, the three had inherited a massive, money-hungry political machine. By the start of the 1990s, the average Japanese MP was spending Y100–200 million ($1.3–2.6 million) on each election campaign, and also paying the salaries of anything from thirteen to 30 extra staff hired to provide the sort of personal service demanded by voters between elections. Only two, and more recently three, staff members are paid for by taxpayers. Politics in Japan, and indeed in much of Asia, is a service industry. Politicians, or staff members in their place, must attend the weddings and funerals of important constituents and their relatives, where they hand over the customary cash gift in a suitably embossed envelope. MPs also provide a range of other labour-intensive services which involve them intimately in voters' lives. They find jobs for constituents' children, help them get into universities and sometimes even hunt out a prospective marriage partner. Most of the time, ideology and ideas do not get a look-in.

'Both techniques—bringing home the bacon and delivering it to the constituents—take a lot of money', said Kazuo Aichi, who was to emerge later as a leading member of the reformist clique in the Tanaka/Takeshita faction.

> That brings in the business element. The closer the relationship between the politician and the industrial sector, the greater the political donations. Most of Japan's prime ministers have been implicated in questionable campaign-funding deals. They may not have liked being caught, but raising money is a pre-requisite for the office in the first place.[18]

(The other, most oft-cited reason, for expensive electioneering

87

and institutional corruption, dubiously so in this writer's opinion, has been the electoral system, an issue we will return to later in this chapter.)

Politicians sometimes felt the need to remind the public of the high cost of running their businesses. The then Transport Minister Keiwa Okuda lost his temper with reporters during their vigil outside Kanemaru's home, and snapped: 'I would like you to know that Y500 million [$6.6 million] is not such a large amount. Politics costs money, and Mr Kanemaru has to secure many things going through his office!'.[19] This much was true. One of the many 'things' that Kanemaru had going through his office were payments to key members of the opposition Socialist Party to ensure the passage of legislation through the parliament. Even though the LDP had a solid parliamentary majority in the parliament, Japanese-style politics still required the ritual of consensus—and consensus required money. 'The flow of political funds was one of the worst-kept secrets in Japan', says political scientist Seizaburo Sato. 'The government and the opposition would gather in smoke-filled rooms, [and] script entire Diet sessions, deciding which bills would pass, and how much the government would amend them, to allow the opposition to keep up appearances.'[20]

With such expensive overheads, a young politician needed not so much eye-catching policies to build his or her career, but the right connections in Tokyo, both within the ruling party, and the powerful ministries. The first battle for new MPs is to attach themselves to the *zoku* or 'tribes' which cluster around ministries with clout and spending power. These MPs became known as *zoku giin*, or 'tribe MPs'. Thus, few MPs have any interest in joining committees concerning foreign affairs, or the Justice or Science and Technology ministries, because there isn't a buck to be made out of it.[21] Instead, most attempt to join the *zoku* attached to the Construction, Transport, Finance and Post and Telecommunications ministries, which oversee either public works spending or regulations which businesses will pay generously to get round or get rid of.[22]

The *zoku* system has had some positive effects, by involving politicians in policy as well as pork-barrelling. It has also increased the power and the leverage that politicians can exercise over bureaucrats, as we will see in Chapter Five. But the *zoku giin* system is a fecund source of corruption for bureaucrats and politicians alike. A senior Finance Ministry official, Eisuke Sakakibara, says most Japanese MPs 'serve, in effect, as executive treasury officers stationed in Tokyo for their various regional institutions' by cultivating strong relationships with rich and powerful ministries. The relationship between the *zoku* MP and the bureaucrat, he says, 'resembles that of business partners'.[23] Politicians openly flaunt their connections, and boast when campaigning for re-election about the big pipe(line) that they have into a ministry in Tokyo, which allows them to funnel benefits back out to their electorates. And it is the length of their pipes, as much as the content of their policies, that gets them re-elected.

Kanemaru was thus doing what was expected of a person in his position—milking businesses and providing favours at one end, and using the proceeds to dispense political patronage to his faction at the other. There are various theories about how and why he was caught, and prosecuted. That one should even ask how and why is indicative of what many commentators consider to be the arbitrariness of Japanese political scandals. Dutch journalist Karel van Wolferen maintains that scandals in Japan play a similar role to the courts in other countries in curbing the excesses of the system. 'Controlled scandals may bring anguish and pain to members of the elite', he says. 'They are like a garden hose; if the water is turned on before one gets hold of the nozzle, the hose may flap about and drench bystanders who were not expecting to get wet.' Van Wolferen's simile scarcely explains all the scandals that afflict the Japanese body politic, but it is true that scandals operate more to rein in individuals who have grown too big for their boots than to enforce a clear legal or moral code. The 'tall poppy' syndrome, criticised so sharply in Australia for discouraging risk·takers, operates potently in Japan to bring to heel people who have grown too powerful. And by the end of 1992, an array of forces were lining up to chop Kanemaru down.

The Finance Ministry, which sits at the apex of bureaucratic power in Japan, reportedly targeted Kanemaru in revenge for his campaign against its sacrosanct tight budget policies. At one point, Kanemaru called for the governor of the central Bank of Japan to be 'sacked' unless he cut interest rates. 'The Finance Ministry hated Kanemaru, and he lost his position after the Tax Agency [which is under its control] got him for tax evasion', said one top bureaucrat.[24] Even though it had little power in domestic political debates, the Foreign Ministry was also gunning for the 'godfather'. Japanese diplomats had been furious when Kanemaru travelled independently to Pyongyang in 1990 and promised the country's then dictator, Kim Il Sung, compensation for Tokyo's failure to establish official relations with North Korea since the war. It took years for the Foreign Ministry to disavow this untenable promise.

Another powerful group out to get Kanemaru was from the public prosecutor's office. Most Japanese white-collar workers wear small company badges on their lapels to identify their corporate loyalties. Japanese criminal prosecutors wear a badge with the motto *shuso-retsujitsu*—meaning 'autumn frost and blaz-ing sunlight'—as a symbol of 'the severe consequences of crime and their own serious duty'.[25] The prosecutors had been witheringly criticised after Kanemaru humiliated them over the Y500 million, and they wanted blood. So too did a public disgusted by the steady stream of corruption scandals. One 26-year-old office worker, (Ms) Uko Masui, wrote to a newspaper comparing Kanemaru's summary trial and tiny fine with her own recent experience at a police station, where she had gone to pay a parking ticket and had been held and interrogated for four hours. A comedian-turned-politician, Yukio Aoshima, gathered a 200 000-signature petition calling for Kanemaru's resignation, including messages from the crews in boats moored off the coasts of Angola and Peru.

Kanemaru might have been able to withstand the storm over the illegal Y500 million donation—the thousands of 'little Kanemarus' amongst the Japanese population have forgiven politicians for much worse—but he couldn't survive the revelation sprung by prosecutors in September 1992, at the trial of the businessman who had given him the money. Hiroyasu Watanabe, the president of a parcel delivery company, Tokyo Sagawa Kubin, said he had used a notorious gangland leader to help the successful campaign of Kanemaru's ally, Noboru Takeshita, to become Prime Minister in 1987. Armed with money from Takeshita's opponents, a small and obscure ultra-nationalist group called Kominto from the island of Shikoku had taken to the streets of Tokyo in sound trucks to campaign against the putative prime minister. Kominto used a tactic known as '*homegoroshi*'—meaning to damn with exaggerated, sarcastic praise—to harass Takeshita. The Kominto trucks circled the Diet, noisily broadcasting: 'Mr Takeshita is the greatest politician of all! Vote for Mr Takeshita! Nobody can raise money like Mr Takeshita! Mr Takeshita is the king of money politics!'. It was never clear who was behind the anti-Takeshita campaign. Some saw it as the handiwork of bitter Tanaka supporters avenging the treacherous coup against their boss. Whatever the motive, Kominto proved difficult to shut up. An envoy from Kanemaru approached the boss of Kominto, and offered him Y300 million ($4 million) to stop the campaign. 'Produce the Y300 million in front of my eyes. Make Kanemaru see if I grab it with my hands or kick it with my feet', the boss snarled.[26] The envoy did not approach him again.

That left just one avenue. Right-wing nationalist groups like Kominto proliferate in Japan and are often indistinguishable from *yakuza* gangsters, and it was to the underworld that Kanemaru now turned. Desperate to prevent the Takeshita campaign from being run off the rails, Kanemaru called on Watanabe, the head of the transport company, to intercede with an infamous *yakuza* boss, the head of the Inagawa-kai (Inagawa gang), Susumu Ishii. Ishii leaned on Kominto; the harassment stopped and Takeshita was elected by his party to succeed Yasuhiro Nakasone as Prime Minister. A few months later, Kanemaru the politician met Ishii the gangster to thank him for his help.

There have been numerous and well-documented links between right-wing politicians and *yakuza* gangsters over many years. But in the climate of hysteria over money politics, the public exposure in 1992 of Kanemaru and Takeshita's use of the underworld to win election to the highest office in the land was too much even for the Japanese system to bear. Takeshita stayed in parliament, but resigned from the LDP, and took himself into lengthy political purgatory to cleanse himself of his sins. Kanemaru was far more exposed. Coming on top of the bribery scandal, the scandal left the 'godfather' with nowhere to turn, and he resigned from parliament in October 1992. In testimony to a Diet inquiry given from his hospital bed, Kanemaru confessed to the *yakuza* connection, but showed no shame. It was another case of *giri-ninjo*, or obligation to one's fellow man. 'If your child falls in the river and nearly drowns, and someone helps that child and you later learn that person was a *yakuza* gang member, you are indebted to that *yakuza* gang member', he said. 'Public opinion says I am wrong for thanking a *yakuza*. But if I were helped by a *yakuza*, I would do so in line with my philosophy of life.'[27]

Kanemaru's kingdom quickly disintegrated around him. Emboldened prosecutors resumed their raids, and discovered a vast underground stash of cash, bank debentures and gold bullion hidden in buildings owned by Kanemaru and his family. The initial donation of Y500 million turned out to be a trifling amount. In the second wave of raids, prosecutors estimated they seized assets worth a whopping Y6.7 billion ($89 million) from Kanemaru. But even that staggering figure did not give anything like a true picture of the 'godfather's' black wealth. When his wife died the previous year, she had left behind Y5.2 billion ($69 million) for Kanemaru, and another Y409 million ($5.4 million) for her sister. Kanemaru had been paid Y23.5 million ($310 000) a year as a Diet member, but had somehow amassed a fortune of around Y12.3 billion ($164 million), not counting the value of his own property holdings. The mystery of who had made up the difference was quickly solved. It had mostly come in the form of cash contributions from a grateful construction industry, sometimes under the cover of the traditional gift-giving seasons, but otherwise as political donations or in exchange for successful bids on public works projects. The sums of money were cutely coded to conceal their purpose. 'Manju', in ordinary parlance a sweet bun filled with bean-paste, was the code word for bribes paid for successful public works bids. 'Coffee money' was a political donation disguised as entertainment expenses.

Prosecutors charged Kanemaru with evading billions of yen in income tax, and locked him up in a 1.8- by 2.7-metre cell in the Tokyo detention centre. The Japanese press reported in lurid detail, with accompanying diagrams, how the 'godfather' had been forced to bend over and undergo the compulsory rectal examination for new prisoners. He was then led off into solitary confinement, and fed a daily diet of cooked rice with barley, a form of low-grade meal common amongst peasants last century.[28] Kanemaru complained about his conditions, but to no avail. One size fits all in Japanese jails. There are no special cells for white-collar criminals, or places like prison farms to ease the pain of incarceration. Kanemaru was treated exactly as any criminal would be. So complete was his fall from grace that even the public ignored the trial that followed. Diabetic and confined to a wheelchair, Kanemaru faced his accusers before an empty spectators' gallery.[29]

Through this final humiliation, Kanemaru protested that the hidden money was not for him personally, but to bankroll the establishment of a new political party. 'Political realignment was my dream', he told the court. And political realignment was what he got, although perhaps not in the way he'd planned.

THE NEW ORDER

Besides the old joke that the ruling Liberal Democratic Party was neither 'liberal' nor 'democratic' was the assertion that it wasn't really a party either. Each of the LDP's five factions operated like small fiefdoms, with their own distinct names and identities, and separate offices, bank accounts and fund-raising drives. For individual MPs, the faction came first, and the party second. The same might sometimes be said of the sharply factionalised branches of the labour parties in Australia and Britain, or indeed in other countries, except for one key difference. The odd marriage of convenience aside, labour party factions are divided according to their beliefs. The LDP factions are divided according to their patrons. That is an over-simplification, to be sure. Strains of various policies can be traced through the history of a number of LDP factions. Some are more in favour of the postwar restraints on the armed forces than others. One is more nationalistic, and less supportive of the US alliance, while another attracts a large proportion of ex-bureaucrats to its ranks. But by and large, MPs clustered under the wing of their chosen feudal chief and financial benefactor rather than seek out a leader whose policies they supported. Ideology, after all, did not pay the bills.

Besides enjoying the spoils of power, which had become a habit over the years, one single thing—anti-communism—had kept the LDP together through its 38 years of uninterrupted rule. A Japanese cartoon at the time of the US occupation showed a package called 'Democracy' descending from the heavens like a relief package into Japan, but it was never to be a democracy of Japan's own making. Established as a grand conservative coalition in 1955 at a time of hysteria in Washington about the menace of communism, the LDP was a classic product of the Cold War—a bulwark of capitalism and the US security alliance in Asia. Dreading the prospect of a left-wing government, Washington both sanctioned and buttressed the LDP against a powerful and occasionally radical left-wing movement in Japan in the 1950s, and covertly funded it during its first years through the CIA.

This, then, became the basis for 'democracy, Japanese-style', or the '1955 system', as it became known. The LDP presided over sound economic management which delivered low inflation, low unemployment and strong growth, and left security policy—and thus high defence spending—to the United States. In return, war-shy voters were mostly willing to overlook its many ugly failings, like corruption and links with organised crime.[30] The fortunes of the opposition party, the Socialists, surged occasionally when voters wanted to protest against corruption or tax increases, but slowly waned with Japan's increasing affluence.[31] The Socialist opposition to the conservative LDP became ritualised over time, and its leaders strangled an already truncated policy debate by refusing to budge from their pure and rigid anti-American positions. Gradually, a clear division of labour was established, with the LDP as the perennial ruling party, and the Socialists as the permanent opposition. This arrangement only partly obscured the two parties' fundamental compact. Both believed that Japan should concentrate on building its economy, and keep a low profile internationally. The only difference was their rationale for adopting such positions—the LDP supported the US alliance, for example, while the Socialists adhered to 'unarmed neutrality'. But for public purposes, the ideological confrontation between the two parties was highly structured, and so, as we have seen, were their day-to-day dealings in the parliament. During Kanemaru's time, if not before, Socialist leaders were drawn deep into the web of money politics, and directly corrupted by bribes from LDP bosses. Politics was largely about dividing the spoils of Japan's wealth, and policies were rarely debated seriously.

In the 1990s, however, the pillars supporting the LDP and 'democracy Japan-style' began to crumble. The Berlin Wall collapsed, the bubble economy burst, and a political establishment traumatised by Japan's inability to contribute anything but money to allied forces in the Gulf War opened a furious debate on the postwar constitution's restrictions on the military. The electorate, too, was changing. The power of the rich agricultural lobbies was declining in parallel with the size and wealth of farming communities. Younger urban voters with little or no connection to Japan's rural ethos were demanding a voice, and new parties, like the Japan New Party under Morihiro Hosokawa, had sprung up to represent them. Television, too, began to have an impact. How Japanese politicians looked and behaved suddenly mattered.

The Prime Minister at the time when such pressures were reaching a boiling point, Kiichi Miyazawa, was powerless to control the chaos spreading through the political scene. Miyazawa was not your typical Japanese politician. He didn't spend large amounts of his time, as did so many of his colleagues, raising cash so he could rush back to his electorate to spread it around. In fact, just before the election which followed the collapse of his government, he hadn't visited his Hiroshima electorate once in over a year, an outstanding display of indifference to all the demands for personal services. The internationally minded Miyazawa spoke fluent English and had an intimate and unparalleled involvement in fashioning postwar economic policy, beginning in 1950, when he joined the Finance Ministry. But the qualities that won Miyazawa respect overseas and in parts of Japan were the same ones that caused him to be disliked and ineffectual within the ruling party.

Miyazawa's faction in the ruling party was known derisively as *kuge shudan*, or the court nobles' group. Comprising many former senior bureaucrats, it was less corrupt than its rivals, but for the very same reason less powerful. Miyazawa had a reputation amongst his colleagues as elitist and arrogant. I once attended a discussion in English at a luxury Tokyo hotel between Miyazawa and his 'good friend' Henry Kissinger where the pair perched up on a stage and chatted about issues ranging from the collapse of the Soviet Union to the imperial role of Deng Xiaoping in China, each alternately complimenting the other on his erudition. Spread below them in the large hall, an audience of scores of Japanese politicians sat through this geopolitical tour de force, stiff and stony-faced, with large clumsy earpieces attached to the sides of their heads like Mickey Mouse ears to listen to the interpreter. At the end of the session, a pair of politicians sitting next to me ground their teeth as they got up to leave. 'Mr Miyazawa may be able to speak English, but can he speak Japanese!?' one snapped.

Miyazawa had long been an enemy of Kanemaru, and during one late night drinking session said he wished the 'old man would drown himself in Yamanashi River' (in his home prefecture). Kanemaru was not amused, and Miyazawa had to grovel to win the support of the kingmaker and his faction to become Prime Minister. He declared, 'I will not do anything that differs from the intentions of Mr Kanemaru', and received the godfather's blessing. But when Kanemaru was arrested in early 1993, there was no one with the power or stature to mediate in the combat that erupted inside his faction in his absence.

The two groups struggling to gain the upper hand in the LDP after Kanemaru's demise were ostensibly divided along two fault lines. One camp demanded a new electoral system to replace the money-hungry multi-member electorates, and supported a broader international role for Japan's armed forces, while their opponents broadly backed the status quo. Out of public view the two groups waged a battle that was just as crucial, for control of the faction's wealth and donor networks in the construction industry and the like. The fight was also bitterly personal, and it became impossible to separate the personalities from the policies, mainly because of the man leading the 'reformist' clique—Ichiro Ozawa. Ozawa's powerful personality, as we shall see, fired the entire political debate.

When the hapless Miyazawa, under pressure from Ozawa's enemies, delayed the bill introducing the new electoral system, the rebel leader immediately declared that his 35-strong band of MPs would quit the LDP and back a motion of no-confidence in the prime minister. By itself, Ozawa's defection was not enough to bring the government down, but his daring action galvanised other LDP rebels who sensed the party was crumbling, and a host of other ginger groups scattered across the political spectrum. The momentum in favour of the so-called reformers swelled day by day, and when the no-confidence motion was put to a vote at 8.16 pm on 18 June 1993, 55 ruling-party MPs crossed the floor to support it. The motion was passed by 255 votes to 220, and Miyazawa dissolved the parliament to call a general election. It was a moment of high drama and history—the insular, cash-addicted political system which had ruled over Japan's spectacular postwar rise had finally cracked.

THROW THE BASTARDS OUT!

Now, at last, the people would have their say. Here was their chance to vent suppressed anger about corrupt politicians and cast a vote to 'throw the bastards out'. The climate of condemnation of the LDP's crooked cliques that had prevailed for months, if not years, prior to the poll meant that new politicians like Yuriko Koike, a well-known woman television newsreader, should have no problem beating old ruling-party fogies like Kenzaburo Hara, to usher in a new political era in Japan. Or so many pundits thought when they set out on the election trail that summer.

The glamorous, multilingual Koike had given up her high-profile newsreading job to join the hippest and most popular of the multiple parties that had sprung up across the political landscape, the Japan New Party. The party had everything going for it—a handsome, charismatic leader, Morihiro Hosokawa, loads of media coverage and support, and even a semblance of some real policies. The Japan New Party marketed itself as a clean break from the old ways of Japanese politics—it backed electoral reform to reduce corruption, and wanted to wrest power from the unelected bureaucrats in the capital and give it back to the people in the provinces. But most of all, the Japan New Party was *new*, an essential quality for anyone launching a political career at that time. Koike's opponents dismissed her out of hand as an 'airhead' because of her television background, but she proved to be a feisty, if melodramatic, campaigner. Standing on the stump at Takarazuka, the home of a famous all-woman theatre company near the city of Kobe, Koike warned passers-by who stopped to listen that Japan faced a new 'Pearl Harbor' unless its leaders explained the country's policies to the world. 'Our first and final goal', she said later, 'is to get rid of the LDP'. Determined to be untraditional at every turn, Koike and others in her party refused to wear the white gloves that are de rigueur on the campaign trail in Japan as signs of cleanliness and purity. 'We banned that,' she told me. 'And bowing down and using certain words to beg for votes. I won't be attending any weddings either, but I am not invited anyway.'

Not so one of her opponents, Kenzaburo ('Ken') Hara. At 86, and running for election for the nineteenth time, Hara was notorious for his old-style stumping for votes. During each campaign, he shed tears and fell to his knees, prostrating himself before the voters and wailing, 'Make me a real man [by electing me to parliament!'. His wife would often follow him onto the stage, and perform a similar routine begging for votes. She crouched and bowed so low that her nose would touch the ground. At meetings around the constituency, Hara often left money under cushions as small gifts. According to a rival campaign worker, Hara would also distribute cash to various community 'bosses'—elderly people, leaders of women's groups and some housewives. A teary Hara told crowds that this poll was 'the most important election of my life!'. He wasn't joking. A victory this time around would give him 50 years service in parliament, and qualify him to have his statue built and placed permanently outside the Diet building in Tokyo.

Novice politicians like Koike weren't the only ones to base their entire campaigns around anti-LDP themes. When I met Kenichiro Sato, one of the 55 LDP rebels who had quit the party, he eagerly told me he was spending only Y40 million ($880 000) on his campaign—the maximum legal limit—rather than the Y200 million ($2.6 million) he usually outlaid. How many politicians do you meet who boast that this time they wouldn't be blatantly breaking the law to be re-elected! At campaign rallies in his electorate south of Tokyo, Sato emotionally recounted how he'd made up his mind to quit the ruling party during long hours tending his dying mother. 'Japanese politicians usually have no time to think, because if they did, they'd want to do all sorts of things. The ones who don't think usually rise through the ranks quickly.'

The LDP old guard was really running against its own corrupt legacy in the election, no one more so than Noboru Takeshita, the man who had become the dark symbol of money politics in Kanemaru's wake.[32] Takeshita undertook a humbling schedule during the campaign, returning to the isolated back-blocks of his rural electorate in Shimane Prefecture in western Japan to speak to tiny groups of voters for the first time in more than two decades—even his resignation as Prime Minister in 1989 (in another corruption scandal) hadn't sent him scurrying home to shore up support. His black chauffeur-driven car whisked him from rally to rally, weaving though the narrow twisting streets of a small fishing village when I caught up with it, before pulling up abruptly outside a Buddhist temple. Flanked by his special police guard, the diminutive Takeshita jumped out, slid off his shoes and entered the temple, clasping his hands to bow to the Buddhist icon before turning to the group of 20-odd supporters gathered to hear him speak. 'It's been a long time!' he declared. 'Twenty-four years!'

Takeshita's public utterances had never been easy to divine. An Australian diplomat, asked after he had met with Takeshita how he would describe the politician's message, replied, 'Delphic, but not content-free'. Even on this occasion, Takeshita did not go into detail about the accusations against him. Instead, he apologised to the small group for causing 'great sorrow at home' and appealed to them to trust 'his personality'. 'It is extremely difficult to deny something that has never happened. All I can ask you to do is trust me', he said, speaking in clear and gently forceful tones for which he was renowned. 'In the last 50 years, I have never got angry and lost my cool, but this time, I must fight the election head-on.' After a few more lines about all the world leaders he knew, Takeshita was whisked back into his dark car with its tinted windows, before zooming off to the next of the day's 30-odd rallies. The priest of the temple, Tatsuno Sekan, was both resigned and satisfied with the explanation. 'As far as the scandals go, I believe that he couldn't help it as a politician', he said. 'I trust his personality.'

Looking out of the window of the plane flying into Shimane earlier that day, I had a feeling at first I was arriving in another country. Green hills rolled down to the banks of a placid lake, and there at last, for the first time in Japan, was a river with what appeared to be its own natural banks, rather than concrete ones, meandering through the countryside. (I later realised that I must have been wrong about the river's natural banks. Japan's 'construction state' had left the country with just *one* major free-flowing river, Nagara River in Mie Prefecture—that is until work began to dam it in mid-1990.) Shimane is indeed beautiful, but mainly because it is sparsely populated. The district is covered with new bridges and smart roads. Even the rice paddies are criss-crossed with freshly tarred bike paths. Thanks to Takeshita's pulling power in the capital, the construction companies have not spared Shimane. The prefecture has the highest annual expenditure per head of any region in Japan. Near the Buddhist temple where he had stopped to talk to voters was one of Takeshita's gifts, a glistening museum displaying the unique 'singing sands' of the area's beaches. After seeing the museum, our party adjourned to a pretty beach close by to inspect the real thing, only to find that the sands had been completely concreted over for construction work.

Takeshita's home village of Kisuki, population 4000, is dominated by his family's sake brewing factory, tucked deep into a steep hill thick with bamboo. The head of his vote-gathering network, Kakeya Takeshita, a childhood friend, but no relation, took his foreign visitors across the lane from the factory into a hall filled with pictures of the highlights of Takeshita's career. The vote-gatherer was confident his boss's local network would survive the scandals. 'We have a pretty tight network here in this village. We cover everyone—husbands, wives, children, relatives—so if we hear someone is planning to vote for another candidate, then someone will go and see them to persuade them to vote for Mr Takeshita', he said.

With support from rich construction companies, protected rice farmers and tight village networks, Takeshita's roots were dug too deeply into the soil of Shimane for him to have any chance of losing. When the votes were counted, Takeshita was returned to parliament, and so were all of his colleagues across the country. Nobody much noticed it at the time, but the LDP actually gained one seat during the election. Even 'Ken' Hara scraped back in by the skin of his teeth in his multi-member electorate. So much for the 'throw the bastards out' mood! Voters did elect a wave of newcomers, like Koike, but not at the expense of the LDP. Overall, the resilient conservatives strengthened their representation in parliament, albeit under a range of different banners. The new parties won by taking votes away from the Socialists. The end of the Cold War had been even more dispiriting for the left and its rigid anti-American policies, and voters recognised it. The Socialists lost nearly half their MPs, plummeting from 146 seats in the old parliament to 71 in the new one.

Despite the LDP's strong showing, the media still marked the election down as a major defeat for the ruling party. That was because in the horse-trading that followed, Ozawa's rebels ensured that Japan got its first prime minister in nearly four decades who wasn't a paid-up member of the LDP.

TOKYO SPRING

Japan's new Prime Minister, Morihiro Hosokawa, had an unusual pedigree for a self-proclaimed reformer from outside the system. He was the eighteenth direct descendant of a long line of *daimyo* (feudal lords) from southern Japan. Family members had been stripped of their official titles and powers during modernisation in the 1860s, but they retained their aristocratic aura. The media liked to call him 'Lord Hosokawa'. His grandfather on his mother's side, Fumimaro Konoe, had been Prime Minister just before the sneak attack on Pearl Harbor and the outbreak of the Pacific War. Konoe was best remembered for making political parties in the 1930s give unconditional support to the Emperor, and then committing suicide with poison soon after Japan's surrender.

Hosokawa's aristocratic antecedents were no guarantee of a successful political career, but they gave him a high profile and a head start. After a short stint as an LDP upper-house MP, ironically enough as a member of the Tanaka faction, Hosokawa returned to his home in Kumamoto in south-western Japan in the early 1980s and made his name as a governor willing to battle the central bureaucracy. He regularly complained that he had to get permission from Tokyo to move even a bus stop ten metres. Hosokawa timed his move onto the national stage adroitly, forming his Japan New Party just as the old order was disintegrating. Hosokawa preached that Japanese politics was 'terminally ill', and liked to quote a line from the Hollywood film *JFK*, that 'those who love their country must protect it from the government'. Youthful and attractive, Hosokawa didn't mind Kennedyesque comparisons, as long as they didn't include one of his other reputed qualities—vigorous womanising.

Although his party won only 10 per cent of the vote at the 1993 poll, Hosokawa controlled a pivotal swag of new MPs, and traded their support for the leadership of a seven-party coalition government cobbled together by Ozawa. The LDP, for the first time in its history, was forced into opposition. A lightweight waffler in the eyes of many, Hosokawa nonetheless produced a burst of idealism and optimism about Japanese politics at home and abroad after years of grubby scandals. Editorial writers, foreign journalists and reform-minded Japanese were thrilled by his promises to bulldoze the bureaucracy, reform the oppressive education system, empower consumers and apologise for Japanese war aggression. It was an exciting, exhilarating period, a Tokyo spring, if you like—but just as ephemeral. In retrospect, it is clear that as an individual politician Hosokawa never really had a chance.

For all his qualities, his government never managed to live down the presence of its chief powerbroker and strategist, Ichiro Ozawa, perhaps the most capable politician in Japan, but also certainly the most loathed as well. Ozawa was both Hosokawa's greatest strength, and also his Achilles heel. Ozawa emerged during the time of the LDP split as a shining, born-again reformer with an audacious agenda not only to clean up politics but also to turn Japan's postwar foreign policy on its head. Outside Japan, his prescription that Japan become a 'normal' country—with elected politicians in charge of unelected bureaucrats, and a military liberated from its postwar straitjacket—would have seemed mild, and even mundane. But in a country still traumatised by memories of war, Ozawa was denounced bitterly as a 'fascist' for daring to push change. Ozawa's problem was one of style as much as substance. Not only did he challenge policy taboos, he bluntly refused to conform to the traditional 'consensus' style of politics. He abhorred this lowest-common-denominator policy-making, which weighed up and gave face to all views. Ozawa wanted to lead, albeit from behind the scenes, but Japan and its bureaucratic establishment, and media, weren't ready to let him.

As a political reformer and anti-corruption crusader, Ozawa suffered from a severe credibility problem. Here was a man who had been up to his eyeballs in money politics. His three mentors—Tanaka, Kanemaru and Takeshita—were the corrupt system's greatest architects and biggest beneficiaries. It was, as one commentator quipped, 'an age of discontinuities', but many people were deeply cynical about Ozawa's new clothes. Ozawa had been present at the hotel meeting where Kanemaru and Takeshita discussed using gangsters in 1987 during the prime ministerial election. He later feebly explained to a disbelieving interviewer that he had only been there 'as an attendant [to] change the drinks and clean the ashtrays'. Needless to say, neither were tasks commonly associated with Ozawa's career. Many refused to take Ozawa's conversion from corruption seriously. 'It's like a career thief saying, "I'm getting out of this business", while living in a stolen home', said Hirotaka Futatsuki of the *Nikkan Gendai*.[33]

Ultimately, Ozawa's crash-or-crash-through style brought the anti-LDP coalition tumbling down. First, he manoeuvred Hosokawa into supporting a Finance Ministry plan to more than double the country's deeply unpopular consumption tax and, even worse, allowed it to be announced without warning at a pre-dawn press conference. Hosokawa, who was forced by the uproar to dump the tax a few days later, never recovered from this setback. Neither did the head of the Finance Ministry, who was not forgiven by LDP chiefs for the alliance with Ozawa when they returned to government. Two months after this episode, Hosokawa resigned after the LDP exposed a minor scandal, something that is easy to do in a country where every self-respecting politician has at least one tucked away in his or her closet. Ozawa's choice as the next Prime Minister, his close confidant, Tsutomu Hata, was crippled from the start after the Socialists walked out in fury at one of Ozawa's power plays. On his first day in office, Hata was deprived of his majority on the floor of the parliament. If you blinked, you would have missed the Hata government—it lasted just four months, a postwar record.

Hosokawa did achieve the single reform he had committed himself to, and that had cost his two predecessors office—reform of the electoral system. Under the old multi-member system, three to five MPs were elected from the same district. That meant that LDP candidates battled against other LDP candidates in pricey campaigns bankrolled by their respective factional chiefs, and decided more by personalities and pork than policies. 'Come election time, my colleagues became my competitors', said Kazuo Aichi. 'We compete for the highest ranking, which is determined by the number of votes received. If my ranking slips, my prestige suffers among my constituents and fellow LDP members.' Abolish multi-member electorates, so the refrain went, and you get rid of expensive electioneering and corruption at the same time. This theory has yet to be tested, and in fact the opposite may be true. Under Hosokawa's new electoral system, 300 MPs will be chosen from single-seat constituencies, and 200 by proportional representation. To be elected in a single seat, politicians will need 40 to 50 per cent of the vote, compared to a quota of only about 15 per cent under the old multi-member system. Prominent political scientist Seizaburo Sato, who is closely aligned with the old-guard LDP, says the higher quotas will encourage budding MPs to be even more cautious with policies than before, for fear of alienating voters, exactly the opposite of the new system's intention. 'It is naive to think that tinkering with the election rules will eliminate corruption', says Sato.[34]

Hata's short-lived coalition government was replaced by a cynical alliance between the long-time governing and opposition parties, the LDP and the Socialists. Only a little over a year after the party had been ousted and written off by many pundits, the LDP made a stunning comeback. The party ceded the prime minister's job to Socialist leader Tomiichi Murayama, in return for his party's votes, but that was about all the left got. The LDP kept the major ministries for itself, and then used the pressure of government to force its Socialist partners to dump all their lifelong policies. In the space of a few weeks, Murayama conceded that Japan's armed forces were constitutionally legal, approved the national anthem and flag, supported the dispatch of troops overseas and ditched the party's adherence to 'unarmed neutrality'. All were positions which ran directly counter to the party's pacifist and anti-nuclear policies of decades. It was the equivalent of the Australian Labor Party in the early 1980s dropping its opposition to US bases, French nuclear testing, foreign banks, East Timorese self-determination and uranium mining, all in the space of a week. Even with its leader in the Prime Minister's office for the first time in more than four decades, the Socialists were shedding members and disintegrating irrevocably. The party was now empty at the core. Noboru Takeshita, who had regained his position as the LDP's kingmaker after his 'purification' in the election, remarked sardonically that he had swallowed the Socialists, and now only had to digest them. In early 1996, the LDP leader, Ryutaro Hashimoto, regained the premiership for his party.

On one level, the alliance between the Socialists and the LDP made sense. Both groups had an interest in rebuilding the domestic status quo of the '1955 system', and opposed Ozawa's policies to give the military an expanded role overseas. The neutralist right had joined the neutralist left, if you like. But the greater significance of their union was that it marked the final destruction of the structured confrontation which had been at the core of the political system for nearly four decades. In a familiar display of Western conceit, most foreign commentators confidently tipped that the Japanese system would then inevitably metamorphose into a two-party democracy resembling the ones in their own countries—one in which power periodically changed hands. In other words, the Japanese would continue to become more like us. But events since the collapse of the LDP show that a Western-style two-party system is anything but inevitable.

Sato says the most likely scenario for Japan is a stream of 'unstable and unprincipled coalition governments', followed by the emergence of a new super-ruling party, even bigger than the LDP, and more chronically ensconced in power. Sato blames this, too, on the new electoral system which was meant to reform Japanese politics. Because politicians will need an even greater percentage of the vote to win office, they will jump under the largest umbrella available to keep their jobs, rather than risk alignment with a small and powerless party. This trend is already entrenched in regional politics in Japan, where virtually all the parties, except for the communists, are part of a governing coalition. A new super-ruling party on a national level would be undesirable, unstable and undemocratic—because voters would be deprived of a choice of other parties—but Sato says that it may be all that Japanese politicians are capable of for the moment.[35] So much for political reform! Sato may be unduly cynical, but certainly, by the time the Hata cabinet fell, all traces of starry-eyed idealism of 1993 had disappeared from the political scene.

The upper-house elections of July 1993 gave some superficial support to the proposition that a two-party system would emerge. The conservative parties continued to swallow and digest the Socialist vote, but not in the way that the LDP's Takeshita had envisioned. The Socialists recorded their worst performance in the postwar period, winning only 16 out of 126 contested seats, but most of their vote was snared by the new opposition coalition organised and now led by Ozawa, *Shinshinto* (New Frontier Party). *Shinshinto* matched and, in some areas, outpolled its conservative rivals, and won 40 seats compared to the LDP's 46. Finding a distinctive policy difference to explain this result, however, apart from a desire to cast a vote against the Socialists without supporting the LDP, is not easy.

The starting point for distinguishing the LDP from *Shinshinto* is usually foreign policy. Ozawa and *Shinshinto* have supported a more independent military posture, while the LDP officially supports the present constitutional restraints. But a

109

quick trawl through the LDP would find many senior politicians with the same views as Ozawa on this issue. Three of the country's most belligerently nationalistic politicians, Ryutaro Hashimoto, Shizuka Kamei and Shintaro Ishihara (until his retirement in 1995) were all leading members of the LDP. *Shinshinto* supported deregulation and reform of the bureaucracy more vigorously than the LDP, which was generally comfortable with the present political and bureaucratic establishment. But similarly, you could pick through the two parties on this issue and find a range of incompatible views within each. The two rival political groups were thus polarised not so much by Ozawa's policies, but by whether they were anti or pro Ozawa himself. In Hashimoto's case, this was particularly pronounced, as Ozawa represented a threat to his ambitions to lead the LDP and become prime minister. Competition between the LDP and *Shinshinto*, if they survive in their present form, might yet produce distinctively different policies and healthy, democratic transfers of power from one party to another, but there is no guarantee that this will happen.

Shusei Tanaka, a reform-minded MP who had come to prominence as 'Hosokawa's brain' during the first coalition government, predicted genuine change would take another five to six years, if it came at all. 'To really regenerate Japanese politics, we need people who share the same ideas about history and the future to get together in the same place and party', he said. 'At the moment, parties are full of people with different ideas, and if it doesn't change, it will be a disaster.'[36] But for every reformer like Tanaka, there are MPs like Junichiro Koizumi. Like more than one-third of the LDP MPs, Koizumi had taken over his seat in parliament from a close relative. (Hashimoto and Ozawa also succeeded their fathers in their seats.) In Koizumi's case, he had inherited his seat and his factional allegiance from his father, who had in turn succeeded his father. Unlike many politicians who had inherited political sinecures from their relatives,

Koizumi was a talented and active MP, but naturally, he was also a willing defender of the system that had nurtured him. For Koizumi, politics was a family business that had prospered for three generations. More than that, the absence of ideology that Shusei Tanaka bemoaned was, in Koizumi's opinion, rooted in the very soil of Japanese politics. He told me that just as communities appreciated the families that had run the post office, bath house and local sushi shop for generations, they also liked continuity amongst their politicians. 'Japanese people are comfortable with this', he said. Most were also happy to align themselves with a large and powerful party, rather than capriciously swinging between two, because that was the way to ensure greater benefits for their communities. But even Koizumi's generational certitudes were beginning to desert him. Asked what he expected to happen in Japanese politics in the near future, he frankly admitted he had no idea. The result of important mayoral elections in 1995 in Japan's two biggest cities, Tokyo and Osaka, only confirmed his confusion.

Japanese voters have a long if not so honourable tradition of electing actors, comedians, writers and the like to parliament, usually to the upper house, where they can perform and posture without causing anyone much bother. These *tarento*[37], as they are known, have a head start on the ordinary politicians in Japan's personality-intensive electioneering because of their high public profiles. Even as a third-generation politician, Koizumi has to hire small sound trucks at each election, and fill them with pretty, white-gloved young women, who circulate in his electorate from dawn to dusk, waving and shouting out his name. Such irritating, screeching campaigning is de rigueur in Japanese elections, where name recognition is an all-important factor in winning votes. It is even regulated—noise laws stipulate that the sound trucks cannot begin operating before 8 am. Still, neither Koizumi nor the rest of the political establishment were prepared for the election of two *tarento* politicians as mayors of the two giant metropolises of Tokyo and Osaka. If ever there was a message that the voters were becoming as cynical as the politicians, this was it.

Yukio Aoshima was elected as mayor of Tokyo—a city with a budget bigger than Australia's—against the big guns of the major parties after a campaign which consisted of him sitting at home and doing nothing. His only gesture at mainstream politicking was to employ five voluntary workers, who included two relatives, to put up a few thousand posters. As a member of the upper house, Aoshima had lifted his political profile with his successful petition against the 'godfather', Shin Kanemaru, in 1992. His real pulling power had been garnered years before, however, when as an actor, he dressed up in drag to play the archetypal Japanese harridan—a nasty grandmother—in television soap opera. But Aoshima was a serious and tough politician compared with the buffoonish comedian who became mayor of Osaka. 'Knock' Yokoyama (his mother knows him by his real name of Isamu Yamada) ran a less existential campaign than Aoshima, actually hitting the hustings to promise a 'new politics for the people', and horrified local officials by keeping his stage name when he won. In the upper-house elections that followed the mayoral polls, voter turnout was 44.5 per cent, the lowest in Japanese history for a national election.

There was a clear message for the bureaucrats in this. If the politicians were going to be comedians, and the voters weren't going to vote, then the bureaucrats were going to have to be bureaucrats, and maintain their position in the control tower from which they firmly guided Japan, and its destiny.

CHAPTER 5

THE NANNY STATE

'Have you ever heard an educated opinion from a politician on the current Cambodian problem or our relations with Russia? All they can talk about is how they won a public works project, or something like that.'

Yoshihiko Morozumi, retired bureaucrat

'Weak political leadership [in Japan] is nothing less than an imposition on other countries.'

Ichiro Ozawa, politician

The first thing Japanese workers hear on boarding the bus or train for the morning commute is an announcement to be careful boarding the bus and train. When they get off, there is a recorded message telling them to be careful getting off. If it's raining, the message might also say to grab an umbrella. Some buses run cautionary announcements, interspersed with advertisements, each time they turn a corner ('Please pay attention—the bus is turning the corner'). Then there is the ubiquitous all-purpose 'Make sure you don't forget anything' refrain, an instruction that in some taxis comes in the form of a recorded order triggered by the passenger door opening. From the moment they leave home to the time they return in the evenings, Japanese people are protected by the inescapable embrace of the Nanny State.

On the highest snowy mountain, and in the steamiest *onsen* (natural hot spring bath), the peace is invariably disturbed by a crackling order from a 1950s-style speaker, hidden behind a tree, directing you to follow certain rules. Lift your ski tips. Be careful of the steps. Don't leave anything behind. Even the visit to the local public swimming pool is fraught with rules. The usual compulsory routine requires bathers to wear a cap and have a shower, and then an extra sprinkle before the prerequisite dunk in a tepid, disinfected pool, styled not unlike a sheep dip. On finally reaching the water you get in, and if you've timed your arrival badly, a few minutes later you get out—for the mandatory rest break, which is enforced to ensure that swimmers don't exert themselves too much. It can come as a terrible shock for the uninitiated to look up and see that the pool has emptied itself, as if a shark had been spotted. The swimming-pool regime is exasperating and irritating, but mild compared to an incident I witnessed one year at the annual summer fireworks on the Sumida River at Asakusa, an old quarter of Tokyo. A father, strolling through the crowd on a warm evening across the bridge over the river, gently lifted his young daughter onto his shoulders to give her a better view. No sooner had she settled there when one of the scores of crowd controllers, literally a few metres away, lifted his loudspeaker and yelled into it, 'Please get that child off your shoulders—it's dangerous!'. The child immediately came down, and order was restored.

The pervasive atmosphere of control in society is bolstered by the *koban* (police box) system, which is a feature of all Japan's cities and suburbs. The two or three police officers manning each box do everything from monitoring movements in and out of the area to helping drunks find their way home at night, and even lending them money to ensure they arrive there safely. The police patrol the streets on foot and by bicycle, a habit which has earned them the endearing nickname of *omawari-san*, or 'Mr Go-Around'. Police have access, as well, to the loudspeaker systems which are rigged through the suburbs of every city and town in the country. Ostensibly for use during disasters like earthquakes, the loudspeakers can be activated whenever order needs to be restored. In small villages, they are still used in early-morning broadcasts to tell people what crops should be planted and the sort of fertiliser to be used. This 'friendly neighbourhood police state', which would be considered oppressive in the West, is reassuring for the Japanese and at least partly responsible for the country's much-envied low crime rate.

Noisy orders are sometimes just for show. In some divisions of the mighty MITI, bureaucrats working back at night are bombarded with successive announcements on the hour over the in-house speaker system urging them to go home. The announcements are part of an official campaign, pressed on Tokyo by foreign governments keen to cut Japan's exports and to coax the Japanese to work less and play more. They are broadcast in full knowledge that they will be ignored. The lights still burn late into the night at MITI—after all, the officials have a country to run, and regulations to administer.

Big Brother's cosy web has spun itself into all sorts of odd areas. The Education Ministry, for example, has an elaborate system of about 600 state-sponsored examinations setting standards for everything from 'Improving Competitive Skills' to 'Practising Healthy Exercise'. These do not qualify a person who passes the exam to teach these skills, merely to be able to say that they have acquired them. One popular exam is the 'Test for Home Cooking'; the ministry awards certificates to people who can cut, peel and prepare food for Japanese, Chinese or Western dishes. Just over 1700 Japanese sat for, and passed, this exam in 1993. In fostering a paternalistic exam culture, the public sector sets an example for all manner of private bodies, and even religious organisations. Dancers, actors, flower arrangers, potters and painters all belong to special schools, which emphasise the importance of doing things 'the proper way'. Those aspiring to join one of Japan's most popular new religions, *Kofuku no Kagaku* ('The Science of Human Happiness'), must first sit for an entrance exam, and then pass further tests after being admitted. Success requires intense study of the works of the religion's leader, Ryuho Okawa, a 30-something former trading company employee who considers himself to be the reincarnation of Buddha. So far, Okawa's 151 books have sold around 40 million copies.[1]

Cooking and health skills exams and announcements on public transport may seem trivial items, but they are indicative of the mindset which drives the Japanese bureaucracy on a national level. The bureaucrats consider themselves less servants of the people than their guardians. Their attitude towards their subjects is at once protective and condescending. They are also fearful of the consequences should the people be unshackled, and allowed to run wild and free. Look at the attitude of the top officials in the Transport Ministry to demands that they deregulate taxi fares. When one frustrated company in Kyoto sardonically applied to cut its fares to zero, the ministry naturally refused the application. The ministry's top-ranking bureaucrat, Vice-Minister Michihiko Matsuo, said he feared cutting fares, even during the recession that at the time was leaving hundreds of cabs empty. 'Maybe [cutting fares] would help', he told one interviewer, 'but if you want to liberalise fares, it's necessary to have a society in which people can take responsibility for themselves. I wonder if the present Japan is mature enough for that. If there were ten different taxi fares in Tokyo, people might lose confidence in taxis.'

'You don't have confidence in consumers?' the interviewer asked.

'We could leave the issue to their own choice, but if we did that, we would be criticised by consumers', Matsuo replied.[2]

So Father (or perhaps Mother) knows best, and the children have learnt not only to concur, but to encourage the disciplinary streak as well. None of this would matter if bureaucratic control were just a domestic issue, but Japan's wealth and power means it no longer is, if it ever was. A lack of political leadership capable of checking the bureaucrats, says politician Ichiro Ozawa, 'is nothing less than an imposition on other countries'.[3] The Nanny State was a central theme in Ozawa's 1993 best-seller, *Blueprint for a New Japan*. In the opening passage of the English-language edition, Ozawa recalled his first sight of the Grand Canyon, and his awe at the depth of the natural wonder spread out before him—1200 metres deep, more than four times the height of the tallest building in Japan. But one other thing about the natural wonder made an even deeper impression on Ozawa—something that perhaps only someone from Japan would have commented on. There were no fences to protect the visitors from the views. 'Multitudes of tourists coming to the park annually, but no fences!' remarked Ozawa in the opening. 'In Japan, there would be fences, "no entry" signs and park attendants who come running to warn people away.'

Ozawa tried to imagine what would happen in Japan if there were an accident in a public place because there were no fences. The press would rage at the park management, and demand to know why the authorities had been so negligent. Why weren't there fences? Why weren't there signs? Where were the atten-dants to keep watch? But officials in Japan, knowing this, would have taken every possible precaution to tightly control their piece of turf. Japanese people take for granted that they are being cared for by the government, says Ozawa, even when they're having fun sight-seeing.[4]

THE TIES THAT BIND

The standard cliché about Japan is that while the politicians reign, the bureaucrats rule. If that were true, then the bureaucrats have much to be proud of. Japan's economy has grown spectacularly since the war at a pace probably unmatched in history. But as with most things Japanese, sorting through the myths and realities surrounding the bureaucracy and its powers necessitates a journey through a maze of competing interpretations. The contenders range from the Japan Inc. school, which focuses on the way political, bureaucratic and business elites collaborate to run the economy and the government, all the way to those stressing 'unique' Japanese values such as group loyalties and consensus. The most extreme theories portray Japan as a 'national conspiracy' directed from bureaucratic command posts in central Tokyo. 'The elements that comprise this conspiracy come from every facet of Japanese life—unelected bureaucrats; industrialists; *shinko-zaibatsu* [reconstituted business cartels]; labour union officials; and submissive workers', wrote American businessman, Marvin J. Wolf. It is only worth mentioning Wolf's paranoid stereotype because it is one that many foreigners believe in.[5]

Somewhere between the conspiracists and the culturalists is a milder and more accurate version of Japan Inc. which acknowledges that the country cannot be reduced to a 'monolithic, consensual machine-like organism bent upon national aggrandisement', as the Wolfs of this world do. Politicians, entrepreneurs and workers all played their part in Japan's economic miracle. So too did the United States, which allowed its markets to be flooded with Japanese goods while it simultaneously guaranteed Japan's security. The 'iron triangle' of businessmen, bureaucrats and politicians who comprise Japan's 'conspiratorial' power elite in fact compete as much as they co-operate, in a way that gives the Japanese system a degree of pluralism that is generally not acknowledged. And just as the Japanese state can create and manipulate interests, so too can it also be colonised by them.[6] Agriculture is a classic case of this. The crusty bureaucrats at the Ministry of Agriculture, Fishery and Forests—known as MAFF, or more colloquially the 'MAF-Fia' because of their tough clannishness—are as much under the thumb of their farming constituents as the other way round. The MAFF squeezed an astounding Y6 trillion ($80 billion) out of the stingy Finance Ministry in 1994 to compensate an already heavily subsidised farm sector for the slight opening of Japan's rice market in 1995. This amount was larger, and made available more expeditiously, than government funds to reconstruct Kobe after its earthquake.[7]

But for all the system's malleability and inbuilt competitiveness, Japanese bureaucrats, through their informal networks in business and political circles and their own iron-clad institutional solidarity, exercise a power over economic and political management, industry policy, foreign affairs, education and employment that far surpasses that of their counterparts in any other developed country. Their working conditions, it must be said, do not match their much-vaunted status. The bureaucrats in the key ministries work in almost Dickensian conditions that are a shock for first-time visitors to their offices. They sit crammed side by side at old-fashioned metal desks piled high with papers, with barely a laptop computer in sight. One commentator quipped that the messy sight reminded him of a Mexican customs office. It might look chaotic, but you always knew that they could do you over if they wished.

Naturally, the Japanese bureaucrats' ethos transcends day-to-day discomforts. They are a self-styled and self-sustaining elite—intelligent on the whole, deeply schooled in the ways of their institutions, and committed to them for their working life. The solidarity amongst top bureaucrats is developed early, at the country's main elite training ground—the Law Faculty of

Todai, Tokyo University, which was established in 1880 to train the Emperor's court officials. Just over 70 per cent of the top-ranking entrants to the nine most powerful ministries are graduates of *Todai*, mostly from the Law Faculty. In the case of the Finance Ministry, which sits at the apex of bureaucratic power, the percentage is even greater—a full 90 per cent (18 out of 20)—came from the university in 1994. So influential and entrenched is the *Todai* stream that in 1992 prime minister Miyazawa, himself a Tokyo University graduate and former Finance Ministry official, ordered the ratio of *Todai* alumni entering the elite bureaucracies be cut to 50 per cent. Four years later, the numbers hadn't budged.

This is hardly surprising, as some parents begin preparing their children for *Todai* from the age of five, sending them to primary, high and late-night 'cram schools' which train pupils for the university's rigorous entrance exams. Former *Todai* graduates now working in the ministries also have a strong interest in maintaining the system, because it perpetuates their all-important alumni networks. The bureaucracy, particularly the Finance Ministry, is touchy and defensive on the *Todai* issue these days. When I was checking the latest figures for this book, a ministry spokesman stressed at great length how only about half the latest intake into the agencies under the ministry's control, such as the Customs Office and the National Tax Agency, were *Todai* graduates. In doing so, he only reinforced the point—that the cream of the *Todai* crop all went into the elite Finance Ministry itself. As arduous as the entrance exams are for *Todai*, the institution's worth lies not so much in its educational values, as in its exclusive networks, extending from the highest levels of the bureaucracy, and through business and politics. The exclusivity of the institution makes graduates from *Todai* in particular, and also from one or two other top universities, hot property on the arranged marriage and dating circuit. A Tokyo company started a dating service, the Three Plus One

Club, in 1994, and charged women $2200 to meet exclusively men who had graduated from *Todai*, and Japan's two leading private universities, Waseda and Keio.[8]

The bureaucrats' lifetime commitment to their ministries gives them an awesome institutional memory, used to the starkest advantage in decades of trade talks with the United States, in which Japan has virtually always prevailed by giving only the minimum away. Former US trade negotiator Clyde Prestowitz recalled how 'lean and mean teams' of nine or so US officials would laugh at the large size of the Japanese delegations facing them across the table—sometimes more than 100 officials—until 'we realised the laugh was on us'. 'Their back-up officials were learning while keeping their principals supplied with every possible statistic. On our side, few would even be in government in three years', he wrote.[9] Japanese officials are used to American bluster, with no follow-up. In the Japanese media, senior Tokyo bureaucrats are openly contemptuous of the calibre of US officials. After the 1994 round of bilateral trade talks—when Japan resisted Washington's pressure to adopt numerical targets for imports—a senior Finance Ministry official lamented the weakness of his opposition negotiators. 'Comparing this to Sumo wrestling, we had 14 wins and one defeat', he said.[10] 'When Japan drove the US strongly into a corner, one of the Japanese negotiators sent around a memo reading, "Please stop here; it is so pitiful!".'[11]

Some commentators contend that the dominance of a university like *Todai* is not unique to Japan, and point to institutions like the École Normale d'Administration, the training ground for elite bureaucrats in France, or Oxford and Cambridge, where most of Britain's conservative ruling class is schooled. But there is one crucial difference between Japan and other countries with established bureaucratic traditions. 'In those countries', writes political commentator Takao Toshikawa, 'the supremacy of elected politicians over unelected officials is clearly established, and there is no opportunity for bureaucrats to get the idea that they alone are fit to steer the ship of state'.[12] Many, if not most, Japanese bureaucrats see politicians as little more than 'meretricious players' flitting across the stage of sound administration.[13] The bureaucrats, by contrast, are the permanent government, and consider themselves to be in the service not so much of the political administration of the day as of the state and the Emperor. 'A cabinet minister is often changed in less than one year, so the minister is just a guest in the Government agency. [The bureaucrats] want to say, "A guest should behave like a guest. Don't meddle in another family's business" ',[14] says Akihiko Tanaka of Tokyo University.

When he was put in charge of the Economic Planning Agency during the short life of the Hata government in 1994, former businessman and political neophyte Yoshio Terasawa gained a first-hand taste of how bureaucrats ran their ministers.

About 30 officials would crowd into my office at 7.30 each morning, hand me documents and explain my schedule—'At the eight o'clock cabinet meeting, please make this statement. Then, at the lower house budget committee, MP so-and-so will ask this question. Here is your answer for the part which concerns us'.[15]

The best boss in the eyes of the bureaucrats, said Terasawa, was a minister who knew nothing about economics and just did as he or she was told. An informed minister just meant more headaches.

By and large, the bureaucrats make policy and write the laws. Or, as the old joke goes, the politicians pass the laws, then the bureaucrats write them. (And re-write them, as the occasion demands.) Even during the Gulf War crisis, it was the Finance Ministry which ultimately set the level of Japan's monetary contribution to the anti-Iraq coalition, and told the government of Prime Minister Toshiki Kaifu later.[16] When they are not dictating the answers to parliamentary questions for ministers, the bureaucrats are often on their feet in the Diet answering the questions themselves—in place of their political masters. Ozawa outraged many senior bureaucrats with his radical (for Japan) suggestion that politicians alone should handle questions in the parliament. Tradition-bound public servants fiercely resisted this initiative, because in their view politicians possess neither the skills nor training to discuss policies in detail. 'Have you ever heard an educated opinion from a politician on the current Cambodian problem or our relations with Russia? All they can talk about is how they won a public works project, or something like that', said former MITI Vice-Minister Yoshihiko Morozumi.[17] The prestigious monthly *Bungei Shunju* published a lengthy dialogue between four senior bureaucrats about the upheaval in the political world, and what they could expect from ministers. 'We wouldn't be surprised if the new administration assigns a not-very-capable minister to our ministry, because that is nothing new', said the MITI official. 'Our ministry, too, once had an extremely incapable minister, though of course, no one outside the ministry knew that (laughs).'[18]

In some respects, one can hardly blame the bureaucrats. Japan had nine prime ministers in the nine years to January 1996, and each of them formed at least one, and sometimes two, cabinets. Politicians often barely had time to learn their briefs as ministers, let alone master them, even if they wanted to. Cabinet meetings rubber-stamp policies rather than debate them, and usually conclude their business cypher-like within an hour. Moreover, while the most capable and powerful politicians are usually in charge of the key ministries, ministers have not been generally selected for their ability, but for their length of service as MPs. Everyone who has served in parliament through five or six elections receives a turn. Under the old LDP regime, only a single ruling-party MP who had been re-elected to the parliament five or six times had not been made a minister, and that was only because he had been convicted of bribery. This

MP, Koko Sato, tried hard to make amends, including changing the reading of the Chinese characters that made up his first name to 'Koko' from 'Takayuki'. (The new reading, 'Koko', means filial piety, and was designed to instil a renewed sense of trust in him.) But Sato's show of contrition was to no avail—he never became a minister, unlike many of his less capable colleagues.

The new breed of administrators, like the Finance Ministry's Sakakibara, resist theories of a 'bureaucratic dictatorship'. Sakakibara says that under the LDP's one-party rule, the party's supreme body, the Policy Research Council, vetted all decisions and legislation in 'fine detail'. Activist politicians do leave their mark on policy, particularly in foreign affairs. But the politicians' real power has been in brokering compromises between competing agencies and administrators, rather than in taking policy initiatives. It is also true that the advent of the *zoku-giin* politicians clustering around certain industries and interests like tribes, has increased the power of politicians over the last decade. Through these 'tribes', politicians have been able to develop the networks and the expertise to match the bureaucrats on their own turf. But the relationship is mutually beneficial, because powerful politicians, in turn, are invaluable for guiding the bureaucrats' legislation through the parliament. Far from instructing the bureaucrats to implement specified decisions, the politicians act more like the bureaucrats' bodyguards in shepherding them past their enemies in the legislature.[19]

The bureaucracy's agenda is not hurt by the fact that roughly one-third of MPs, slightly more so in the case of the LDP, are former bureaucrats, whose loyalties and networks largely tie them to their former ministries' interests. In recent years, the mandarins' web of influence has also spread to regional governments. Seventeen former officials of the Home Affairs Ministry are now governors of prefectures, sixteen are vice-governors and

25 occupy the position which controls the budget.[20] (There are 47 prefectures in all.) This back-scratching arrangement allows the central bureaucracy to keep a grip on the policies of the provinces, and has made a mockery of repeated attempts to promote decentralisation. Much of the time of local government officers is spent lobbying the central bureaucracy. Prefectural governments, for example, took an average of 1120 days, or nearly three years, to consider an application to rezone land in their districts, largely because each decisAon has to be approved by the central bureaucracy in Tokyo. The *Asahi Shimbun* reported that in each case, an average of 68 local government officials travelled to Tokyo on 24 separate occasions to visit different ministries in Tokyo to gain their approval for rezoning.[21] The 31 prefectural governments which responded to a survey by a citizens' group reported that they spent Y2.2 billion ($29 million) in the 1993 financial year wining and dining central bureaucrats. If all 47 local governments had responded, the figure would have been much higher.[22]

The long-standing collusive mechanism used by bureaucrats to marry their interests with those of the private sector is the practice of *amakudari*—literally, 'descent from heaven'. This is the custom by which bureaucrats retire into positions in private companies and public corporations, usually ones under their ministry's control. For 30 consecutive years to 1995, the Finance Ministry retired the most number of officials into the private sector, generally to run the very banks and large life insurance companies which they had hitherto regulated, according to lists published annually in the Japanese media.[23] The construction industry is also fond of *amakudari*. Since 1960, one in four retiring Construction Ministry officials have gone onto the payrolls of private companies, entitling them to receive tens of millions in retirement allowances after just a few years service.

The practice is also entrenched and codified in the country's massive defence industries. Here, the private companies accept *amakudari* from the Defence Agency according to the value of government procurement orders. Thus the biggest contractor, Mitsubishi Heavy Industries, has over the years accumulated 70 former Defence Agency officers onto its payroll, followed by NEC with 50, Toshiba 50, Fuji Heavy Industries 40, and Ishikawajima-harumi Heavy Industries with 25. The head of Canon, Ryusaburo Kaku, well known as a straight shooter in the corporate world for his long standing refusal to make political donations, complained that the system was like 'an invisible corporation tax'. 'When we started doing business in the defence industry, we were told that if we accepted one junior officer, we could expect an order for Y500 million [$6.6 million], and a more senior officer, an order for Y1 billion [$13.2 million]', he said.[24]

Japan's premier big business organisation, the Keidanren, is also required to make a contribution to the welfare of retiring bureaucrats. On fifteen separate occasions since 1991, the body has been 'requested' by various ministries to donate money to establish foundations for ageing mandarins. These 'requests' are somewhat similar to a Mafia-style offer that can't be refused, lest an offended ministry decide to take administrative revenge against a reluctant donor. The official amount paid by Keidanren-affiliated companies to these foundations in recent years is Y15.1 billion ($201 million), but the real sum, according to a recent book on the bureaucracy, is probably around Y200 billion ($2.6 billion).[25]

The *amakudari* system has some benefits, as it ensures that the bureaucrats' skills are not thrown on the scrapheap when they retire. But in practice, *amakudari* has come to symbolise an unseemly and often corrupt collusion between regulators and those they regulated. Criticism of the custom led to the introduction of a law which bans bureaucrats from taking jobs in companies closely connected with their work for two years after their retirement. However, the law can be sidestepped if the bureaucrats get permission to join companies two years before their retirement date. In 1994, at the height of the bribery scandals in the construction industry, the government grandly announced that no retiring officials would be joining private construction companies. In fact, it was later revealed the officials were being 'warehoused' by public corporations under the ministry's control until the scandal blew over.

The bureaucracy's distinctive characteristics—such as *amakudari* and the elite graduates steaming out of Tokyo University—are all long standing and well documented features of the Japanese system, and are likely to remain so. But this is a point worth reinforcing. Recent publicity out of Japan heralding epochal change in the country have mostly overlooked the fact that none of these fundamental building blocks of, and feeder systems into, the bureaucracy and its networks have been disturbed. In the case of some politicians, however, it was not for want of trying.

The high point of the politicians' attempts to capture the bureaucracy in the post-LDP era was the dramatic sacking on Christmas Eve 1993 of Masahisa Naito, a star bureaucrat in MITI. The sacking was an event of huge symbolic importance in Japan. Naito was the first senior bureaucrat in the ministry to be dismissed in more than three decades, and his removal had the potential to force an historic split of the bureaucracy along the same lines that now divided the two warring conservative parties. After 32 years and nine months in MITI, Naito was the director of MITI's prestigious Industrial Policy Bureau, and one step from the position of Vice-Minister, the top job, in one of Japan's most powerful ministries. Naito's sin had been to 'improperly' promote a junior official on the eve of that official's resignation from the ministry to run as an LDP candidate in the 1993 general election. In doing this, Naito had followed standard practice established over many years. Such promotions were designed to add prestige to the bureaucrat's election campaign, and make him a more attractive candidate. In return, the ministry benefited from having another former MITI official in parliament. Sacking Naito for making this standard promotion was the equivalent of handing him 'a death sentence for urinating outdoors', said one of his supporters.[26]

Naito's real mistake, however, was his timing. During the rule of the monolithic LDP, this kind of collusive practice was tolerated, and even tacitly encouraged. For all the bitter factional battles over the spoils of office, deals bringing smart bureaucrats into the LDP's fold were all ultimately for the benefit of the single ruling party, the LDP. But by the time Naito promoted the official the LDP had split in two, and his new minister in the incoming Hosokawa government came from Ichiro Ozawa's rebel camp, then called the *Shinseito*.[27] It was any bureaucrat's worst nightmare to find himself on the wrong side of an incoming government. Ozawa immediately began hunting down the 'war criminals' among bureaucrats in the former establishment, and Naito was his biggest scalp. There was no little irony in the fact that the minister who did Ozawa's dirty work by sacking Naito, Hiroshi Kumagai, was a former MITI official, and had himself been promoted prior to leaving the ministry to boost his own election campaign! Even worse, in a world where seniority was all, Kumagai had entered the ministry after Naito, and thus was his junior. Kumagai himself acidly noted this when giving Naito the shove. 'It's rather hard to say this to my senior', he told him, 'but will you resign'.[28]

The sacking had a dual motivation. First, it was a straight political payback for Naito's leg-up to the LDP. Second, it was an attempt by the Ozawa group to grab control of the rich industry associations overseen by MITI. The ministry assigns parliamentary responsibility for about 50-odd associations to select Diet members, who can use them to raise political funds and collect voters. In return, MITI and the industries in question can prevail upon the MP to look after their interests in the parliament.[29] But the impact of Naito's sacking went far beyond a mere political power play to gain control of this lucrative source of money. All ministries maintain a fierce grip on the right to make major personnel decisions themselves. The Ozawa camp had breached the sanctity of this convention in the most crude and public fashion, and triggered a crisis within the entire bureaucracy. Journalist Koei Kaga, in his definitive account of the affair, recounted the details of an emotionally charged meeting between the Vice-Minister Hideaki Kumano and Naito over the sacking. 'The Vice-Minister, while crying, said to his Secretariat Director-General [Makino], whose room was next to his: "What about you, Makino?" Then Makino also started crying and said, "Mr Naito! You are the most respectable senior I know. To be honest, there is nothing like that." The two just kept crying.'[30] His account of their teary conversation sounds like two people discussing a sudden devastating death in the family, and in a way, it was.

Ozawa's intervention in MITI, like most of his actions, was a mixture of cynical power play and principled high policy, and extricating one from the other is all but impossible. But if nothing else, Naito's sacking introduced a new dose of uncertainty and competition into relations between politicians and bureaucrats, something that has already spilled over into subsequent governments. The Director-General of the Science Agency—a position with ministerial ranking—in the LDP-led Murayama government, (Ms) Makiko Tanaka, sacked a bureaucrat in 1994 after he objected to her plans to streamline the number of bodies nominally under her control. 'They are not the minister's personal possession', the bureaucrat, Kinji Atarashi, admonished her.[31] Atarashi chose the wrong person for this kind of confrontation. Tanaka is the daughter of Kakuei Tanaka, and just as tough and competent. She had already broken the mould by being named a cabinet minister in her first term as an MP, and is lauded by some as a future prime minister. After Atarashi challenged her authority, she swiftly had him removed from his post.

Competition between the political parties for power, if it persists, will breed a more competitive relationship with the bureaucracy. It is wise not to exaggerate this trend, as the LDP faction chiefs have long played favourites with their bureaucratic allies. But in a genuine two-party system, politicians will be forced to compete more on policy than personalities, something that will naturally bring them into conflict with the bureaucrats. For the moment, the chaos on the political scene has made the administrators more, rather than less, powerful. But the surest sign that the bureaucracy would not be able to rise above the political fray was given by the LDP powerbrokers in the Murayama government. They took careful note of Ozawa's bureaucratic favourites, and targeted them when they returned to power. The lines were now clearly drawn between the rival political camps, and nowhere were the stakes higher than in the battle for the Ministry of Finance.

THE MEN FROM MOF

The Japanese say that you can tell the man from MOF (Ministry of Finance) just from where he is sitting. When senior bureaucrats entertain MOF officials, it is the MOF official who always takes the seat of honour, even when he is younger and out-ranked by the host, a significant gesture in a hierarchy-conscious society. The same goes for a politician courting a MOF official, particularly one from the all-powerful Budget Bureau. Large banks and securities firms employ people known as *MOF-tan*— literally, 'in charge of MOF'—whose sole job is to cultivate close ties with the ministry. Ideally, the *MOF-tan* should be *Todai* graduates, to ensure that they meet their MOF quarries as equals. The *MOF-tan* visit the important securities and banking bureaux in the ministry on most days, and also discreetly entertain senior ministry officials in the evening in exclusive traditional *ryotei* restaurants. (On average, an evening in a private room at a *ryotei* for a party of six to eight guests will cost around Y350 000 ($4600).)[32]

The rising MOF officials who are sent for a stint in a branch of the Tax Agency outside Tokyo also get the red-carpet treatment, as the guest of honour at nightly banquets sponsored by local business groups and governments, for example. The young bureaucrat is a sound investment for local government officials, especially as preparation for the annual trek to Tokyo to pay homage to the ministry officials drawing up Japan's annual budget. During this time, the halls of Kasumigaseki, the bureaucratic heartland of Japan in central Tokyo, swarm with around 2000 officials and governors from all 47 prefectures armed with gifts and large entertainment budgets.[33] So crude and overwhelming was the gift-giving in 1994 that the government's chief spokesman, Kozo Igarashi, stepped in and demanded that local officials exercise 'self-restraint', a polite Japanese way of saying 'Desist'.

When the local officials depart, the real action begins. Bureaucrats from spending ministries scoop up spending requests from regional offices, consult with the *zoku* MPs, and crowd into MOF corridors to present their demands. Once again, the official from the spending ministry requesting the money is always one rank higher than the MOF official who receives him. The fallen 'godfather' of Japanese politics, Shin Kanemaru, upbraided MPs for their timidity before the mighty MOF mandarins, and told them in a speech in 1988 how to really go about lobbying for money. 'You can't get money out of the government when all you've got are representatives who think they are kingpins! You can't keep everyone happy unless you are prepared to lay your life on the line, and go about overturning the desk of the Director-General of the Budget Bureau at MOF!'[34]

The reason that cultivating the ministry and its officials is so important is simple. MOF sits at the pinnacle of power in Japan's hierarchical society—quite literally, writes economic journalist Eamonn Fingleton, it is 'the most powerful economic organisation on earth . . . combining under one roof a degree of concentrated power unheard of in the West'.[35] MOF controls the national budget, collects taxes, supervises Japanese banks and life companies, which are the largest in the world, oversees the savings system, regulates the sharemarket and manages the macro-economy. It has a hand in allocating Japan's massive foreign aid budget, again the world's largest, and setting defence policy through the officials it posts to head the Defence Agency. The MOF controls the terms on which virtually all public and private Japanese investment is made. Its mastery of the budget gives it unparalleled access to information held by other ministries, and through that, control over them. It also has a large say, through the central Bank of Japan, in setting monetary policy. 'In other words', says Fingleton, 'it controls the three basic functions of government—taxing, spending and national security'.

The characters which make the Japanese name of the ministry, *Okurasho*, literally translate as 'Ministry of the Big [fireproof] Storehouse'. Within Japan, the ministry is sometimes compared to a village elder who oversees the harvest and makes sure it is shared through the whole village. Its officials, however, are far from humble and benevolent village types. They are proud, horribly hard-working and convinced of their mission as guardians of the public purse. They are also adherents to Margaret Thatcher's TINA (There Is No Alternative) principle of political management. A senior MOF official once lamented in a conversation with me the difficulties being faced by his colleagues in the Foreign Ministry as they grappled with a thorny diplomatic issue. The issues confronting the Foreign Ministry, he said, were tough because they involved making ideological choices, whereas the MOF's work was free of such loaded decisions and debates. In other words, economic policy was value-free! Just about everyone else, from the president of the United States down, took a very different view in the tax debate that dominated the political scene throughout the first half of the 1990s.

MOF has long resisted demands from politicians and foreigners for income tax cuts for two reasons. Its fiscal rectitude and loathing of deficit financing is legendary, and the ministry fights strenuously to protect the tax base. MOF also has no desire to spur consumption and empower consumers by putting more money into the pockets of ordinary Japanese. MOF would prefer that Japanese saved, and made their money available for industry to invest. Correspondingly, the ministry has taken every chance for the past two decades to increase consumption taxes. The 3 per cent consumption tax introduced in the face of strong public opposition in 1989 momentarily exhausted the ministry's political capital, and was the primary cause of a sharp electoral setback for the LDP in upper-house elections that year. In 1993, MOF spotted another chance to lift taxes—ironically, at precisely the time when Japan was coming under severe pressure from Washington to cut taxes to boost consumption and cut the trade surplus.

Unlike the Foreign Ministry and MITI, which had to respond quickly to demands from Washington, MOF's then head, Vice-Minister Jiro Saito, and his ministry, were relatively impervious to pressure from the Americans. Saito once refused for four months to meet with the most important foreigner in Japan, US Ambassador Walter Mondale, a man who could count on being received immediately in almost any other forum in the country. Mondale wanted to push the case for a Japanese income tax cut before a summit meeting between Hosokawa and President Clinton in December 1993. The counter-suggestive Finance Ministry saw the introduction of an income tax cut as the perfect chance to renew their push for a consumption tax increase. A few days before the summit meeting, the ministry did a deal with Hosokawa's chief strategist, Ozawa. The MOF would allow a temporary cut in income taxes, but only if the difference was made up by a permanent hike in the consumption tax later.

Hosokawa was powerless to oppose the plan, and was cornered into suddenly announcing the deal at a pre-dawn press conference, without having consulted the cabinet. He called the additional impost on consumption the 'people's welfare tax', because it was earmarked to pay for Japan's expanding elderly population, but the sugar-coating did not help quell the uproar which followed. Hosokawa fumbled the announcement badly, and was unable to explain why the new tax was being set at 7 per cent. He lamely suggested it was a 'rough estimate' of what might be needed. Members of his own cabinet, drawn from a fragile seven-party coalition, threatened to walk out of the government, and a few days later Hosokawa dropped the plan. Hosokawa's humiliating backdown crippled his leadership forever, but the greater significance of the episode lay in the role of the MOF, and Saito.

As administrative Vice-Minister, Saito's job was to broker agreement between the ministry's different bureaux, a job which made him more powerful than his minister (and in many respects the prime minister as well). Saito established his supremacy early in the term of the Hosokawa government, ambushing an attempt by the Prime Minister to hasten completion of the national budget. After securing the support of the Finance Minister on this crucial issue, Hosokawa and his senior advisers had scheduled a meeting late one evening to conclude the agreement. Saito, however, refused to let the minister attend, and surprised Hosokawa by turning up, unannounced, himself. 'The atmosphere completely changed', one of Hosokawa's advisers recalled. Saito bluntly rebuffed the initiative for an early budget, and it died a quiet death.[36] When it suited him and the ministry's agenda Saito did deals with powerful politicians like Ozawa, and when it suited him he kept them at bay.

The mistake that many make in analysing the MOF is to equate its awesome powers with an infallible ability to micromanage the economy. Dutch journalist Karel van Wolferen says Westerners would 'declare you insane' if you suggested you could agree with your bankers that your land 'is worth two to three times as much as you had calculated half a year before, or that you can enhance your productive capacity with free capital. But the Ministry of Finance may endorse these notions with enthusiasm because it can make them come true'. Van Wolferen says that to the extent that economic reality is a result of what people believe about it, the Ministry of Finance is the ultimate arbiter.[37] Van Wolferen's point about the MOF's lack of accountability is well made, but his dual contention about the ministry's ability to sustain these surreal asset valuations is not. Reality bit the MOF mandarins sharply in the 1990s because of their monumental mismanagement of the bubble economy. After a decade in which all the levers of policy had been under the ministry's tight supervision, MOF's legacy by 1995 was an economy hovering on the edge of a catastrophic deflation, a financial system begging for taxpayer-funded bailouts, and a currency which had careened out of control, and permanently damaged Japanese industry. Ministry officials had also been implicated in a number of sleazy scandals, which caused severe harm to the institution's prestige. The low point came with revelations in early 1995 that one of the shadowiest entrepreneurs of the bubble period, Harunori Takahashi of EIE International, had corrupted two senior ministry officials, including the deputy chief of MOF's most powerful and prestigious agency, the Budget Bureau. In mid-July in the same year, a senior MOF bureaucrat resigned after confessing to starting a business with a consultant to EIE. 'Here were ultra-elite officials

. . . being rather easily seduced by a man no better than a street corner gangster, offering them a few free eats and drinks', commented *Tokyo Business Today*. 'To many, it was a symbol of how far the ministry had sunk.'[38]

Saito's high-profile interventions in the sensitive tax issue, the failure of the economy to respond to repeated attempts at stimulus, and the scandals involving ministry personnel unleashed an unprecedented burst of MOF-bashing by politicians and the media. *Tokyo Business Today* was not alone in suggesting that breaking up the ministry, and stripping it of its enormous powers was now 'a serious consideration'. But as MOF's opponents discovered, while bashing the ministry was easy, dismembering it, and reducing its powers, was not. The LDP used the scandals to force Saito to resign early as head of the ministry. This was reported as a ground-breaking symbolic blow by the politicians against an arrogant and all-powerful ministry, but in the broader scheme of things, it is difficult to see it as anything other than a token punishment. Saito had already managed to lengthen his usual one-year term to two, and left his post only one month before his extended stewardship was due to finish. Saito also ensured that a hand-picked successor took his place.

Under the fashionable banner of 'deregulation', the LDP tried to punish Saito and MOF further by merging two of the public corporations under their control, the Export-Import Bank, and the Japan Development Bank. The merger proposal barely contemplated changing the operations of the two bodies, which lent money to developing countries, but it would have been a symbolic body blow to the ministry's prestige. The merger would also have deprived the ministry of a precious *amakudari* post where it could place retiring officials. It was not as if the government did not have a blueprint for change. Businessman Eiji Suzuki, who had been handpicked by Hosokawa to head an inquiry into reforming the bureaucracy, had identified the

MOF monolith as the biggest single obstacle to reform. 'Unless we change the network of ministries and agencies and the colossal authority they have acquired—in short unless we hack up the Ministry of Finance—we can't reform the bureaucracy', he pleaded.[39] But when the politicians turned up the heat, MOF simply refused to bend, and bluntly rejected the merger. In lobbying against the merger, MOF's powerful reach extended overseas, and it managed to enlist even foreign powers, such as the Mexican government, to intervene on its behalf with the administration in Tokyo. By the time the dust had settled in the ministry's battles with the politicians and the media, the MOF had lost a smidgin of its prestige but virtually none of its sweeping powers.

The broader battle over deregulation, however, extended way beyond the personal vendettas of politicians against the Finance Ministry, and is in many respects much more important. It involved the group often accurately tagged as the His Majesty's real opposition to the government of Japan—foreigners—plus a new breed of Japanese who are also battling to break down the walls of Japan's bureaucratic citadels.

BREAKING THE RULES

Deregulation is something that Western free-marketers assume is a good thing for an economy, and by extension, society. The less the government is involved in an economy, the more room is left for individuals to build businesses and create wealth. The proverbial Martian arriving in Japan at any time during the last decade could have easily assumed that the Japanese heartily agreed. From the Maekawa Report of the mid-1980s, named after a former Bank of Japan chief, all the way to the 'epoch-making' report authored under the guidance of big business chief Gaishi Hiraiwa in 1994, Japan has officially supported 'the concept of an economy being open in principle and closed only by exception'.[40]

If it were true that the economy was 'open in principle and closed by exception', it would be a radical about-face for Japan. Even more than their counterparts around the globe, the first impulse of the Japanese bureaucrat is to regulate and control whatever is part of his patch. 'To put it a bit simplistically', says former US trade negotiator Glen Fukushima, 'in the American system, things are assumed to be permitted unless they are explicitly proscribed, whereas in the Japanese system, things are assumed to be proscribed unless explicitly permitted'.[41]

The bureaucrats' tentacles are spread into all sorts of minute, petty areas. Every convenience store and new building across Japan, for example, is required to have the same green and white-coloured fire exit sign. All glass bottles with 400 millilitres capacity or more have to be individually checked for safety, following two small accidents in the 1970s. The Agriculture Ministry specifies two levels of quality and five sizes for tomatoes—and if they don't fit, they have to be thrown out. The Transport Ministry insists on inspecting rooms before licensing them to be used for the luggage storage business, and then also sets the prices to be charged. And so on.[42]

The stakes got higher, and the contradictions sharper, when the peak business body, the Keidanren, made deregulation the body's top priority in 1995. Deregulation emerged simultaneously as the solution to all Japan's domestic and international economic problems. Stripping away rafts of bureaucratic rules was the panacea to increase imports, cut the trade surplus, revitalise business activity and decisively end the five-year economic slump. There was some truth to this theory. The Japanese economy and consumer exhibit incredible vitality when bureaucratic obstacles are removed from their path. A classic case was the decision of the government in 1994 to allow people to buy cellular phones instead of just renting them. Cellular phone prices subsequently halved, and sometimes even dropped to zero, as new companies rushed to sign on subscribers. Within a few months, sales of the phones were four times those of rental phones earlier.

But this kind of decision was as much the exception as the rule. Almost immediately after launching the great deregulation push, the Keidanren's head, the chairman of Toyota Motor Corp., Shoichiro Toyoda, was hoist on his own petard on the issue of government regulations. At the same press conference where he supported the removal of bureaucratic shackles, he said that the rigorous safety inspections for cars and car parts— something that Washington insisted was a major barrier to imports—should be maintained.[43] His assertion that deregulation was a good thing for every sector except his own shattered his credibility, and that of the Keidanren, on this issue. There was a degree of irony in Toyoda's dilemma. The inspections hindered the importation of foreign cars into Japan, but their effect on Japanese domestic car makers, like Toyota, was exactly the opposite. The rule, in fact, had long been considered a conspiracy between Japanese car makers and the government to increase sales of new vehicles. Because inspections had been made so tough and expensive for cars only three to four years old, people were easily persuaded to buy a new one instead. 'Many people buy new cars because of a pending inspection. By lengthening the time between inspections, it will be even harder to sell cars . . . and contrary to economic stimulus measures', admitted a senior MITI official.[44]

In truth, the push for deregulation from both outside and inside Japan was always powerfully resisted by the bureaucracy and business, even as they continued to pump out reports in its favour. There were exceptions, of course. The ministry which had guided and protected Japanese postwar industry, MITI, increasingly backed cutting bureaucratic red tape, as it realised it was the only way to return the economy to growth. MITI was acutely aware that deregulation was necessary to develop new areas of business and maintain vitality and innovation. As the ministry responsible for dealing with perennial complaints from foreigners about Japan's unfair trade practices, MITI also knew that deregulation was the key to defusing frictions with the country's international partners. MITI adopted the well-worn tactic of generating pressure from abroad to force change at home in Japan, by cajoling Tokyo-based foreign businessmen to join a committee, the Import Board, to tally complaints about regulations to other ministries. But even this failed to get results. Many of the businessmen were deeply cynical about the worth of the committees—not surprisingly, as during a decade of similar exhortations for Japanese businesses to import more, beginning in 1982, Japan's current account surplus had increased seventeen-fold! The American representative on the committee despaired when the Japanese government refused to allow a US-made power hammer, which was much cheaper and more portable than its Japanese competitor, to be sold in Japan. Japanese bureaucrats classified the hammer as a potential weapon under the Gun and Sword Law, and refused to allow it to be used for construction. When the Americans complained to the Japanese trade ombudsman, the bureaucrats triumphantly pointed out that it had been used to attack a villian in one of Hollywood's *Lethal Weapon* movies.[45] MITI's best efforts aside, the whole process was fatally flawed from the start, because the politicians had entrusted the process of deregulation largely to the bureaucrats, whose careers depended on doing the regulating.

The bureaucrats, however, could not stand in the way of the massive discounting wars that broke out after the bursting of the bubble economy. Price cutting had been traditionally frowned upon in Japan because it created 'confusion in the marketplace', a code for the disruption of the close-knit interests, and mark-ups, of manufacturers, distributors and storekeepers. Manufacturers refused to sell to any stores that discounted their products, and the government's competition watchdog, the Fair Trade Commission, until the early 1990s largely ignored the complaints of putative price-cutters. But the recession, and the surge of cheaper imports on the back of the strong yen, swept aside many of these traditional barriers. A declaration by Isao Nakauchi, the head of Japan's largest super-market chain, Daiei, that he could cut prices in half if all government regulations were removed struck terror into the hearts of many old-style retailers.[46] In one single month in 1994, the prices of 26 imported products surveyed by the Finance Ministry fell, with 20 of them recording double-digit drops. Nakauchi and a number of other discounters became celebrities for their efforts to reduce prices and, most importantly, consumers loved it. 'A myth had grown up, propagated by manufacturers, that consumers value service and quality above everything else, and don't care about price', said prominent market researcher George Fields. 'But nobody bothered to ask consumers what they wanted—it was a producer-driven market.'

It wasn't only producers who didn't like discounting. For years, foreigners who had already penetrated the Japanese market had been able to sell their goods at inflated Japanese prices by licensing—illegally—the import rights to a single Jap-anese company. Many an odd alliance between foreign companies and their Japanese suppliers sprang up behind the scenes to lobby against any changes opening the market wider to imports. But more interesting was the sharp philosophical and nationalistic backlash against deregulation, and in defence of the Japanese system. A group of prominent academics and commen-tators published a paper titled 'The Nightmare Called Deregulation' claiming that a reduction in bureaucratic power was incompatible with Japanese capitalism, and also posed a threat to social order. 'Deregulation aims to weed out inefficient industries, lower prices and stimulate the economy, but what it will do first is wreck the lifetime employment system. It will cause major turmoil in wide-ranging areas', the group said.[47] This school presents a relaxation in rules almost as a form of ethnic deregulation of Japan's homogeneous society.

Another academic, Professor Tsuneo Ida, condemned deregulation as Darwinian and destructive, and argued strenuously in favour of the virtues of a Nanny State instead. 'A society consists of many incompetent people. I think that a society discarding such people cannot be healthy. Can we say that today's American society is better than ours?' he said.[48] Much as consumers are learning to love lower prices, this is a position with broad support in Japan. 'Society would be happy with minor reforms of the bureaucracy', says Ed Lincoln, an American academic who has also acted as an adviser to the US Ambassador in Tokyo. 'They don't really want deregulation or major reform. They simply want the bureaucracy to behave better so that trust is restored.'[49]

Ultimately, radical challenges to bureaucratic authority in Japan are doomed to failure for another reason. Those Japanese and foreigners who do want change lack one crucial avenue of review available in other democracies—the law and the court system. In Japan, the bureaucrats have made sure that they not only write the laws, but interpret them as well.

TAME COURTS

When the Japanese vote at a general election, they also sit in judgement on the country's Supreme Court justices. The names of the judges sitting on the bench of the country's highest court are listed on the ballot paper, and any one of them can be sent packing if enough people mark a disapproving 'X' by his or her name. Translate that situation to the United States or Australia, and imagine the consequences. The Chief Justice and his learned brethren on America's Supreme Court, or Australia's High Court, would be sitting ducks in any poll for savage campaigns by their numerous vocal critics—campaigns which, if they didn't unseat the judges, might at least intimidate their office, and weaken their independence. But in Japan, the judges glide back into office easily in election after election. Not one single judge has ever been voted out, because most Japanese have no idea about who they are, or what role they fulfil.

Few institutions so strikingly illustrate the deep differences between Japan and other democracies as its legal system, and the court that sits at its apex. According to the constitution, Japan's Supreme Court is the 'court of last resort' which determines the constitutionality of all laws. The judges' chambers are sited symbolically in central Tokyo, commanding Olympian views across the deep moat surrounding the Imperial Palace. Theoretically, the court is all-powerful and independent. But unlike its namesake in the United States or the High Court in Australia, it virtually never challenges the decisions of bureaucrats and politicians. The court sticks to the subterranean role allotted it in the Japanese political system by the Justice Ministry, which oversees and controls it. Most Japanese don't know the names of the judges, let alone the decisions they take. 'Even lawyers don't know that much about them—I can't name all the justices', confessed Seiichi Yoshikawa, the president of the Second Tokyo Bar Association.[50]

The system of putting the judges up for election after they have been appointed gives the system a democratic lustre, but it is a complete illusion. In 1989, for example, the court ruled against the government in just 28 of the 1547 cases brought before it. In other words, only 1.8 per cent of the anti-government litigants succeeded. This pattern is mirrored in all jurisdictions, particularly in the criminal courts. In 1990, Japanese courts found 107 of the 1 271 395 people brought before it innocent, according to official Justice Ministry figures—a mere

0.01 per cent. 'Not guilty' verdicts always cause great shock and consternation. After one lower-court judge, Shinichi Tateyama of the Tokyo High Court, discharged a number of prisoners with verdicts of innocent, the press said he was suffering from 'not guilty disease'. There are no such loose cannons on the Supreme Court. Seiichi Yoshikawa laughed when asked if he could remember any dissenting opinions in the court's judgements. 'I'll have to check, because it's rather rare.'

Yoshikawa blames the court's tameness mostly on its stealthy but steady takeover by the Justice Ministry during the many years of the Liberal Democrats' one-party rule. Neither the ruling party nor the bureaucracy had any interest in encouraging an independent centre of power outside their own orbit. 'The court has a very powerful secretariat, and in order for young judges to be promoted, it's very important for them to be members of it', Yoshikawa says.

But the secretariat is an institution of the bureaucracy—they do not discharge judicial functions. They look after budgets, personnel and issues like how to keep up the courthouses. So in a way, promotions of judges to sit in important positions lies completely with the bureaucrats. The whole judiciary has been run by these people.

The cabinet is only nominally involved in appointing the court's fifteen members. In practice, the choices are made by the Justice Ministry, which carves up the positions according to a somewhat obscure convention. At least six of the court's fifteen members are career judges, trained to sit on the bench from a young age and promoted on the basis of seniority. Another four positions are split between former bureaucrats and prosecutors. There is always one law professor and also one ex-diplomat. In the United States nominees undergo harsh and partisan gruelling by senators before confirmation; in Australia the careers of new High Court judges are raked over by the media in search of ideological leanings; but appointments in Japan don't make big news, because the judges and their decisions are considered to be predictable. 'Most of the judges nominated by the Government are . . . people who don't feel compelled to eliminate administrative control', says Yoshikawa.

The role of the Japanese judiciary has always been limited. 'Before the war, under the old constitution, the emperor was the supreme power, and by taking over this framework, the military ruled the country. There was very little opportunity for the judiciary to participate in the political process,' says Yoshikawa. 'After the war, the whole thing was changed over to the American system, but of course, people don't change so quickly.'

The courts enjoyed a brief period of feisty independence after the war, but this wilted in the 1960s when the ruling party and the bureaucracy began attacking it for a number of 'biased decisions'. At times, the court appears embarrassed about its constitutional powers. In a landmark case in the 1960s, the court was asked to rule on whether the American military stationed in Japan breached the country's constitutional ban on armed forces. The court decided the issue was too hot to handle, and abandoned its prerogatives. The sitting judges said that 'highly political' issues such as this could not be decided by judges—a stance that, incidentally, many critics of activist higher courts in the West would endorse. Gradually, the courts became the creature of a political culture, in which the bureaucrats have successfully equated an aggressive assertion of individual legal rights with a sort of anti-social egotism. 'The system has turned into a bureaucratic organisation similar to administrative offices where orders are passed from top to bottom', says the *Asahi Shimbun*.[51] When difficult cases are listed, members of the ministry's secretariat make their views known by calling on judges, arranging conferences and sending them huge volumes of reference documents. It is a brave judge who strikes out on his own. Judges and the courts have long learnt to value civil order over civil liberties.

Even if ordinary Japanese were 'culturally' predisposed to conciliate rather than litigate their disputes, as the official line contends they are, the bureaucrats have ensured they have no choice. As we have seen, the Justice Ministry strictly restricts the supply of lawyers by allowing only about 2 per cent of the students who sit the annual Bar exam to pass. The test is so difficult that it takes the successful applicant at least six attempts on average, and many hours at special cram schools, to pass it. As a result, Japan has one lawyer per 6331 people, compared with the US, which has one per 320; Australia, one per 560; the United Kingdom, one per 693; Germany, one per 981 and France, one per 1784.[52] Lawyers are thus in short supply, and expensive. Not surprisingly, the small elite who do pass the gruelling bar exam are not in favour of their achievement being undervalued, and are conspicuously silent in supporting moves to increase the numbers of lawyers. 'Severely restricting new-comers is symptomatic of the protectionism and over-regulation that plagued Japan's economy in the past', complained Yoshio Suzuki, the head of a legal think-tank. 'And never was there as much of a closed shop as the legal profession.'[53]

The number of judges and court staff is also kept deliber-ately low. The Supreme Court's fifteen judges process thousands of cases every year. A *Mainichi Shimbun* journalist who visited the Supreme Court in 1994 reported that the results of 65 cases were dispatched in just eleven minutes. In all cases the court ordered the plaintiffs to bear the costs, and gave no reasons for the decision! Criminal and civil cases can take as long as 25 years from the initial trial to the final appeal, hardly encouraging for litigants, particularly as they are likely to have their claims rejected in the end anyway. With the odds so heavily stacked against potential litigants, it's no wonder that one of the fastest growing areas of law in the West—challenges to the legality of bureaucratic regulations and decisions—is a no-growth industry in Japan. The capture and control of the court system by the bureaucracy dovetails neatly with its predilection for drafting vaguely worded laws and regulations that it alone can interpret and enforce. Former MITI chief Yoshihiko Morozumi admitted this was done because it was considered 'too time-consuming' to explain the legal ins and outs of issues to politicians. 'Instead, we came to depend on administrative guidance, whereby the ministries and agencies regulate industry through dialogue and persuasion. No doubt one element of this was the feeling that laws can tie your hands', he said. Japan, like so many Asian nations, has developed a culture that enforces rule by men, not laws.

As the Japanese make the slow transition from subjects to citizens, they should, according to Western standards, expect disputes to be decided not by informal bureaucratic fiat but by clear, well defined rules. 'What's the good of a court that acknowledges greater discretion for bureaucrats, and refuses to play the role worthy of a watchdog?' the *Asahi Shimbun* complained in an editorial. In recent years, there has been some movement in that direction, with the passage of new laws allowing people to sue for defective products and take action as shareholders against company management. 'Japan will become somewhat more litigious, a birth pang of emerging from this cocoon of mutual back-scratching and collusion', claims Yoshio Suzuki.[54] But the jury remains out on this question. Japan may have gained some new laws, but it still has the same old Justice Ministry, and its raft of controls designed to ensure that the courts don't become messy and unpredictable. There is also little pressure from the public for change. The Japanese legal system may look repugnant and unfair through Western, libertarian eyes. But from Japan, the view is different. Many commentators there cast a cold eye on a deregulated society like the United States, which is overflowing with expensive lawyers and rising crime, and conclude that a strong bureaucracy and a controlled legal system are two of the secrets to their success.

Morihiro Hosokawa, who came to office promising to roll back the power of the mandarins, was in fact well liked by the bureaucrats—in some respects because neither he nor many of his neophyte ministers had the power or the networks to push them around. A high-ranking Foreign Ministry official could not have been nicer when I asked him over an informal lunch one day about Hosokawa. The bureaucrat replied that he saw him as a clean, fresh face to represent Japan to the world—a symbol of change for a world which was demanding it. 'But there was one thing which greatly worried us for a while', he confided. That was when Hosokawa boldly declared soon after becoming Prime Minister that Japan had waged a 'war of aggression' against its neighbours more than half a century before. The official said the ministry immediately dispatched its top bureaucrats to warn Hosokawa that such statements could support legal compensation claims against Japan.

'And', he said with emphatic satisfaction, and not the least shame, 'Mr Hosokawa has never used those words since'.

CHAPTER 6

THE WAGES OF WAR

'I regret that Japan was defeated in the war, but people in Asia were able to be liberated from colonial rule by the whites and achieved their independence.'

Seisuke Okuno, conservative MP

'It destroyed me both physically and mentally. Even if I were given all of Japan, I still wouldn't be able to regain my younger days. I cry every day without my family.'

Kimiko Kaneda, a Korean woman conscripted to work as a prostitute for the Imperial Army

He is a gentle ageing man, with a soft, round face, and a tranquil, happy air reminiscent of a traditional Chinese Buddha, welcoming visitors warmly into his comfortable home in the suburbs of Tokyo with green tea and cake, before sitting down to recount how he and his fellow Japanese students slaughtered scores of Chinese just over half a century ago. Koki Nagatomi tells his story calmly—about how in a fit of patriotic fervour, he had rushed over to China as a 22-year-old student to witness his country's glorious civilising war against its neighbour, travelling around from city to city until one freezing winter's day in December 1937, when he found himself in the central square of the captured capital of Nationalist China, Nanjing. A Japanese officer lured a group of cornered Nationalist soldiers out of the crowd with promises of safety and sanctuary, and the students volunteered to escort them away. The Chinese soldiers should have known better.

'When we stopped near the railway line, there was one narrow passageway which led to the station, and it was filled with corpses—hundreds or even thousands of them, all frozen', says Nagatomi.

> The Chinese got out of the truck, and they were made to lie down on the ground, and then one of the Japanese officers told us: 'You, students from Tokyo, kill them as you like'. Someone tried to do it with karate, but it failed, and the officer stepped in and said: 'Watch me!' He pulled out his sword and sliced the man's head off, and the blood spurted out from the Chinese man's neck.

Nagatomi threw both his hands away from his neck as if to mimic the flow of water from a fountain. 'One of the Chinese soldiers was running away, and I grabbed a pistol and killed him. I was just a student from a right-wing university, and if I couldn't do it, then I would have been seen by others as timid. In those days, I believed it was a sacred war for the Emperor—I never thought of it as a war of aggression.'[1]

When Japan surrendered, Nagatomi bunkered down in Shanxi Province with a hard-core group of Imperial Army officers dedicated 'to re-building the Japanese Army' and fighting Mao's surging communist revolution. The communists took him prisoner, and he was sentenced to thirteen years in jail for war crimes. His remorse and regret came slowly, during grinding interrogation and 'struggle sessions' with his Chinese captors about Japanese atrocities, but once it set, it set in deeply. He returned to Japan after serving his sentence, and he joined the 'Liaison Council of Japanese Who Had Returned From China', a national organisation formed by former Japanese POWs found guilty of war crimes in China. Eventually, in his seventies, he began to purge his conscience by speaking publicly—about murder, rape, the military's use of 'comfort women' (the Japanese euphemism for women forced to work as prostitutes for the military), and anything else he could remember about his wild youth in China. 'I must suppress the sense of shame and speak up before an audience', he said. 'I have to tell what I and others did during the war, or Japan will become alienated in the international community.'[2]

Shigeto Nagano was also in Nanjing during the war, and like Nagatomi didn't start talking about what had happened there until decades later, on the occasion of his swearing in as Justice Minister in the Hata cabinet in 1994, when he was 71. Nagano had gone to Nanjing as a young officer of the Imperial Army 'immediately after' the incident, he claimed. He fought the war out in China, and later had a distinguished career in Japan's postwar military (renamed the Self-Defence Forces), rising to the top rank of chief of staff. He went into politics in 1980, and was made a minister for the first time in 1994. It was not an auspicious time to begin unloading his thoughts on Nanjing. In an interview to coincide with his appointment, Nagano told the *Mainichi Shimbun* that the so-called massacre was a 'fabrication'. In the interview, Nagano acknowledged that the Imperial Army had killed some civilians, but said these actions were by-products of the inherent 'evils' of war. In any case, he said, Japan hadn't invaded China, and hadn't wanted to annex Nanjing. Japan had been fighting for its survival in a hostile world dominated by white colonialism. 'It is wrong to say that the war we waged in China and Asia was one of aggression. Japan was serious about liberating the Greater East Asian Co-prosperity Sphere [from colonialism]', he said.

Nagano's statement provoked an uproar, but outside Japan more than at home. Born in 1922, Nagano was fifteen years old at the time of the massacre. Challenged later about how he had got to the city as an army trainee 'immediately after' the incident, the flustered minister admitted he had not actually gone there until August 1941. Prime Minister Hata at first merely scolded Nagano for his 'inappropriate' statement, but strident protests from the ungrateful neighbouring countries which Japan had waged war to 'liberate' forced his resignation, and a half-hearted apology three days later.[3] According to writer Naoki Inose, the Nagano imbroglio followed a familiar pattern—'an important person makes a fool of himself with an outrageous statement, apologises profusely and then steps down. The media brews a tempest in a teacup, but never really delves into Japan's responsibility for the enormous suffering in the war'.[4]

What was especially telling about the Nagano incident was that Prime Minister Hata, like Morihiro Hosokawa before him, had purported to be leading an enlightened, liberal government with a new vision for Japan's relations with the region and the world. The dashing post-LDP era was to begin with a genuine attempt to come clean about the past. Nagano's frankness illustrated the hollowness of that position, and displayed on a wide screen the unresolved contradictions spread across the entire spectrum of conservative politics on the war. As historian Gavan McCormack points out, Nagano was not exceptional in his views. Amongst conservative bureaucrats and politicians, they were more or less taken for granted, even if most—but not all—of them were smart enough to hold their tongues in public forums. A few months later in 1994, another senior politician, Shin Sakurai, was forced to resign as Environment Minister in the new LDP-dominated cabinet after saying Japan had liberated Asian countries through the war. Ryutaro Hashimoto only just survived the international furore that greeted his statement that Japan had not waged an 'aggressive war' against the Western powers of American, Britain and the Netherlands.

Veterans like Nagatomi and politicians like Nagano exemplified the strange, discordant debate about the Pacific War in the 1990s in Japan. The further the conflict receded into history, the less people were able to agree on what had happened. The blood-curdling memories of some, like Nagatomi, provoked denial in others, like Nagano. The Asian and Allied victims of the war became more resentful the longer the debate went on, and their demands for apologies and compensation grew shriller and sharper. That, in turn, provoked more right-wing politicians to defend Japan's record, which inflamed the victims and liberal Japanese even more. The war debate also fuelled the factionalism that characterises Japanese politics, as British journalist Charles Smith discovered when he attempted to find out the truth of the Nanjing Massacre after Nagano's resignation.

After two months of research and fifteen interviews, Smith had met everyone from scholars who had evidence that the Japanese Imperial Army had carried out a systematic massacre of civilians—the official Chinese death toll estimate is 300000— to 'old soldiers' who insisted that only a few hundred people had been killed by random acts of violence. But what struck Smith even more was the cast of characters who had studied and taken up the issue. Japan's 'experts' on Nanjing ranged from a professor of linguistics at a private university in Tokyo to the president of a family-owned company that made *sembei* (rice cracker) moulds. Professional politics and war historians in Japan are a rare breed. The area is too fraught with dangerous, uncertain politics, so much so that Tokyo University, the elite incubator for future leaders of Japan, did not have a single professional modern historian on its staff until 1955.[5] Instead, history is written by members of a myriad of 'professional' organisations with sharp political axes to grind.

Japan needed a figure of national standing, like former German president Richard von Weizsaecker, who could transcend the political fray, forge a consensus, and then speak from the heart to the world about the feelings of his entire nation. But no such person existed. Not even the Emperor, or especially not the Emperor, could take up that role; the war was far too dangerous and political an issue, particularly as it involved family.

Successive revolving-door governments in Tokyo during the early 1990s squirmed as they confronted these conflicts, and found themselves constantly on the back foot, alternately defensive, evasive, prickly and nationalistic on the issue. The bold, unprompted declaration by Morihiro Hosokawa in 1993, at one of his first press conferences as Prime Minister, that Japan had waged an 'aggressive' war in Asia seemed momentarily to be a circuit-breaker ushering in a more frank discussion of the past by political leaders. But the bureaucrats quickly got to him, and he retreated into semantic obfuscation. Japan had not waged a war of aggression, he said, but a war with acts of aggression.

For every politician who demanded that Japan apologise and make amends there was another who raged that Japan had fought a just war and had no need to say sorry any more. When political leaders did express contrition, the details of the statement were invariably bitterly disputed in public beforehand, and direct words such as 'apologise' eliminated. Whatever words were allowed appeared to be carefully and cynically calibrated to suit the ceremony at hand. As a result, the exercise was futile in all directions—it angered both the nationalists in Japan, who objected to any apology, and the people to whom it was directed. Sitting uncomfortably in the middle of this debate were the bureaucrats, who struggled to square off the conflicting demands of managing Japan's sensitive relations with Asian nations, dealing with aggressive politicians and interest groups, and looking beyond their own paranoid bureaucratic impulse to avoid explicit political accountability and resist compensation claims from victims. Occasionally, when the government and the bureaucracy did manage to strike the appropriate tone about the war, and begin to build a modicum of trust and consensus, someone like Nagano would open his mouth to reveal Japan's 'true feelings', and bring their carefully constructed edifice crashing down.

The 'apology' debate reached its climax during the build-up to the fiftieth anniversaries of the dropping of the Hiroshima and Nagasaki bombs, Japan's surrender and the end of the war. The Socialist Party under Tomiichi Murayama, the Liberal Democrats and a third group, New Party Sakigake, had agreed to make an official parliamentary apology for the war when they became the governing coalition in 1994. The agreement quickly fell apart, as hundreds of MPs in an array of conservative parties reverted to type and rallied a mass movement against what they called 'masochistic history', culminating in an extraordinary rally in central Tokyo in June 1995.

More than 50 years before, in the middle of the war, Japan's Prime Minister, General Tojo, had hosted a similar feast of pan-Asian propaganda at a mass rally staged in Tokyo. The Assembly of Greater East Asiatic Nations featured a mixture of genuine Asian nationalists and quislings masquerading as independence leaders. The assembled Asian visitors lauded Japan's war against the white colonial powers, and likened it to a struggle of East versus West, and ultimately, blood versus blood. The then Burmese leader, Ba Maw, evoked the solidarity of 'a thousand million Asiatics', and urged participants to 'think with their blood'. His idealism lasted only a few years, and by the end of the war he was denouncing the Japanese for their 'brutality, arrogance and racial pretensions'.[6] Many of his hosts, however, had not learnt any lessons at all.

The 1995 rally at the martial arts stadium, the Budokan, was convened by a group of Diet members 'for immortalising the true history' of the war and a number of prominent ultra-nationalist fellow travellers. The powerful returned soldiers group, the Japan Bereaved Families Association, rounded up its members, and filled the spectacular hall with a 10 000-strong crowd. But the star attraction for the day, billed (for the foreign media, in English) as 'A Celebration of Asian Nations' Symbiosis—A Tribute, Appreciation, Friendship', was again a cast of Asian leaders. A mixture of flattery and yen had been enough to persuade someone from just about every Asian country to attend, with the exception, not surprisingly, of Korea, mainland China and Singapore.

The hall lights dimmed to allow the Asian delegates to make a grand entrance. Like athletes being led into an Olympic stadium, they marched into the hall and along the aisles towards the stage behind banners bearing their countries' names. One by one, they mounted the stage and, to wild applause, bowed Japanese-style to the audience. They then turned, in unison with the Japanese dignitaries, to face reverentially the chrysanthemum-clad altar for the playing of the stirring national anthem, 'Kimigayo', a tune heavy with militarist associations. A group of Korean journalists behind me folded their arms, and stayed seated in disgust. The prime mover in the Diet against the apology, a former minister in LDP governments, Seisuke Okuno, mounted the stage, and reassured the audience that Japan hadn't fought the war against Asian nations, but in self-defence after the encirclement by the 'ABCD powers'—wartime Japan's nomenclature for America, Britain, China and the Dutch colonialists in Indonesia. 'I regret that Japan was defeated in the war, but people in Asia were able to be liberated from colonial rule by the whites and achieved their independence', he said.

The Asian guests then took to the stage. They had been well chosen—a former Thai Foreign Minister said Japan should be 'proud of liberating other Asian nations' (wild clapping!); and the Indonesian Ambassador thanked Japan for helping make his country independent (loud applause!). The Asian delegates were a mixed bunch—not surprisingly, since it was a group thrown together haphazardly for propaganda purposes. The former Thai Foreign Minister is best known these days for supporting the murderous Khmer Rouge, something that apparently didn't disturb the Cambodian Ambassador sitting by his side. The Indian speakers were the sons respectively of Sabhas Chandra Bose (a misguided patriot driven out of India and granted refuge in Japan during the war as a 'nationalist') and of Judge Radhabinod Pal, who delivered the only dissenting judgement at the Tokyo Tribunal trial of Japan's wartime leaders. The judge, his son said, loved Japan, and had wanted to live there 'forever' (more applause!).

The Japanese politicians, including former Justice Minister Shigeto Nagano, and the audience no doubt went away immersed even more deeply in their delusions about Japan's 'liberation' of Asia. But inside Japan, their views carried weight. The rally organisers had gathered 4.56 million signatures against the Diet apology. More importantly, Okuno and his cronies had won the support of 202 out of the 270 LDP members of the Diet. In a country where consensus reigned, they had scuttled the hope of any meaningful gesture coming out of the Diet, and Japan's best and last chance in 50 years to put the war behind it. But if the anti-apology activists thought they had put the war in its rightful place, once and for all, their movement was a failure. It was far too late for that. The original debate over the apology had been propelled by a steady flow of appalling war stories from veterans and victims alike. Ugly and horrifying tales of sex slaves, biological warfare, death railways, vivisection, begrudging apologies, and distorted textbooks had all piled up in the Japanese and international media in gruesome, uncensored detail day after day for a few years beforehand. The stream of revelations that began trickling out in the 1980s became a torrent in the 1990s. There were two reasons for this—the death of the Showa Emperor, Hirohito, in 1989, unlocked many taboo topics that couldn't be openly discussed while he was alive; and ageing and retired victims and veterans began to psychologically unburden themselves of the traumas they had mostly repressed for the past half a century.

And once they started talking, they couldn't stop.

THE VETERANS

Japanese veterans had lived out their lives in a society in which the war and their memories had been pushed into a dim and often ambiguous recess of the collective consciousness. For young people born after the conflict, the war barely registered beyond its depiction as a period of dark and insane violence which had turned Japan into a unique 'peace-loving' nation. But whatever their government might teach children at school about the official story, old soldiers in Japan vividly remembered their role in their nation's sacred mission to liberate Asia from the white colonialists. Stranded between official ambivalence and youthful indifference, most of them behaved as veterans around the world do, meeting on the one day of the year for a reassuring reunion to drink until they were drunk and swap tales about the old times. These weren't completely informal occasions. With an enduring Japanese sense of hierarchy, the ex-soldiers still addressed each other according to the ranks they had held 50 years before, and then divided into their old units when they bunked down for the night. The ones that did break ranks, like Hiroshi Abe, were not popular.

Abe had been tried and sentenced to death after the war for his brutal role as a guard on the notorious Thai–Burma railway. About three in four of the 1600 British and Australian prisoners died in the conditions he enforced for their labour, a death rate which far exceeded that in camps nearby. The prisoners who survived never forgave or forgot Abe. After my interview with him was published in Australia in 1993, a number of diggers wrote angry letters detailing the horrors he had inflicted on them, such as brutally dragging sick and dying men out of hospital to work in the steamy disease-ridden jungle. 'Many appeals and petitions were made to Lieutenant Abe, but he treated them with contempt', one digger wrote bitterly. 'His death penalty was well deserved.' The *Straits Times* newspaper in Singapore in 1947 labelled Abe and his fellow interns on death row in the Changi Prison in Singapore 'the evil devils of the Burma–Siam railway' and urged people to come and watch their hanging. Abe felt not the slightest tinge of guilt. 'At the time of my arrest and sentence, I never had any idea I had done anything wrong. I would like this fact accurately conveyed to the British and Australians', he told me. 'If my execution had not been called off, I would have died without a guilty conscience.'[7]

Nearly five decades later, after he had retired and allowed all his suppressed memories of the war to rise to the surface, Abe had become so possessed with guilt and remorse that he could talk about little else. The experience seemed to excite and uplift him, and give him a new burst of life. When I visited him at his small farm on the outskirts of Tokyo, I didn't meet an elderly man stricken with angst, but a boisterous, cheerful 72-year-old who would take any amount of time out of the day to noisily tell you damning, horrific stories about not only his behaviour in the war, but that of his colleagues and the entire Japanese nation. A few days afterwards, he agreed to make the long trek into central Tokyo to be photographed in front of the locomotive from the 'death railway' perched outside the city's war museum. Propped up by his walking stick, Abe stiffened his back proudly, and gazed steadfastly at the camera with a perverse mixture of dignity and shame.

Abe's outspokenness had already caused a rift within his family. One brother-in-law had told him how he'd cut off the heads of Chinese during the frenzy of the war, and had been mystified when Abe then severed all relations with him. After all, his brother-in-law had said, this was what happened in war! But it was with his wartime comrades that he was causing the most trouble. Abe had affronted them by suggesting that they invite some of the Allied survivors to their reunion that year. 'I have just started to talk to the other veterans about this, but they have no idea to listen. I frankly admit that I am beginning to dislike the Japanese, even though I am one', he growled.

> I myself am a bit sceptical about having a ceremony only amongst the Japanese survivors. It should be expanded to outsiders. These Japanese have no intention to reflect on the causes of the war, and regret for the terrible things they have done. And when they get together, they still keep all the old ranks and levels of respect they used to have. I can't abide that.

The venue chosen for the reunion was a strikingly beautiful Shinto shrine in the centre of Tokyo, adjacent to the war museum and the 'death railway' locomotive. Yasukuni Shrine—literally, 'peaceful country shrine'—is the resting place for the souls not only of millions of Japanese killed in battles since 1853 but also of a number of Japan's most notorious war criminals from the Pacific War. General Tojo and other wartime leaders executed by the Allies were formally enshrined there by the temple's head priest, quietly and without any public announcement, in the late 1970s. The news of the secret enshrinement caused an uproar amongst anti-war groups in Japan and throughout Asia when it leaked six months later. This inability to distinguish between honourable service and vicious warmongering had made Yasukuni a potent symbolic battleground for the politics of the war. Japanese left-wingers and Asians attacked it as a sanctuary of nascent militarist values, while conservatives defended it as a legitimate sacred place. Very quickly the disagreement lapsed into a sterile, ritualistic stand-off of the kind that ran through all the debates about the war in Japan—a stubborn dialogue of the deaf. So too did the battle involving Abe and his former comrades-in-arms' refusal to invite foreigners to their reunion.

The one-time secretary-general of the Thai–Burma Veterans' Association, Yoshio Otsuki, was prickly and defensive about the veterans' decision to keep their distance from their former enemies. 'People don't appreciate what happened. They only attack the Japanese soldiers—it's unfair', he pleaded.

> Some POWs had cattle, and whenever they moved up the line, they were able to eat meat. The Japanese only ever had vegetables. That sort of thing is never reported. The Japanese soldiers are always the evil ones. What I think of during the service is my friends who died at that time. Seventy of them died and I cannot forget that.

The day of the reunion was a precious indulgence for Otsuki and his colleagues. 'Some of the veterans repeat the same stories every year without realising it. I live with my wife and my daughter who don't want to hear what I experienced, so it's good to have a chance to talk to old friends. We get really noisy!' he laughed. A few days later, mindful of the need to be seen doing the right thing, Otsuki phoned back to stress that even if the veterans won't invite any foreigners, they will be praying for them. 'In our hearts, we are praying and remembering everyone', he said. But his suspicions about foreigners were close to the surface, and easily roused. When asked for a copy of the photograph taken at the reunion in front of the railway locomotive, Otsuki demanded to see a copy of the article translated into Japanese first, a difficult and time-consuming request. When told this was impossible, he lost his temper and harshly slammed down the phone. 'Journalists are the worst type of human beings!' were his parting words.

Abe's ghost haunted Otsuki and his colleagues. So too did those of other veterans, like Seiji Yoshida, a transport clerk in the Shanghai area during the war. In 1983 he published a ground-breaking book about the military comfort women called *My War Crimes: The Forced Draft of Koreans*. With only his own diary records to go on, Yoshida had written to 40 former colleagues seeking information, but all of them refused. Yoshida pressed on, and produced a book which was crucial in exposing one of Japan's most shameful wartime practices. No veteran, however, could match the crazed fervour of Kenzo Okazaki, the subject of a riveting film documentary, *The Emperor's Naked Army Marches On*, in the 1980s. Okazaki ran an eccentric, resolute and on occasions violent one-man campaign against the Emperor and the old wartime establishment. He had once been jailed for firing spitballs at the Imperial Palace in Tokyo. The film-maker's shaky, handheld camera follows Okazaki and his noisy, festooned sound truck across Japan as he flees his parole officer and searches for the truth about the fate of two young soldiers from his platoon in Papua New Guinea, who had been shot in mysterious circumstances. You cheer Okazaki on as he visits his ageing former colleagues in his manic quest for the truth, but duck and cringe when he hits and kicks these elderly men, and their wives, when they don't tell him what he wants to know. By the end, he has discovered that the two men were shot to allow the remaining members of the war-ravaged platoon to cannibalise them. Okazaki sets out to extract his final revenge, but when he can't find the platoon commander, he shoots his son instead, and is caught and jailed.

Not all former veterans felt as defensive and ostracised as the Japanese survivors of the Thai–Burma railway, and not all of them were hunted down and attacked by former colleagues like Okazaki. The deeds of some, like the surviving kamikaze pilots, transcended the divisive debates and foreign scoldings about the war. The adoration of the kamikaze ('divine wind') spirit held up a mirror to the true feelings of the ruling elite about both the glory and the tragedy of the war. To understand this you only had to see the roll-up at an extraordinary reunion of all the surviving members of Japan's special attack units in central Tokyo in 1994.

The ceremony was held on the first day of spring, just as the cherry blossoms had begun to bloom. The cherry blossom symbolises purity in Japan and, like the kamikaze, is romanticised as a symbol of the fleetingness of life. The surviving pilots and their supporters make a point of commemorating the war not in the sticky heat of August at the time of Japan's humiliating surrender, but under the fragile cherry blossoms of early April. All the associations clustered around the numerous different suicide squads, and their thousands of members and supporters, frail and hunched with age, met for the first time in 1994 under a single umbrella label—the Association in Memory of the Souls of Kamikaze Pilots. There were the kamikaze pilots themselves, the ones who failed to find their targets or ran out of planes and enemy soldiers to fall on; and the tens of men who survived the even more radical *Oka* (Cherry Blossom) planes. These planes were attached to the bottom of larger aircraft before being let go to glide towards their targets, propelled only by a solid-fuel rocket booster during the final fatal phase of their flight. A few surviving pilots of the *Kaiten*, tiny one-man cigar-shaped submarines carried to their destinations by mother submarines and then launched on kamikaze attacks, also came. So did families, friends and supporters—of pilots both living and dead. 'They are all part of the divine wind', said Gen Saito, a kamikaze pilot who had been horrified to find himself alive when the war suddenly ended. First, his unit ran out of planes and petrol. Saito had then tried a different tack, training to strap explosives to his own body to launch a suicide attack directly at the Americans if they invaded Japan. The Americans sent *Enola Gay* over Hiroshima to drop the A-bomb instead, and added half a century to Saito's life.

The guests of honour at the reunion provided a good guide to the value of the kamikaze pedigree. They included top industrialists, a host of the most powerful right-wing politicians in the land, and two former prime ministers from the LDP— Yasuhiro Nakasone, an outspoken nationalist, and Noboru Takeshita, who as a young man had trained to join a suicide squad. Ryutaro Hashimoto also attended. The last guest to arrive was the Imperial Family's Prince Mikasa, the younger brother of the Showa Emperor, Hirohito, the 'living God' whose voice was heard by his subjects for the first time when he broadcast Japan's surrender. Prince Mikasa's clothes, as was customary on such occasions for the Imperial Family, mimicked turn-of the-century Western formal wear—he wore a pompous English morning suit, and carried a top hat and gloves in one hand. Walking into the ceremony grounds, every ten steps or so he would stop and nod slightly towards each part of the crowd, each time setting off a ripple of deep bows in response. He stayed seated through the ceremony, and said not a word.

The ceremony was a mixture of syrupy nostalgia and solemn remembrance. A schoolgirl choir sang a famous sentimental war song, a sort of Japanese 'We'll Meet Again' called 'Home Town in Autumn', about a mother waiting for her son to return home, that brought tears welling to many eyes. The patron of the association, and one-time adviser to Nakasone, businessman Sejima Ryuzo, presented a brace of chrysanthemums and made the keynote speech. 'During the war, young people of around 20 years of age made a grave decision to go on suicidal attack missions and sacrifice their lives for their nation and friends', he said, facing the flowered altar like priests used to when saying mass, with his back to the crowd. 'The number of people who killed themselves this way was 6952. You won't find this sort of thing anywhere else in the world. It's our duty to remember the significance of what they did.'

The then Prime Minister, Morihiro Hosokawa, had sent only a junior minister with a dry, perfunctory message to deliver to the veterans—a nod towards sensitivities in Asia about any official Japanese glorification of the war. So it was left to Shigeru Kawamura, the head of Japan's peak veterans' body, to strike the most poetic tone. 'The suicide squads', he said, 'had to sacrifice their lives like they were falling cherry blossoms in enemy territory'. The pilots who avoided this glorious death, like Taketoshi Miyasaka, carried with them a shameful sense of anti-climax. 'Japan was in a very difficult situation, and before we went, we were ready to die', he told me. 'However, fortunately, or unfortunately, because of the lack of planes, we were transferred and we survived.'

Fortunately or unfortunately?

'Unfortunately', he says, after a short pause. 'We wanted to die like the senior pilots. We could not help but feel guilty.'

The pilots were not all cut from the same cloth, but none at the reunion looked back with the clarity of half a century of life, and expressed bitterness at their country's demanding that they kill themselves—quite the reverse. Gen Saito compared the pilots to the samurai, the warrior class in feudal Japan, an analogy which seems romantic to Western ears, but one which still resonates in Japan. 'In the original samurai model, the samurai defended the village and the community', he says. 'The nation was just an expanded village. So if someone attacks the nation, then it's only natural that you should give up your life.'[8] As to their ghastly fate, they shrugged their shoulders and said it couldn't be helped—'*shikataganai*'—an expression typically used by the Japanese in situations where they feel powerless.

So this was Japan's war: the glorious mission, the shame of survival and defeat—and in the end, the helplessness of the individuals fated to fight it out, not to mention the victims who got in their way.

THE VICTIMS

One Monday in July 1992, the Tokyo government's chief spokesman, Koichi Kato, apologised for Japan's 'mistake' in conscripting more than one hundred thousand women to work as prostitutes for the Imperial Japanese Army during the war. Some 'mistake'. Kimiko Kaneda, a Korean woman who used the name given to her by the Japanese colonial and military authorities, left her job as an eighteen-year-old housemaid for a missionary couple and travelled to China on the promise of being given a job in a factory. Instead, she was put into a two-metre-square room and made to have sex with 20 to 30 soldiers a day. She said later that she felt pain after just three. On her third day at work, she was stabbed with a bayonet after she refused to service one soldier.[9] Over the next six nightmarish years, she was carted from town to town, and comfort station to comfort station in northern China, and forced to have sex with the soldiers over and over again. She took up opium smoking to ease the pain, contracted venereal disease on at least one occasion, and was only able to return home after a sympathetic officer persuaded the Japanese military police to let her go after she suffered a collapsed uterus. She lost contact with her family forever, and never married. For years, she needed tranquillisers to sleep. 'It destroyed me both physically and mentally', she said later at a public meeting in Japan. 'Even if I were given all of Japan, I still wouldn't be able to regain my younger days. I cry every day without my family.'

The story of the comfort women had been suppressed for decades. The Japanese government, of course, has never encouraged it to be told. The few Japanese veterans and left-wing scholars who chronicled their story were ostracised or studiously ignored. In South Korea there was little chance to publicise the tale, as the military dictatorship kept a lid on all forms of democratic expression and dissent. The dictatorship fell in 1987, on the eve of the Seoul Olympics, but it wasn't until a few years later, when the women themselves, with the support of citizens and feminist groups, demanded redress that their plight became an issue.

Kaneda was the first comfort woman to testify in a Japanese court in June 1992. Even at that late stage, the Japanese government was still resisting a full acknowledgement of its involvement in the brothels. When Kaneda and a number of other comfort women had first come forward the previous year, government spokesmen sorrowfully sympathised with their pain, while washing their hands of any responsibility. The brothels were privately run, they said. The officials protested that they had continuously expressed regret for the war, and that various demands for compensation had been settled—in South Korea's case, by a treaty and some money in 1965. By the time they were forced to admit the Japanese government's deep involvement, the comfort women case had destroyed the credibility and smeared the image of these politicians and bureaucrats indelibly, and became a significant factor in provoking the victims of Japanese aggression all over the region to stake their claims for compensation.

The Japanese government was hung out to dry by a couple of short days work in the library of the National Defence Agency. That's all it took for a history professor, Yoshiaki Yoshitomi, to find damning documentary evidence of the military's role in the prostitution racket that the government had claimed didn't exist. The results of his research were published in the left-leaning *Asahi Shimbun* on 13 January 1992. The Japanese government was caught red-handed. The Prime Minister, Kiichi Miyazawa, then preparing for a trip to Seoul, apologised on arrival, actually using the Japanese word for apology—*owabi*—for only the second time ever in the history of Japanese expressions of remorse for Japan's colonial and wartime aggression. (The only other times the word *owabi* was used was in another apology, also to South Korea, and in a 'private' apology by Prime Minister Murayama on the 50th anniversary of the war's end.) Miyazawa also promised an investigation, which produced a report six months later, and Kato's belated admission that Tokyo had made 'a mistake' in sending around 130 000 women from all over Japan and Asia to work as prostitutes on the frontlines.

The 127 documents uncovered from six ministries showed that army and civilian bureaucrats established the brothels and wrote regulations for the recruitment of women, the use of condoms, medical check-ups and the issuing of IDs for staff. With typical Japanese thoroughness, one ministry even laid down rules for lighting in the rooms, and the wages, conditions and holidays for the women. Even so, there were many influential people who were less than apologetic. Don't get emotional, they warned. Put the issue in its 'historical context' of the legal prostitution of the day, and the war. An editorial in the conservative *Sankei Shimbun* said the comfort women issue belonged to what the Japanese call *kahanshin*—the lower half of the body, or sex. Every country has such dirty tales, and there was no need to revive them. These conservatives also considered that in keeping the women's systematic rape a secret, they had protected the women from their own shame.

The initial inquiry had been frank by Japanese standards, but still fell deliberately short of anything like full disclosure. The investigation was restricted solely to government archives, and no surviving comfort women were interviewed. Koichi Kato claimed that the government had not wanted to violate their privacy, even though 74 women had come forward offering to tell their stories, and a number had, like Kaneda, already given

Nationalistic and proud, outspoken Finance Ministry bureaucrat, Eisuke Sakakibara, expounded theories of a new 'post-western civilisation' freed of dictates from the United States.

Malaysian Prime Minister, Mohamed Mahathir, spreads his pan-Asian message in a lecture to students at a Tokyo university.

Fuyuhiko, an elite banker and his wife, Miwa, struggle with his *maza-con* (mother complex) in one of the most watched television dramas in Japanese history, 'I Have Been in Love With You for a Long Time'.

Justice Minister for a day, Shigeto Nagano resigns after telling a journalist in an interview to mark his swearing in as a member of Cabinet that the Nanjing massacre was a 'fabrication'.

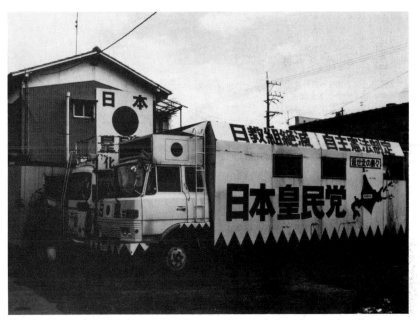

Kominto, an obscure ultra-right wing group, used the ultra-nationalists' traditional weapon, sound trucks, to harass politician Noboru Takeshita and stop him from becoming prime minister. A yakuza gangster group was called on by his supporters to shut up the protestors.

Manga artist,
Yasunori Kobayashi.

'Cameramen and women!' screams one of the characters in Kobayashi's manga comics, urging them to get a real close-up if they are going to peddle pictures of women's bodies.

Kiichi Miyazawa (left) became prime minister with the nod of the ruling party's grizzly kingmaker, Shin Kanemaru, but was powerless to hold the government together when his patron was arrested for corruption.

Ichiro Ozawa was reviled as a fascist and extreme nationalist for ignoring postwar taboos in favour of policies that would have seemed mundane in other advanced countries.

Imperial Army veterans gathered outside Yasukuni Shrine in central Tokyo to celebrate the war, not commemorate Japan's defeat.

The Emperor plants rice seedlings in an annual ritual to underline the grain's importance. Rice plays an intimate role in the Emperor's sacred and mostly secret enthronement ceremony.

After a brief reign, which promised much but delivered little, Morihiro Hosokawa and his wife farewell supporters at the prime minister's annual cherry blossom party in the spring of 1994.

evidence in the courts. Large files held in the United States were ignored. The inquiry also conspicuously avoided conceding a crucial point—that the women had not volunteered to be prostitutes, but had been coerced. Sharp criticism at home and abroad sent officials reluctantly back into the archives, and compelled them to interview a number of the comfort women. About a year later, on the final day of the Miyazawa LDP government, on 4 August 1993, outgoing Foreign Minister Yohei Kono admitted that many of the women had been coerced, deceived and intimidated into working as sex slaves, and apologised abjectly. 'We shall face squarely the historical facts instead of evading them, and take them to heart as lessons of history', he said.

For the women's Japanese lawyer, Kenichi Takagi, a mild-mannered, gentle man with a devilish goatee beard, this was the breakthrough he had been counting on. Takagi is one of those Japanese whose work had set him for life against a system that gave little or nothing away. For the previous 20 years, ever since he passed the Bar exam, Takagi had been fighting compensation cases on behalf of Asian victims of Japan's war. He also considered he was cleaning up after the Allied occupation, which he says conspired to prosecute only those war crimes committed against Americans and Europeans. The most notorious example was the indemnity given to the Japanese leaders of Unit 731, who operated on live human beings in a vast project established in China to develop biological weapons. 'Virtually all the Asian victims were ignored', Takagi said. International publicity for the lawyer's efforts had severely embarrassed the Japanese government, but he had precious little else to show his clients. In two decades, he had had just one qualified success, when the government had agreed to pay compensation to conscripted Korean labourers stranded on the island of Sakhalin after the war. That victory had come not so much through the courts as through the intervention of sympathetic politicians. When I interviewed him in mid-1993, he remained optimistic, and said he believed that the chances of winning a genuine settlement had never been better.

> The biggest problem has always been the Japanese bureaucrats. Generally speaking, they want policies to be consistent with the past, present and future. To change something, someone has to take responsibility, and no one wants to do that. But now the Government's position on the comfort women, for example, has changed. First, they said it didn't happen; then they said they had no information and then they said it was all done by private operators before they finally admitted it. When they finally apologised, everyone understood that the next step would be compensation.

Everybody, that is, except for the government itself.

The Japanese establishment was incensed at the revival of the war as a nasty political issue. They blamed left-wing activists like Takagi, and cynical opportunism among politicians in China and South Korea in particular. Former senior diplomat Hisahiko Okazaki said China and other countries had ignored the war for four decades, and were only now grasping it as a 'convenient lever' to use against Japan. His partner in a dialogue about the issue in a weekly magazine, political scientist Seizaburo Sato, went further, and claimed that Japanese masochism could spark a nationalistic backlash. 'Because excessive masochism is the reverse side of arrogance, exclusionist nationalism will mount in Japan', said Sato. 'In fact, criticism of Japan by Japanese is making Japan's relations with Asian nations worse. It is about time to liquidate this stupid, and moreover, criminal thing.'[10] Liquidating 'this stupid thing' in a way which satisfied the political demands of Japan's critics proved exceedingly difficult, however.

In preparation for the 50th anniversary in 1995, the government formed in August the previous year a committee called

'The Committee to Tidy Up Postwar Issues'. As one commentator remarked, you only had to look at the committee's name to see that it embodied the fatal flaw that had characterised Tokyo's official policy to date—'chronic avoidance of political accountability'.[11] Prime Minister Murayama followed the committee's recommendations faithfully and completely excluded official government compensation for individual war victims. Instead, the government decided to set up two funds. The first, to express remorse for the comfort women, was called 'The Asia Peace and Friendship Fund for Women'. A group of leading businessmen and TV personalities were shanghaied to head a body which would raise funds from the private sector and then distribute it to individual comfort women, all at arm's length from the government. The fund was also meant to pay for projects supporting 'women's rights in Asia'. The woman nominated to launch the fund, Mutsuko Miki, the wife of the late 'Mr Clean' of Japanese politics, former prime minister Takeo Miki, dropped out because of the government's 'lack of repentance'. The second fund, dubbed the 'Peace, Friendship and Exchange Initiative', was to translate 'Japan's repentance over atrocities and damage into fiscal action'. One Japanese bureaucrat told Kyodo News Service that the government had taken on the project 'spontaneously'. The value of the fund—Y100 billion ($1.3 billion)—was a nicely rounded and grand-sounding figure, but not nearly so impressive when compared with the outstanding claims against Japan.

By 1995, it was getting difficult to keep a count of these claims. Thousands of Chinese forced labourers, scores of comfort women from a number of different countries, Australian, British and Dutch POWs, and Hong Kong residents who had lost their savings had all commenced legal action since 1989. Takagi, the lawyer, had 22 different actions on his books alone. The *Mainichi Shimbun* calculated that the compensation demands of Asian war victims totalled Y19.3 trillion ($257 billion), most of which was

171

from actions being brought by Chinese who had been made to work as forced labourers.

Another way to put the Y100 billion into perspective is to compare Japan to Germany. Not only does Germany have an excruciatingly honest official history of Hitler and the Holocaust, it also puts its money where its mouth is. Since the war, the government and private companies have paid out a total of 86.4 billion marks ($164 billion), with a further 33.6 billion to be paid up until the year 2030 ($61 billion). Japan's payout, by contrast, amounts to a measly Y250 billion ($3.3 billion).[12] Stung by constant international criticism, the Japanese government has increasingly pushed the line in recent years that its massive overseas aid program is de facto war reparations. 'Most of Japan's aid goes to Asian countries because of the public sentiments regarding the physical damage and spiritual suffering Japan inflicted on those countries through war and colonial domination', said the Director-General of the cabinet External Policy Office, Sakutaro Tanino, in 1994.[13] In a sense, Tanino is right. China, for example, rescinded its right to claim official reparations, and has accepted aid instead. But the ambiguous formula of aid in the place of concrete above-the-board payments of reparations was artfully constructed, once again, to avoid explicit responsibility or accountability.

The same goes for Japanese private companies which were up to their necks in the profitable war economy. Whereas German private companies such as Daimler-Benz have published frank histories of their involvement in the war, and also paid out cash, Japanese companies steadfastly refuse to confront the past. In the most important test case, 486 Chinese working as conscripted labourers were killed in an uprising at a mine run by the construction giant, Kajima Corporation, during the war. More than 100 of them died from torture after the rebellion was put down. Kajima did not openly acknowledge the incident, or offer an apology of sorts until 1990, and makes no mention of the incident in its two-volume official company history. The company eventually agreed to pay Y50 million ($660 000) towards the cost of a cenotaph on the mine site, but rejected out of hand demands that it pay compensation to surviving individuals and the families of the dead workers. A company spokesman said that using these 'contract workers' was national policy at the time, and that compensation wasn't necessary. (This was a neat reversal of the initial formula used by the government to explain away the comfort women—that they had been recruited and run by private operators.) Kajima received strong backing from corporate Japan. If it had agreed to pay, another 35 Japanese companies, including household names like Mitsubishi, which also used forced labourers, would also have been liable.[14]

Despite the government and private sector's implacable stance, Takagi had dug in for the fight. To win in court, Mr Takagi had to persuade Japanese judges to override their bureaucratic masters, and agree for the first time to compensate foreigners for 'crimes against humanity', something that he knew would be well-nigh impossible. Japan's tortuous legal system can take up to two decades to hear a case to its final appeal—many of his clients would be dead by the time the judges ruled on their claims. This perhaps would have been the neatest bureaucratic solution of all.

There was perhaps an even bigger obstacle standing in the way of Japanese like Takagi who wanted to force their rulers and fellow citizens to confront the victims of the war. On reflection, most Japanese didn't agree that these Asians were victims who deserved compensation. Through a mixture of skilful propaganda, historical circumstance and congenital introspection, many Japanese had come to think they, and not anyone else, were the real victims of the war.

THE OTHER VICTIMS

Japan's most famous film-maker, Akira Kurosawa, met members of the press and the public in late 1991 in Tokyo after the screening of his latest movie. It was a rare and eagerly anticipated public appearance by the revered director, and his fans applauded when he entered the theatre with the sort of enthusiasm that one does when in the presence of greatness—with a sort of restrained, respectful intensity. Kurosawa, tall and lanky for a Japanese, politely doffed his trademark sailor's cap in appreciation. But it soon became apparent that the only people in the theatre clapping were Japanese. The large contingent of foreign journalists attending the preview sat in their seats in a stony silence. Kurosawa's film—*Rhapsody in August*, about the suffering of a family after the atomic bomb was dropped on Nagasaki—had left them furious. One scene in particular got up their nose—when the actor Richard Gere, who played a Japanese–American coming back to his mother's home town, begged forgiveness from his ageing grandmother for the Americans' use of the A-bomb.

A British journalist sitting in the front row fired the first question. 'Do you think the Japanese *zaikai* [big business] would have financed your movie if you had mentioned the Rape of Nanjing, and the slaughter of the Chinese?' he sneered. 'All we heard about was the bomb this and the bomb that', hissed an Italian colleague next. 'You never said *who* started the war, and *why* the bomb was dropped.' The Japanese in the audience gasped and squirmed in a mixture of anger and embarrassment. Kurosawa muttered a few vague answers about the horrors of war, and his film being misunderstood. Now in his eighties, Kurosawa has the status of a *sensei* in Japan—a word of respect, which loosely translates as 'master' or 'teacher'. The Japanese tried hard to make amends for the rude foreigners in their midst.

'*Sensei*, could you please tell us why you kept using the music of Verdi in different scenes. It was very beautiful', asked one politely. But it was too late. The occasion limped to an awkward close.

For Kurosawa, and countless other Japanese of all political persuasions, the atomic bombings of Hiroshima and Nagasaki were the defining events of the war—not the attack on Pearl Harbor or the Nanjing Massacre or any murderous aggression by the Imperial Army, but the martyring of innocents in both cities. Right-wing nationalists latch onto the bombings to illustrate the perfidy and cruelty of the West, and also use it as a convenient moral equivalency to douse criticism of Japan's own atrocities. The left is keen to focus on the bombings for another reason, seeing in them the symbolic, apocalyptic death of Japanese militarism, and the dawn of a new era of universal peace. Socialist supporters compare the devastation of Hiroshima to the Nazis' extermination of the Jews. 'Along with Auschwitz, Hiroshima is one of the crucial events in the history of mankind that we must learn from. This lesson, that war is never the answer, is the spirit of Hiroshima', says the Socialist MP for Hiroshima, Tadatoshi Akiba. 'We are a nation that has renounced war. If we abandon our peace constitution, we will defile the memories of the victims of the bombings of Hiroshima and Nagasaki. Without it, we will lose our way in Asia and the world.'[15] This message has sunk in with young people. The youth magazine, *Denim*, asked 500 '20-something' men and women what came to mind first when thinking of the war. The answers: the atomic bombings, 149; Pearl Harbor, 83; the non-atomic bombing of Japan, 49; kamikaze attacks, 42; the Japanese invasion of Asia, 22; and the Battle of Okinawa, 21.[16]

Hiroshima, more than Nagasaki, has reconstructed itself as a shrine to selective victimhood, and self-absorption. The devastation of the city is laid out in excruciating detail in the city's main tourist attraction, and Japan's best-attended national museum, the Hiroshima Peace Memorial Museum. No detail is too small, no image is too horrifying for the museum's permanent exhibition, which includes pictures of charred corpses; shreds of maimed skin preserved in bottles of acid; the pathetic remains of a child's burnt-out lunchbox, and the side of a building with streams of black rain running over it. But Hiroshima has done much more than just display the devastation of the bomb, even though it has done that admirably. It has turned itself into a mecca of peace for the world, and created a thriving peace industry in the process. The *Hiroshima Handbook* lists 40 peace groups with chapters in the city, twelve full-time government groups devoted to the bombing and its victims, and another eleven private organisations set up for the same purpose.

All visitors to the city are asked to imbibe the 'spirit of Hiroshima'. School children, after lectures from the fifteen or so A-bomb victims permanently working at the museum, approach foreign visitors outside the museum to ask them whether they support 'peace'. The city government has applied to have Hiroshima's signature building, the bombed-out dome, added to the United Nations World Heritage List. 'Hiroshima peace is a global issue, and we are responsible for it', says the museum's director, Mr Hiroshi Harada. 'Our attitude directly affects world peace and international relationships, so we feel a heavy responsibility.' Harada is a career municipal bureaucrat taking his turn in one of his city's most important jobs. He has not forgotten his roots—for about the first 20 minutes of a 50-minute interview, he talks proudly about the 'Hiroshima garbage system', introduced first in his city and then nationally as a way to control refuse. But as museum director, he has had to leave garbage behind and bear the weight of world peace that has shifted onto his shoulders. He reels off the lists of foreign visitors—trade unionists from Finland, diplomats from Africa, politicians from New Zealand, musicians from Spain, all passing through to breathe deep 'the Hiroshima spirit'. Visitors to the museum seem to leave with this spirit thoroughly absorbed, if the book at the exit containing their comments is any guide. 'War is Terrible!', says one. 'F_ _ _ the Americans!' 'Give Peace a Chance.' It is as if everyone had just come out of a John Lennon concert, circa 1970.

Until recently, there was one other striking thing about the 'Hiroshima spirit', as embodied by the museum. It only told one side of the story. Here's how the museum describes the attack on Pearl Harbor: 'In 1941, a surprise attack on the US base at Pearl Harbor hurtled Japan into the war'. That's it. Note the use of the passive tense—Japan is 'hurtled into the war', as if by some unknown force. Not a word about the vicious fighting which followed, or any of the atrocities which made many people, Asians and Europeans alike, exclaim on hearing news of the blast, to quote historian Paul Fussell, 'Thank God for the Atomic Bomb!'. Mr Harada is prickly on this point. He is puzzled by my question about the brevity of the Pearl Harbor description, and says that people who complain about the museum's emphasis on Hiroshima alone are 'rather few'. 'The point is that the museum is for Hiroshima, not for all of Japan', says Mr Harada. 'The main stress is what happened in Hiroshima— that's the reason for the character of the museum.'

Author Ian Buruma visited Hiroshima when researching his book, *The Wages of Guilt*, which contrasted the different responses to the war in Germany and Japan. He observed that while it is impossible for Germans to feel victimised by the legacy of Auschwitz, the Japanese were able to identify themselves with the victims of Hiroshima. The vicious bombings, he wrote, had dissolved the Japanese sins 'in the sins of mankind. This allows the Japanese to take two routes at once, a national one, as unique victims of the A-bomb, and a universal one, as apostles of the Hiroshima spirit. This, then is how Japanese pacifists, engaged in Peace Education, define the Japanese identity'.[17]

The Hiroshima museum has changed since Buruma visited, in small but significant ways. The museum re-opened in mid-1994 after a complete overhaul and refurbishment of the permanent exhibition. In the new exhibition, Hiroshima's role as a military base and Japan's war against China, including the Nanjing Massacre, were displayed and discussed for the first time. One picture shows the citizens of Hiroshima celebrating in a lantern parade after the fall of Nanjing. The description of Pearl Harbor is the same in both the old and new museums, but the motives for the Americans using the bomb are laid out in a restrained and balanced fashion in the new one. The reasons listed—a desire to test a new weapon, restrict Allied casualties to a minimum and keep the Soviets out of the war—say nothing about the oft-levelled accusation by many Japanese that the bomb's use was racially inspired—in other words, that it was saved specially for use against 'the Japs'. To outsiders, this new display may seem the minimum that is reasonable in the circumstances. But it outraged the Hiroshima victims' groups, who thought that it diluted the sacred message about the bomb. 'Japan was certainly involved in wars in Asia as an oppressor, but that is one thing, and the A-bomb is another', said Mr Amato Uemune, the secretary-general of the Atom Bomb Victims Association. 'The new museum mixes these things up. Japan's responsibility for the war has nothing to do with the bomb dropped by the Americans. Putting [these new displays] in is almost like exempting the Americans of their responsibility for what they did.'

The changes were more significant, though, for another reason. They brought the museum into line with what many conservatives were striving to have institutionalised as the core, mainstream view of the war.

THE OFFICIAL STORY

Most Japanese distinguish between the war against China (which began in 1931 or 1937, depending on your interpretation) and the occupation of the Korean peninsula, and the war against America and the white colonial powers in Asia which started with Pearl Harbor in 1941. The war against the United States was suicidal, but the Japanese argue their country had a legitimate *causus belli*—Washington's imposition of an oil embargo. The attack on Pearl Harbor was not aggression, but self-defence, and thus there is no need to apologise. This line of argument was the basis of the statement by politician Ryutaro Hashimoto in 1995 that Japan had been guilty of aggression against Asia, but not the West, and that the world should not impose a 'life sentence' on Japan for crimes which have been forgiven or forgotten when committed by Europeans.[18] Not only is there a greater degree of genuine remorse for Japan's war in Asia, but more than that, there is an overriding imperative for Japan to fix the issue politically in the region, or find its diplomacy forever hobbled.

In recent years the media have mounted a number of officially sanctioned campaigns along similar lines. Before the historic visit of the Emperor to China in 1992, a trip hysterically opposed by supporters of the Japanese monarchy, the national broadcaster, NHK, broadcast a series of grisly TV documentaries showing rarely seen footage of the Nanjing Massacre, the bombing of civilians in the defenceless city of Chungking, and the use of poisonous gases. A few weeks after Shigeto Nagano resigned as Justice Minister, after pronouncing the Nanjing Massacre a 'fabrication' in 1994, the nation's leading conservative newspaper, the *Yomiuri Shimbun*, carried a large front-page story detailing eyewitness accounts of the Imperial Army's atrocities in China in what appeared to be another official effort get a more balanced history on the public record. The witness was particularly significant in this case—Prince Mikasa, the late Emperor Hirohito's younger brother.

The most protracted battles over the official story have been fought over the content of school textbooks—for many years, Exhibit One for those pushing the charge that Japan's history had been whitewashed. The most celebrated series of cases involving a tenacious Tokyo academic, Saburo Ienaga, began in 1962, when the Education Ministry refused to authorise Ienaga's radical, anti-establishment textbook, *New Japanese History*, and continued for more than three decades. The ministry said in 1962 that Ienaga's book was 'inadequate' in 323 places, but it objected most strenuously to passages concerning the Nanjing Massacre and Unit 731. Ienaga challenged the ministry in the courts on a number of fronts—on historical detail, on the damage to his standing, and on the constitutionality of restricting textbooks. By 1995, he had had just one small victory—a decision by the Tokyo High Court to award him Y300 000 ($4000) for 'mental anguish' for the ministry's rewriting of his textbook. But as with Takagi and the comfort women case, his lack of success in the courts was inversely proportional to the international attention he had drawn to the textbook issue.

In some ways, there is more to the textbook issue than meets the eye. For many years, Japanese school textbooks were written with a left-wing bias to curry favour and sales with the communist-dominated Japan Teachers' Union. In turn, the conservative ruling party would pressure the Education Ministry to remove the offending passages through its screening process.[19] This stand-off polarised the issue, and turned it into a typically rigid test of wills between two uncompromising groups which could never maintain a dialogue with each other.

The ministry's screening processes, like bureaucratic decision-making all over Japan, have been subject to little genuine scrutiny, and the personal views of the ministry officials were rarely, if ever, enunciated, until a retired senior textbook screener, Shigeru Tokinoya, granted a newspaper interview in 1994.[20] For fifteen years until he retired in the mid-1980s, Tokinoya's job had been to wade through the textbooks submitted to him, and ensure that they fitted the facts, or at least a version of them that he could stomach. Some textbooks, for example, correctly said that Japanese soldiers had killed hundreds of women and children in Okinawa who were in the way of combat operations in the final days of the war. Tokinoya said he had told the writers it was unthinkable that Japanese soldiers would kill citizens, and told the writer 'to base [their] accounts on reliable sources'. The reference to the well documented slaughter was deleted, and the book was cleared for children to read. But Tokinoya made one change too many when in the early 1980s he insisted that Japan's 'invasion' of China and Korea be changed to 'advance'—on the grounds that it was wrong 'to insert value judgements' into the description of factual events—before certifying the book for use in schools. China and South and North Korea erupted in fury, and threw their weight behind an army of local critics of the ministry's screening system. The campaign they waged, and Japan's response, was, like the comfort women case later, a major factor in reopening the war as a political issue in Asia.

The diplomatic manipulation of the issue, by China in particular, was the trigger for a gradual reform that has left much of the stereotypical criticism of Japanese school textbooks out of date today. Following the outcry, the Education Ministry declared that textbooks henceforth should take into account the 'feelings' of other nations. As a result, most Japanese school students in 1995 learn that Japan did *invade* China, and slaughtered thousands of innocent women and children. They are taught that Taiwanese, Chinese and Koreans were transported to Japan as forced labourers, and made to work in horrific conditions. They learn that Okinawans were killed by Japanese soldiers. All—or nearly all—the taboo topics are in the books, in one form or another, something which pains the Tokinoyas of this world. 'It's a terrible shame. Japan is being painted unfairly as bad, evil', he complained in the interview. 'Postwar texts depict only negative aspects of Japan's history. There's too much self-flagellation. The incident [with China] showed that the political atmosphere is not conducive to scholarly independent research.'

Take the Nanjing Massacre, which in many respects has been a litmus test of the ability of the Japanese to be honest about their past. The textbooks used by primary and junior high school students now flatly contradict people like Nagano, even if the entries do bear the scars of the loaded debate that persists over the details of how many people were killed.[21] The Tokyo Shoseki social studies textbook, one of the most popular for teaching 14–15-year-olds, says, 'The Japanese Army massacred a large number of Chinese, including women and children. Japan came under attack from foreign countries for the Nanjing massacre, but the general populace in Japan knew nothing about it'. A footnote to this section adds, 'The number of dead in and outside the city, including women and children, reached 70 000–80 000 people in a couple of weeks. If the soldiers who had surrendered their weapons are included, the number is said to have reached 200 000'.

When the same textbook deals with South-east Asia, it says this: 'The Japanese military imposed oppressive rule on the occupied territories, including Singapore and Malaysia, where the Japanese Army killed many people of Chinese descent'. Once again the number of dead is footnoted in a way which leaves the figures up in the air. 'Studies to determine the actual number killed are still in progress; estimates are over 6000 or between 40 000 and 50 000 in Singapore and more than 7500 or 100 000 in Malaysia.' The textbooks also deal with the other sacred tenet of the ultra-nationalists opposed to the Diet apology resolution—that Japan waged war to free Asia from the white colonialists. 'Claiming that the war was aimed to rid East Asia of western influence and create a new prosperity through co-operation among Asians, Japan referred to the war as the "Greater East Asian War" ', says the *Kyoiku Shuppan* text for junior high students. 'In fact, however, the true aim was that Japan should replace the nations of the West in controlling Asia.'

At great expense, the Foreign Ministry in Tokyo translated these social studies textbooks for primary, junior high and high school students into English, Chinese and Korean. The large glossy books feature the Japanese text on one page, and the translated text on the opposite page. 'We needed to cope with criticism from overseas that Japanese children are not learning modern history. We want [foreigners] to read the facts before they criticise', a spokeswoman for the publishers told me. Her comment is instructive—the changes were made to cope with overseas criticism, or to use the Education Minister's formula, the 'feelings' of foreigners, rather than to address the intrinsic moral dilemma. It's a mindset which goes some way to explaining why the stories the textbooks contain have not sunk in, with either the older or the younger generation.

Toshiaki Yamamoto, a Sydney-based correspondent for a major Japanese news wire service, set out a view typical of the postwar generation in a 1995 article in *Nichigo Press*, a paper published for the Japanese community in Australia. Yamamoto said he had been to China and other Asian countries and knew what Japan did there. But he bore no personal scars from the conflict, nor did he feel any individual responsibility for the sins of his fathers (and mothers) at that time. So when he read yet another story of grisly Japanese atrocities, he didn't see himself or his peers bending and bowing with a craven sense of guilt. Rather they thought—'Enough! Why keep on with this 50 years after the war?'. Later, in the same article, he wrote, 'There exists a deep-seated view in Japan that the Tokyo Tribunal [on war crimes] forced a version of history written by the winners, who were mainly white, over the losers'.

Yamamoto has a point, as did some of the speakers at the Budokan rally opposing the Diet war apology, who called the continuing demands from Westerners for apologies hypocritical. Did Great Britain apologise for waging war so it could sell opium in China, they ask? Did the United States say 'Sorry' for massacring the Plains' Indians last century? Did Australia apologise for wiping out large numbers of Aboriginals? (The answers are No; No; and Yes—more than 150 years after the event.)

Yamamoto says he feels a real distance between himself and the conflict, and considered he was not qualified to make any judgement about who was right and who was wrong. The foreigners' version of the war, which depicts Japan as wholly evil, and the West as singularly good—a sort of black-armband view of history imposed by outsiders—sits uneasily with him. He says he suspects most of the postwar generation agrees with him, and there is some evidence to bear him out. Japan's youngest MP, Ms Sanae Takauchi, 34, of the conservative party, *Shinshinto*, whose leaders officially supported the Diet war apology, insisted there was no need to do any soul-searching. 'I, at least, cannot be said to count amongst the war generation, and that's why I don't feel remorse, or anything like that,' she said.

But war and history can never be dismissed so simply. Even if the Japanese don't teach the war thoroughly in their schools, and it fades from the media as a live political issue, the Chinese, Koreans, Singaporeans and many others will make sure every child who grows up in their countries knows all about it. Yamamoto and his kind ignore this. They expect that when the older generation dies, they will take their war memories and guilt with them to the grave. The next generation will then be able to live in peace, and the war will drift off into the haze of history. Everyone will then be able to get on with enjoying the kinder, gentler Asian co-prosperity sphere that Japan now powers. In fact, the opposite may be the case. If the Japanese persist in dealing with the issue only when they are politically required to do so, then their Asian neighbours will grow up with the worst stereotype of Japan.

In the meantime, a sort of ennui is setting in with younger people in Japan. The changes to the school textbooks are too late for the present generation of young adults. And in any case, formal education is no match for the power of popular culture. For many men in their twenties and early thirties, reading real history is rather dull compared with the scores of fantasy war-time novels and comics now on sale in Japan. These books—'entertainment war novels' or 'simulation war novels'—pander cleverly to the national penchant for make-believe. One major publishing company, Chuokoronsha, sold four million copies of 60 different war simulation novels in 1993 and 1994—more than half of their mainstream paperback sales. A commentator on military issues, Haruo Fujii, puts their popularity down to generational change. 'Most Japanese today were born after World War II, and they have no idea how dreadful war is', he said.[22] These books simulate and re-fight the big battles of the Pacific War with real characters, like the famous naval commander Admiral Isoroku Yamamoto who led the attack on Pearl Harbor, and real themes, like the 'liberation' of Asia. In this proliferation of popular pulp fiction, Japan acts honoura-bly. There is no sneak attack on Pearl Harbor. Elections are held in Manchuria. Asian countries are treated equally and the Imperial ultra-nationalists are held at bay.

And most important of all is the result—Japan wins. Small wonder that Japan's neighbours look on it with so little warmth or genuine affection.

CHAPTER 7

THE ODD COUPLE

'The incomprehensible and persistent frequency with which it is hinted, insinuated or openly stated that Japan has sinister designs on Australia is one of the greatest marvels of the 20th century.'

Katsusaburo Tamaki, Japanese Consul in Sydney, in 1921

'We had to start from scratch, and the physical constraints were beyond comprehension. In terms of per capita national assets, ours were about one seven-hundredth of Australia's. So you were born lucky and we weren't.'

Eishiro Saito, Nippon Steel

German leader Helmut Schmidt once famously remarked that Japan was a country 'without a true friend'. Even though he was a diplomat practised at finding friends where none truly existed, the Foreign Ministry's Kazuo Ogura almost proved Schmidt right when he sat down in 1992 to try to find one. In an article in the Foreign Ministry's in-house journal, Ogura, then the high-flying head of the ministry's Economic Affairs bureau and later the author of the influential paper on Japan and Asia (see Chapter Three), cast his eye over the globe in search of a friend and partner for Japan. He wanted a country which was willing 'to expend blood, sweat and tears' with Tokyo in forging a new regional diplomacy.[1] Not too difficult a task, you might have thought. Here was the world's second biggest economy, with the richest people according to per capita income, and the most generous aid donor on the globe. Japan was the kind of country that other nations should be pursuing with offers of warmth and friendship, but it wasn't.

Two things intervened between Japan and other countries from the very beginning. One was what Ogura called the logic of regions. Thus Europeans stuck with Europeans, Americans with Americans, and South-east Asians with South-east Asians. The 'scars of history' had the same effect. France, Germany and Britain were bound together because they knew the horrible consequences of falling apart. Likewise, several of the countries of ASEAN, Malaysia, Indonesia and Singapore, had learnt to build a common economic destiny the hard way, after dangerous military confrontations in the 1960s. The United States was no good either. Washington was too hypocritical, amongst other things, demanding that the government in Tokyo intervene less in the marketplace, and at the same time order specific industries to buy a certain percentage of US goods. Besides, Japan and the United States were too gigantic to form just a 'regional' bond. Theirs would be nothing less than an overwhelming global alliance.

By this stage, Ogura was starting to run out of countries. Latin America wasn't on the horizon. India was, well, India, and not really pushing to be a close partner with anyone. That left just a single possible nation with close ties to Japan—one way down at the bottom of what the Japanese have historically called the *nan'yo*, the South Seas—Australia. 'Japan and Australia possess common values of democracy and freedom', Ogura wrote.

They both support, in general, market principles and free trade. They have a very deep relationship of economic interdependence and they possess common interests in security and political aspects. Could not Australia and Japan form a partnership which goes a step further than that? The European Community began with steel and coal. The US and Canada began from a common market in automobiles. A similar approach may be possible between Japan and Australia.

Apart from the fact that men in both countries love sport and regularly get blind drunk, at first glance two more different nations and peoples would be hard to find. Japan is an ancient culture with its own deep traditions and mythologies, officially homogeneous and overflowing with theories of its own uniqueness. Schoolteachers drum into children from their first years that they live in a 'small island nation with no natural resources'. Internalised from a young age, this theme breeds a neurotic insecurity and vulnerability that is barely comprehensible to outsiders, who see Japan as an overweening economic colossus. The old cliché—rich Japan, poor Japanese—still holds true. Anyone who lives in the country can only marvel at the daily— and in many cases, six days a week—exacting economic effort still extracted from almost the entire population of this 'rich' country.

Australian values and attitudes stand in stark contrast with Japan's. Just a single generation after barring Asian migrants to protect its own white identity, the Government in Australia now actively promotes ethnic diversity, and even encourages people to rake through other cultures in search of one of their own. Australia also looks at the world through a very different economic window. Australians learn that they live not on an island, but on a vast continent with abundant natural resources. But Australia feels insecure too, not because of a lack of resources, but because of inept management of a surfeit of them. Whereas the Japanese are rich but feel poor, Australians are blessed with wealth, but sense they are squandering it. Australia's isolation—as a small group of mostly white, relaxed people in a region teeming with energetic, ambitious Asians—breeds a sense of vulnerability as well, soothed only slightly by the country's blissful distance and boozy lifestyle. The differences between Australia and Japan are easily reduced to personal stereotypes, of the short, hard-working and group-oriented Japanese, who speak as one in sets of delphic pronouncements, and the large, easy-going Aussies, who are congenitally brash, loud and unguarded—and ultimately naive. These contradictions make Australia and Japan an odd couple, and indeed have done so for over a century.

In both countries, industrialisation and modernisation in the nineteenth century were accompanied by racial policies which fenced them off from surrounding Asian countries. Australia's founding identity was as a determinedly white and British bulwark in Asia. Japan's famous rallying cry for its copycat catch-up modernisation, as we have seen, was 'Out of Asia and Into Europe'. Just over 100 years or so later, when Paul Keating travelled to Japan spouting Australia's newly resplendent Asian sensibilities, one clever Japanese headline-writer turned the slogan on its head to sum up the new course as matching Japan's—'Out of Europe and Into Asia'. For Ogura, Australia's reorientation made it potentially the perfect partner. But he diplomatically left out of his article one important factor which made Australia especially user-friendly to Japan. Unlike just about every other country, advanced and developing in the world, bar the oil-producing states, Australia had for decades run a large trade surplus with Japan. That wasn't because of Australia's industrial prowess, but because of the different strengths of the two economies.

Australia had raw materials and wide open spaces, and for the most part had efficiently exploited both to build large export industries in mining and farming. By contrast, Australia's manufacturing industries had dwindled under a deadly mixture of indolent policy, protective tariffs, slack work practices and suspicion of new technologies, and struggled to export a single widget. The Japanese economy was a mirror image. Japan had no raw materials to speak of, and so set about strategically sourcing them after the war from Australia, Indonesia and the oil-producing states. Japan fed the raw materials into its manufacturing industries, inventively sheltered these industries from foreign competition, and encouraged them to export all over the world. It also protected and subsidised its agricultural sector, while at the same time allowing it to wither slowly, along with its population of ageing farmers. These things, together with the population imbalance, meant that Japan had a massive appetite for raw materials, and Australia had a small market for manufactured goods. The result was a large structural trade surplus for Australia, and the basis for a beautiful friendship. Most countries seethed at Japan's mercantilist trade policies, and couldn't deal with Tokyo without these tensions getting in the way. Australia was different. 'It's fun talking to Australians—you can't blame us for having a huge trade surplus', chuckled Kazuo Nukuzawa, the acerbic managing director of Japan's peak business body, the Keidanren.[2]

The head of the Diet's Japan–Australia Friendship League, a senior conservative politician, Kabun Muto, was slightly more complimentary, but also patronising, in praising relations with Australia. 'Frankly speaking, if I compare negotiating with the Australians and the Americans, it is easy to negotiate with Australians. Those people have the same ancestors, but these days, they are quite different', he said.

> Australians aren't hard negotiators, unlike the Americans. There is a confidence that we can trust each other. I am not saying we don't get on with the US, but in terms of the degree of friendship and trust, the Europeans are the most difficult, then comes the

190

Americans and then the Australians. The Australians are much easier, because they have clearcut views. I think the two countries are co-operating with each other because they match each other economically. Australia is rich in resources—coal, oil, iron ore, LNG, wool, wheat, most of which cannot be produced in Japan. Japan is a high-tech country and can supply Australia with advanced technology—so both countries are mutually supporting each other. So we're partners in this sense.[3]

But a partnership along the lines envisaged by Ogura was something else altogether. Many senior officials in the Foreign Ministry and also MITI, deeply pessimistic about the long-term prospects of the Australian economy, were scornful of Ogura's thesis. One senior MITI official said that nothing irritated the US more than Japan getting Australia to speak to Washington on Japan's behalf. An anonymous bureaucrat in the Foreign Ministry's pro-American mainstream was even more dismissive. 'What on earth would be the merit of committing a double suicide pact with Australia?' he said.[4]

Australia for its part consciously set aside its complaints about various sectors of Japanese industry that still conspired to keep out its products and, from the late 1980s onwards, used its tension-free trading relationship to build a regional political dialogue. More than Japan, Australia needed a regional partner to cement its position in East Asia. Japan, for its own good reasons, ignored the naysayers in its own ranks, and flattered Australia by reciprocating. By the time Paul Keating visited Tokyo in May 1995, Prime Minister Murayama was moved—by his speech-writers—to say that his nation desired to enter the twenty-first century 'walking alongside our Australian friends as best mates'.[5]

At times, Canberra was both naive and dishonest about the trade surplus, and allowed it to be paraded as evidence of Japan's open markets. 'That is like Saudi Arabia saying its massive oil exports to Japan prove that it, too, is an industrial giant on par with Japan', said Tokyo-based Australian academic and commentator, Dr Greg Clark.[6] A Japanese prime minister could not often get away with visiting another country, as Kiichi Miyazawa did in Australia in 1993, and emerge with a front-page headline about both countries pledging 'to work together for free markets'.[7] Few places on the globe associated the word 'Japan' with 'free trade'.

Japan and Australia had long had a loose, low-key political alliance in the region, but it was now mutually convenient to lift it onto a higher level. It was a practical Asian alliance between the two least Asian countries in the region. Australia openly sided with Japan in its increasingly nasty trade disputes with the US, and Japan returned the favour by publicly embracing Australia's new Asian identity. Tokyo irritated European nations, and Canberra's Asian nemesis, Malaysia, by lobbying strongly for Australia to be included in summits of European and Asian leaders. Japan even claimed that Australia could make the running for it in important regional initiatives which the burdens of history constrained Tokyo from taking on itself. Australia, for example, proudly boasts that the Asia Pacific Economic Co-operation (APEC) forum was created on its initiative. From its inception in 1989, APEC has grown into the most important regional body, and the vehicle for an annual summit of Asia–Pacific leaders. But in Tokyo people tell a different story about its formation. MITI officials say they produced a concrete plan for APEC in 1988, but felt unable to launch it themselves because of lingering distrust in the war-scarred region about Japan's motives. So they encouraged Australia to run with the issue instead. This is an interesting concept—Australia as a Trojan horse for Japan's designs on Asia! Australia's most senior diplomat at the time, Richard Woolcott, says MITI is partly right, but that Australia had always wanted something wider than the Japanese. He also points out that while MITI supported the idea, the Foreign Ministry in Tokyo at first didn't. Turf wars between these two ministries are so common that APEC participants joke that the body has three Chinas (mainland China, Taiwan, Hong Kong), and two Japans—MITI and the Foreign Ministry.

Japan and Australia also used each other shamelessly to snooker temporarily the East Asian Economic Caucus, Malaysian leader Mahathir's rival to APEC. Australia was excluded from the Asians-only EAEC from the start, and infuriated Mahathir by campaigning strongly against Japan joining the body. For his part, Mahathir constantly needled Australia about its Asian pretensions, and pounced on Paul Keating's offhand remark about being 'recalcitrant' in boycotting the first APEC summit in 1993, and cynically whipped it into a full-blown diplomatic brawl. The initial emotional response of the Japanese press was to side with Mahathir. 'After all, Japan is a fellow Asian nation', wrote Masahiko Ishizuka in the *Nikkei Weekly*. Mahathir maintained the rage after this incident, denouncing Australia's regional ambitions again in his Japanese-language book-length paean to pan-Asianism in 1994, with the full backing of his co-author, ultra-nationalist politician Shintaro Ishihara (see Chapter Three). Asians can communicate tacitly, using only a few words, Ishihara wrote, unlike rude and emotional Europeans like Keating. 'This is why Mahathir has attacked Keating, asking how he as a white person, could understand the heart of the coloured Asian people', Ishihara said.[8]

Up until the end of 1994, bureaucrats and politicians in Tokyo flirted with the EAEC, and the business community very nearly embraced it. Business was at the front line of both the trade war with the United States and the redirection of the Japanese economy into Asia. The politicians, as ever, lagged well behind, and business had a more urgent need to protect its interests in Asia. Kazuo Nukuzawa of the Keidanren played down Australian fears of the Mahathir plan. 'Mahathir is just like a pebble in your shoe', he said.

My advice to the Australians is not to press Mahathir, or the east Asians in the manner that I belong to you, therefore you have to invite us in. Let the east Asians congregate amongst themselves for a while. It's just comparing notes. If you press too much it will be de facto asking them whether Asians are wedded to Asian racism or not. It's a hard question. There may be a racial element. But there's also an element that we Asians have to [get together] because the western civilisation is hitting with all its power. Pretend that it's just weekend hiking with some of your girlfriends—it's not going to be a marriage. It doesn't go anywhere because it doesn't give any tangible benefits to the Japanese.

Mahathir had other, more virulent supporters of his anti-Australian line in Japan, most notably former Foreign Ministry official Eiichi Furukawa, a self-proclaimed and single-minded roving lobbyist for the EAEC. 'I know Australians—they're nice people, but not civilised', he told me. 'The Australians say that not allowing them into the EAEC is racist. But as long as Australians promote democracy and human rights and interfere in the domestic affairs of Asian countries, they won't be accepted.' But each time the Japanese got up to the starting line on the EAEC, the Americans turned up the pressure to ensure Tokyo stayed out. So rather than say 'no' to Mahathir, Japan played coy and non-committal, and quietly pressed Australia's claims for membership as well. When Mahathir forced the issue, Tokyo looked for a way out—and found a convenient one in Australia and New Zealand. Japan insisted that if it was to attend EAEC-style meetings, then Australia and New Zealand, as 'Asian nations', should be invited too. Australia was overjoyed, and Mahathir was furious. The self-appointed standard-bearer of Asian values did not enjoy being 'out-Asianised' by the inscrutable Japanese.

To understand the import of Japan's gesture, you only had to look beyond Mahathir to the attitudes of other South-east Asians to Australia. One of the most poignant illustrations of

Australia's dilemma unfolded at an Asian Young Leaders' forum in the Philippines in late 1994. Representing Australia was Kevin Rudd, then the youthful head of the Queensland cabinet office, aspiring Labor MP, and a fluent Mandarin speaker. But Rudd wasn't alone—a full 20 out of the 100 delegates were Australian, and a journalist from the Singapore *Straits Times* reported, they 'stuck out like the proverbial mile'. Rudd jokingly informed the other 'Asians' that Australia was there to stay. 'You won't be able to get rid of us!' he said.

More seriously, Rudd told the audience that he was frustrated by the outdated debate about whether Australia was part of Asia. 'It may still be an interesting subject for academics and for Australia, at least, continues to represent an ever-reliable topic to be set for undergraduate papers', he said. 'It may even make for interesting after-dinner conversation among our region's foreign policy elites. It's time to stop theorising. It's already happened. Australia is part of the region. And it's time simply to get on with it.'

The other young leaders were not so convinced. A number countered with well-worn points about Australia being in the region, but not of it, and a bit too pushy and obtrusive anyway. But a Filipino delegate punctured Rudd's confident dissertation, and brought the house down at the same time, with a one-liner. 'You guys are so white!' she said, provoking much laughter.

That, Rudd confessed later to a local reporter, went straight to the heart of the matter. And it always had.[9]

GREAT SOUTHERN LAND

Almost as soon as Japan began to modernise in the mid-nineteenth century, its scholars and travellers gazed southward to the *nan'yo*, the South Seas, at Australia and its vast natural wealth. All the themes that still cloud the debate today—on the

Japanese side, about Australia's wealth and the need to secure it; and on Australia's, the mixture of paranoid dread and ignorance of, and respect for, Japanese power—filled the earliest exchanges between the two countries. The father of modernisation, Yukichi Fukuzawa, first popularised Australia in a book in 1869, rhapsodising about its gold mines, which were 'incomparably rich, surpassing even those of California'.[10] A researcher, Manjiro Inagaki, sent by his information-hungry government around this time to study at Cambridge University, suggested prophetically in his thesis that 'Japan should import raw materials from Australia and industrialise herself to augment our nation's economic potential'.[11] In 1875, the Japanese Navy began training cruises in the Pacific. One passenger was Shigetaka Shiga, an early supporter of Japan's southward advance. Described as a 'political geographer', Shiga was overwhelmed by Australia's proximity and wealth. 'How odd it is until today that we have paid no attention to our southern neighbour, Australia', he wrote. 'The Australians are the bravest and most audacious among the Anglo-Saxons. It is incomprehensible why we have so far had no dealings with this flourishing and civilised people close to us in the south.' The speed with which ships under both steam and coal could reach Australia especially impressed Shiga, as it still does the Japanese buyers of Australian raw materials today. The 5300-mile journey to Sydney could be completed in 35–50 days. 'There', he wrote, 'the ship's arrival will be announced in Sydney's evening papers. The bravery and adventure will be praised, they will be hailed for their speed and single-mindedness, and their goods will be sold in no time'.[12]

This first euphoric assessment of Australia's wealth quickly gave way to the second, nastier theme that has also run like a thread through Australia's relations with Japan this century— that of race. The first diplomatic exchanges of any significance between Australia and Japan were over the White Australia Policy, one of the nation's founding principles. As the nationalist magazine, the *Bulletin*, so brutally put it: 'No nigger, no China-man, no lascar, no kanaka, no purveyor of cheap coloured labour is an Australian'.[13] When the Immigration Restriction Act was passed by Australia's new parliament in 1901, it also meant that no Japanese, or as the *Bulletin* would have put it, no 'Jap', could be an Australian either.

Japan objected strongly to the new law, not so much because it discriminated against Asians, but because it put Japanese people on a par with Asians. Japan wanted the 'respect due to a great power and a highly valued ally of Great Britain' and expected Australia to discriminate between it and 'the backward and dependent Asian peoples'.[14] The attitude of Australia's then Prime Minister, Alfred Deakin, was just as instructive—he wanted to keep the Japanese out, not because he thought they were inferior, but because they were different, and in some respects superior. Japan wanted a status similar to that granted to them in South Africa under apartheid, as honorary whites. (Not, it should be noted, honourable whites.) Under pressure from Great Britain, Australia felt it had to give face to the Japanese complaint. The government slightly modified the dic-tation test requirement used to keep non-white people out in a way which eased the affront to the Japanese. Honour appeared to have been satisfied, even though the whites-only policy did not change in any practical fashion.[15]

Japan's victory in the war against Russia in 1905, culminating in its stunning annihilation of the Russian fleet in the battle of Tsushima in May of that year, didn't immediately raise alarm in Australia, but attitudes gradually hardened from that point. Historian David Sissons says that Australia's 'fears of Japan became acute and widespread' in the years after the military victory, even though the two countries were technically friends and allies for at least a decade after. As an ally of Great Britain, the Japanese Navy escorted Australian troopships across the Indian Ocean during World War I, and stood by to protect the

Sydney when it sank the German light cruiser, the *Emden*, in the Allies' first naval victory in 1914. None of this pleased Australia's bellicose Prime Minister, Billy Hughes, who was horrified at the quid pro quo demanded by and granted to the Japanese by Great Britain in return for its valuable naval support. Britain supported Japan's claims to German islands north of the equator—the Marianas, Carolines and Marshalls—and Japan agreed to back Britain's, and thereby Australia's, claim to German islands south of the equator—Samoa, New Guinea and Nauru. Hughes was alarmed, but could do nothing to stop the deal. But he bided his time, and carefully prepared the ground for the campaign he was to launch against the Japanese after the war.

In his speeches in Australia, Hughes began warning about the threat from 'a thousand millions of coloured peoples'. Hughes also used Japan as a bogeyman in his crusade in favour of conscription, saying Australia had to help Britain now, to ensure its support later, at the end of the war, when Japan would attack the White Australia Policy. Hughes had his showdown with Japan at the Versailles Peace Conference in Paris in 1919, when he engineered an ignominious defeat for Japanese demands that the principle of racial equality be inserted in the Covenant of the League of Nations. Hughes considered that the principle of racial equality could fatally undermine a White Australia. A watered-down Japanese motion was passed by 11 votes out of 17, but the chairman, US President Woodrow Wilson, declared that it would not be adopted because it was not unanimous. It was a bitter and humiliating experience for the Japanese, who insisted they had earned the right to equal status with other great nations. Thanks to Hughes, it was also the one time that Australia had a material impact on Japanese history. Tokyo's humiliation significantly strengthened the position of the nationalists and militarists in Japan. They were the people who wanted to take on and match the Western colonial powers in Asia, and who ultimately propelled Japan into the Pacific War.

The hysteria about Japan continued in the immediate years after the Paris conference. In February 1921, the *Sydney Morning Herald* reported that thousands of Japanese travellers had been seen landing on offshore islands in northern Australia over the past year. An exasperated Japanese Consul in Sydney, Katsusaburo Tamaki, sent a stinging response to the paper, writing that 'The incomprehensible and persistent frequency with which it is hinted, insinuated or openly stated that Japan has sinister designs on Australia is one of the greatest marvels of the 20th century'.[16] But no sooner had the hysteria been whipped up than it died down. After the Washington Naval Conference of 1921 set limits on the respective navies of Britain, the United States and Japan, Australia immediately relaxed about its northern neighbour. The government closed down the sole bureaucratic branch set up to monitor Japan, recalled its one officer monitoring events in Tokyo, and even sacked the only full-time lecturer in Japanese at the Duntroon Military College. Historian Henry Frei says Australia slipped back into the same old kind of Nipponese ignorance that the country had suffered before the war. 'The cancellations revealed a singular superficiality of Australian policy vis-a-vis Japan and her understanding of Asia, and seriously handicapped Australia in the lead-up to the Pacific War', he said.

Australia and Japan did, in fact, enjoy a golden age for the next decade. The virulent, racist rhetoric of Billy Hughes was replaced by the sort of syrupy speeches that are uttered today. 'The destinies of two peoples in the Pacific lie together', said Prime Minister Stanley Bruce in welcoming the new Consul-General in 1925. 'Our civilisations are complementary, and we shall mutually enrich ourselves in receiving and giving what is best in them.' Trade grew rapidly, doubling in value in the first half of the 1930s. Very quickly, Japan ranked second only to

Britain as a customer for Australian goods.[17] But very quickly after that, the two countries were at war, an experience that would take them years, even decades, to get over.

WAR . . .

Few countries were as bitter as Australia immediately after the Pacific War, and the Japanese knew it. Australia, along with England, pushed hardest for Emperor Hirohito to be tried as a war criminal. The External Affairs Minister, 'Doc' Evatt, called Hirohito 'the No. 1 war criminal'. The Australian judge who headed the Tokyo Tribunal which tried Japanese leaders for war crimes, Sir William Webb, also wanted to summon Hirohito to give evidence, but was overruled by the American prosecutor.

Australia's hostility was no secret to the Japanese, particularly to the ultra-nationalist groups who had little respect for this crude British outpost in the South Seas. The nationalists had been particularly affronted by the campaign to try their sacred Emperor. Members of the right-wing Chrysanthemum Flag Association rated Australia close to the bottom of a list of countries they liked or respected, in a survey of sixteen nations in 1951, ahead only of 'the Negro people', Korea and Russia. A more general survey taken in Tokyo around the same time turned up remarkably similar results. Asked to list sixteen countries in terms of preference, Australia rated ahead of the Russians, Koreans and 'Negroes', and behind the Filipinos and Annamites. It was a long way from the results of surveys conducted by the Australian Embassy in Tokyo in the 1990s, which found that Australia was the country that Japanese most wanted to visit, even if most of them didn't actually do so.

Full reconciliation didn't really start until the first visit of a Japanese Prime Minister to Australia in November and December 1957. A lot was riding on the visit of Prime Minister

Nobusuke Kishi. It was to mark the end of a black, violent period in relations and the beginnings of a new era. At a symbolic meeting in Canberra, Kishi and Australian Prime Minister Sir Robert Menzies were to seal an agreement putting trade between the two countries on a normal footing. A couple of years earlier, Japan had joined the international body which set the rules for world trade—the General Agreement on Tariffs and Trade (GATT)—and demanded the same access to the Australian market as other GATT members enjoyed. After much agonising about the impact on its own manufacturing industries, Australia agreed, in return for continued access for its wool, and new purchases of wheat from Japan. The agreement was the launching pad for the lucrative resources trade, and positioned Australia for decades to sell the raw materials which powered Japan's economic miracle, then on the verge of kicking into high gear.

When Kishi arrived on 30 November, Australia was being plagued by one of its periodic severe droughts, but even that downturn did little to conceal the gulf between the two countries. The Australian economy was more than double the size of Japan's, and the individual Australians' earnings far outstripped the money paid to Japanese workers. But any sense of superiority felt by Australians was skin-deep. Many workers and unions feared the dedication and industry of the Japanese, just as they had at the turn of the century. And hovering menacingly over the trade issue was the lingering bitterness and intense distrust over the war. Menzies was well ahead of Australian public opinion, and the opposition Labor Party, in inviting Kishi to Australia to do a deal on trade, and a nervous Japanese Ambassador in Canberra, Tadakatsu Suzuki, knew it. Just how nervous can be gleaned from Suzuki's confidential cables in the Foreign Ministry's archives in Tokyo. Menzies told Suzuki that he had issued the invitation to Kishi over the head of 'many objections', and worried that Kishi's presence would seriously set back his government's careful rapprochement with its former enemy. On the eve of the trip, Menzies watched apprehensively as anti-Japanese Labor MPs raged against a trade deal with the old enemy, and bitter returned soldiers demanded that the Japanese leader stay away from the war memorial.

'There are many people who suffered at the hands of the Japanese army, and we need to pay close attention in dealing with public opinion', Suzuki cabled Tokyo. 'Above all, we should be careful not to upset these people.' Suzuki's cables express alarm about the initial refusal of New South Wales Labor Premier Joe Cahill to attend official ceremonies, and worried that the federal leader, Dr Evatt, would not show up at the visit's centrepiece function in Canberra. In the end, both men attended ceremonies for Kishi, but in Cahill's case in particular with a distinct lack of enthusiasm. Many in the ALP opposed the agreement to give Japan equal access to Australia's markets for the same reason they supported the White Australia Policy. Japan, and Asia in general, were sources of cheap labour and goods, and a threat to Australian workers' conditions, and by extension, the ALP's own political base.

'There is opposition to the trade agreement from local manufacturers and the Labor Party, which maintains that Japan benefited from the agreement, and that Australia lost', Suzuki reported. 'If Japan starts buying less Australian products, then anti-Japanese feeling will be ignited.' Just weeks before Kishi arrived, the Labor MP for Parkes, Les Haylen, made a speech in parliament attacking 'the wily Japanese', 'the Japanese factory coolie', and 'poachers in sampans'. 'It is the same old Japan, the leopard does not change its spots', Haylen thundered. 'The Jap is engaging in snide trading tactics, taking full advantage of the benefits of favoured nation treatment [while engaging] in his old buccaneering trade practices.' A quarter of a century later, Labor Prime Minister Paul Keating managed to paint the conservative opposition into a corner by branding them as anti-Asian. But up to the 1970s, the opposite was true. The conservative parties, partly because they were in government, partly because they embodied some genuine liberal traditions, and partly because of the economic interests they represented, were far more progressive in their policies towards the region. The deal with Tokyo in 1957 was sealed only because the Menzies government had the will to ignore the dyed-in-the-wool racists who filled the ALP's ranks. So too did a select group of far-sighted politicians and bureaucrats in Canberra who saw the long-term benefits from trade with Japan, and backed the agreement from the beginning. A healthy dose of self-interest helped. A threat by Tokyo to reduce Australia's burgeoning wool exports if Canberra didn't treat Japan as an equal trade partner helped concentrate conservative minds in support of the agreement.

As well as advising Kishi what to say, Suzuki also counselled his Prime Minister on subjects he should avoid. One taboo topic was the White Australia Policy. Suzuki warned that the thin-skinned Australians were hypersensitive to criticism of the country's racist immigration laws. 'Recently, a few critics of the White Australia Policy have emerged amongst academics', Suzuki reported. 'However, Australians hate foreigners criticising this policy. We should be sensitive to this issue, and remember our need for exports.' Kishi's own speech reflected the contradictory view Japan held of the former British colony. In his setpiece address to the parliamentary luncheon, Kishi praised Australia as a 'great British democracy'. He could hardly be blamed for thinking Australia was still British—after all, the then Governor-General, Field Marshall William Slim, was British. In the same speech, he attributed Australia's regional aid program, known as the Colombo Plan, to the country's 'awakened Asia-mindedness'.

In defeat, Japan had forgotten its nationalist indignation about being treated just like any other Asian country, and Kishi was willing to put aside his objections to the 'whites-only' policy, if he had any, to pursue a practical and businesslike relationship. The same went for the Australians like Trade Minister Sir John McEwen and his departmental head, Sir John Crawford, who didn't allow themselves to be shackled by the war in building close ties with Japan. Despite his notorious Anglophilia, and distaste for Asia, Menzies was also a strong supporter of closer relations with Tokyo.

All that then needed to be dealt with was the war.

Forewarned by Suzuki, Kishi's advisers inserted a form of apology into the most important speech of his visit to a parliamentary luncheon in Canberra. Beforehand, Suzuki reported, Menzies frankly confessed he was nervous about reaction to the speech. But Kishi rose to the occasion. He spoke of 'the tragic interruption' in the friendship between Australia and Japan, a friendship forged by 'our association with your immortal Anzacs' in World War I. Then came the apology. 'It is my official duty and my personal desire', he continued, 'to express to you, and through you to the people of Australia, our heartfelt sorrow for what occurred in the war'. The Japanese leader's pedigree couldn't have helped his credibility. As a key member of the Tojo cabinet during the war, Kishi was in charge of Japan's munitions industry, and as a minister signed the official document declaring war on the United States. He spent three and a half years in an American occupation prison after Tokyo's surrender as a war crimes suspect before his release.

Despite this baggage, Suzuki reported to Tokyo that the speech had received a generally favourable response. The press reports had been 'cool, but not hostile'. And Menzies told him he considered the speech to be a *ballon d'essai* (trial balloon) on the war issue, and was relieved that it had been a 'big success'. The Governor-General was equivocal about the contents of the apology. 'Strictly speaking, it was vague, and who caused the war was not mentioned', he told Suzuki. 'But it left a deep impression anyway.' Alan Rix of Queensland University, the leading historian of this period, said the speech was 'a reasonably standard Japanese Government apology of the kind that they thought the Australians would expect. But it was not an apology in the true sense of the word. The Australian papers reported it as an apology, but I don't think that was quite right'.

Considering the depth of the bitterness against the Japanese in some quarters after the war, one wonders how such a vague, indirect apology could succeed so admirably. In truth, it may not have had much impact at all, and Menzies' response and Suzuki's upbeat reporting may have just been wishful thinking. It is also possible that Japan's low political profile and relatively small economy at the time muted Australian reaction. Kishi's words, however, are still cited to this day, as evidence of Japan's good faith on the issue of the war. 'The friendship and interdependence we know today had its origins in the late 1950s', said Australian Foreign Minister, Senator Gareth Evans in 1994, 'the stage being set by farsighted actions on both sides, such as the visit by Prime Minister Kishi in 1957, whose apology for the war was accepted on both sides as a formal reconciliation'.[18] It is not surprising that Evans should latch onto this statement. Although the Australian government in public counsels Japan to be franker about its wartime aggression, its private message is often different. One Australian official recalls Evans telling his Japanese counterpart in a meeting in Tokyo to 'forget all about this *awabi* business'. On this occasion, Evans' statement needed some creative interpretation. *Owabi* means apologise; *awabi* means abalone.

Kishi's apology, or more accurately, his expression of 'heartfelt sorrow', was Kishi's *tatemae*—an appropriate diplomatic facade massaged to fit the expectations of the audience. The reaction to it might not have been so positive, or so widely quoted years later, if his *honne*—his real feelings—about the war were known. Kishi's own personal opinion wasn't publicised until his prison diaries were published in 1994.[19] After his arrest

205

as a war criminal following Japan's surrender, Kishi's former university teacher—in Japanese terms, his senior—wrote him a *haiku* poem, urging him to commit suicide. But Kishi refused to adopt this course. 'I will not be committing suicide—I will keep talking about the correctness of the war', he replied. Elsewhere, he called the conflict 'a just war', and 'a sacred war'. Kishi denounced the Tokyo Tribunal as 'nothing but political revenge', and said his bad treatment in jail rendered American democracy a fraud. There was not a word about apologies, and 'heartfelt sorrow', or anything to suggest that either he or Japan had done wrong. Kishi said in his diaries that he would reflect on the war—on losing it, that was, and in no other way.

It's possible that Kishi changed his views after he was released from prison, and elected to parliament in 1953. But it is more probable that he didn't. Kishi was one of many key wartime politicians and bureaucrats who were able to regain their positions of power after the conflict because their conservative views fitted the prevailing anti-communist ideology of the American occupation. Kishi didn't have to change. He simply learnt to manage an economy rather than a war, and mouth 'heartfelt sorrow' whenever it was diplomatically required. In this sense, his apology to Australia, and the ones he issued to other South-east Asian countries and New Zealand on the same trip, stand as the first of many insincere expressions of remorse that Japanese leaders have periodically mouthed ever since.

But no matter, because in the end Kishi's visit to Australia was a political success. It boosted Japan's standing, and if we are to believe one light-hearted aside in Suzuki's cables, it also helped Tokyo's old wartime ally, Germany. Bonn's Ambassador to Canberra told Suzuki that the first German consulate to open in Sydney in the 1950s had been a regular target for anti-Nazi attacks. But as soon as the Japanese diplomats arrived, he said happily, Australians had forgotten about the Germans, and concentrated all their enmity on the Japanese.

. . . AND PEACE

For an insight into how Japan and Australia went from worst enemies to best friends, take the case of Eishiro Saito of Yawata (later Nippon) Steel, one of the first Japanese businessmen to return to Australia after the war in 1951. The trip took three days, by propeller plane from an airforce base near Hiroshima, via Singapore and Darwin. Waiting for him was a pack of hostile reporters at the airport, and a city full of hotels that refused to take him as a guest. 'There was so much of hostility and antipathy', he recalled more than 40 years later.

> The reporters demanded to know whether I had come to sell something or buy something. Sales of iron ore in those days were strictly banned at that time, and there was no way to give an exemption to a former enemy nation. The real purpose was to sell certain steel products we had been making for export. Australian reporters seemed to find it hard to accept that the major purpose was not to get our hands on iron ore.
>
> Under the occupation by the Australian military, the Japanese had already experienced how difficult it would be to get along with other countries. The fact that they were hostile and even quite arrogant had already been driven home to us. But the anti-Japanese feeling was so strong in Sydney that I couldn't even get a hotel room. I managed to get into the Australia Hotel, and then only because Kanematsu [a trading company], and Heine Bros, who had done a lot of business with Japan, intervened to get me a room. I also had terrible experiences in department stores because of the hostile attitude of the staff, and being called a bloody Jap, and being spat on in the street.[20]

At the time I spoke to him in 1994, Saito was chairman of

Nippon Steel, the world's largest steel company and by far the biggest single importer of Australian raw materials. He had just retired as head of the Keidanren, Japan's peak big business council. Saito headed the Australia-Japan Business Council, and was also Bob Hawke's much-ballyhooed pick to head the Japanese end of the ill-fated city of the future in Adelaide, the so-called Multi-Function Polis. If anyone refused Saito a room at a hotel, or spat on him in the street in Australia now, they would be prosecuted, and everyone from the Prime Minister down would issue grovelling apologies. Saito spoke with pride about Japan's achievements. He also spoke with great friendship and affection for Australia, and admiration for the Australian mining company executives he had dealt with over decades. But behind the twinkle in his eye was a touch of disdain for Australia, and the easy ride the natural wealth had given it. 'The background of our two countries is completely different', he said. 'We had to start from scratch, and the physical constraints were beyond [Australians'] comprehension. In terms of per capita national assets, ours were about one seven-hundredth of Australia's. So you were born lucky and we weren't.'

In a single generation, Saito and his peers had gone from courting a hostile Australia for business to being energetically wooed by it. They had also established a firm control over resources like iron ore that Australia had refused to sell them in the immediate postwar years. Japan had carried out its resource diplomacy with an application and organisation unmatched on the Australian side—so much so that the structure of the annual resource talks is Exhibit One these days for the charge that Australian businessmen and bureaucrats have little idea about how to deal with Japan, and by extension Asia. The free-wheeling, individualistic Aussie miners pitted themselves against the cohesive, organised Japanese, and over time, so the argument went, they lost out.

Ever since the resources trade started in earnest in the 1950s, the Japanese steel mills have negotiated as a single group under their lead negotiator, which these days is Nippon Steel. The Tokyo bureaucracy encouraged and supported such cartels, because it considered they served the national interest. Inside Japan, the steel companies competed in a controlled sense. But when they dealt with outsiders, they presented a united Japanese front to their foreign suppliers. The Australian producers, by contrast, were openly antagonistic to any guidance from Canberra and negotiated mine by mine, company by company. There is, and was, a degree of co-ordination, but essentially the miners stuck resolutely to themselves. Moreover, as journalist Michael Byrnes wrote,

> Negotiations are always performed on Japan's home ground, in Tokyo. The timing of the decision is always in the hands of the Japanese negotiators. The game of extra tonnages for the first Australian company to agree to the mills' pricing demands is placed on Japan's terms from the start. The psychological pressure of extra sales or reduced tonnages, of last minute negotiations, of Australian negotiators having to spend hours waiting by a telephone which may not ring, of the rejection of individual Australians who are said to contravene Japanese cultural requirements, is intensified by the game being played in Japan.[21]

Organising a cohesive single group of miners from countries as diverse as Brazil, India and Australia—in the case of iron ore—to talk to the Japanese might be impossible. If Canberra were to mount such a campaign, it might find Australia's dominant market share on the table for discussion as well. The surest sign that the Japanese fear a united front of the kind they mount themselves is their savage reaction when they see one coming. In 1987, iron-ore producers from three countries, including Australia, sent a letter to the Japanese warning that prices were falling so low as to make investment in new mines not worth the expense. On the face of it, this was a mild exercise in orchestration, but the Japanese decided that something more was afoot. They held Australia's Hamersley Iron responsible, and ruthlessly cut its tonnage in half that year, at a cost to it, and Australia, of hundreds of millions of dollars. Similar letters have not been sighted since. Apart from officials of the miners' unions, the Tokyo-based head of Austrade in north Asia, Greg Dodds, is one of the few people in authority willing to contemplate doing unto Japan as it does unto Australia in the resource negotiations. 'The application back to the Japanese of the same ideas and arguments they use on us is one of several good litmus tests of whether you are getting screwed or not. If they show any discomfort with the formula they are applying to you, then there's probably something worth looking at', he said.[22] In Canberra, however, using Australia's power as a dominant producer to negotiate as a nation, rather than a series of mines, is a dead issue.

To be sure, Japan remains highly dependent on Australia for a host of strategic resources. In many key commodities—coal, wool, iron ore, wheat, aluminium, beef—Australia is either the number one or number two supplier to Japan. In some cases, it supplies 70 per cent of Japan's needs. 'In other words', says academic Gavan McCormack,

> every house, bridge, beer can, space rocket and car, every kitchen larder and indeed the energy that lies behind every movement of the Japanese system, has a substantial if invisible component [from Australia]. The bread, meat and noodles on Japanese tables are likely to be substantially Australian. Some of the rice, fruit, flowers, fish and wine too.[23]

Australians underestimate the value of their country to Japan, but so do most Japanese. 'Australia is like the air that we breathe', one Japanese diplomat told me. 'We barely think about it—but without it, we would be dead.'

But the reason the Japanese barely think about it is because the supplies are secured, and the manner in which they are purchased is settled. The application and organisation of the Japanese, and ironically, the hard work and efficiency of Australia's miners, has entrenched the semi-colonial structure of trade relations between the two countries—one in which Australia digs the minerals out of the ground, sells them to Japan, and then imports the finished value-added products. Donald Horne in his book *The Lucky Country* recounted an exchange at a dinner party in the 1960s where he asked the hostess what aspect of Australia she is most proud of. After a moment's hesitation, she replied, 'Our mineral resources!'. Most Australians would now have little trouble in naming more worthy national attributes. But Dodds says the syndrome lingers in both business and official circles, 'where the hard work and success of our mining companies is somehow transformed into a cause for pride and satisfaction for all of us'.

Even worse, the way Australia's miners have succeeded in Japan has set a bad example for other prospective Australian exporters. The miners have played little role in the marketing and placement of their 'products'—that has always been done for them by Japanese steel companies and trading houses. The miners, and the steel companies and trading houses, have also always dominated the peak bilateral business forums. That is why you will never see representatives of cutting-edge Japanese companies like Sony at the annual Australia–Japan Business Conference. You are more likely to meet the representative of 'Blast Furnace No. 2' from Kawasaki Steel. Access to the top levels of Nippon and Kawasaki Steel once meant an entree to the most powerful businessmen in Japan, but not any more. The importance of heavy industry in Japan has steadily waned in the past 30 years, and will continue to do so. That means Australia is locked into a contracting centre of influence and power in its most important regional partner.

Dodds says that the businessmen and women who might

build a new set of bridges are spooked by the overly well-documented difficulties of doing business there. 'There is a widespread fear of Japan—almost a feeling that it is too big, too hard and too expensive, and that the Japanese are too clever, particularly when it comes to manufactured and processed products', he says. 'If expense is the first thing you think about, you are probably going to find that Somalia is the best place to do business in. It will certainly be cheap. And even when people try to sell to Japan, they use the services of the trading companies, who aren't experienced with smaller niche products.' Dodds says that the areas of trade policy into which Canberra puts the most intense effort, large forums like APEC and the body which sets the rules for global trade, the GATT in Geneva, can have the same potentially harmful impact.

The other consequence of the GATT and APEC stuff is that it can reinforce in Australian business circles that there are very serious problems [in entering markets], and that you are really wasting your time to go and do something. They might think: 'When was that date (by which regional leaders agreed to drop trade barriers)? 2015. OK—let's just put that in my desk-top diary, and gear up, and in the meantime, I'll find something else to do at home.' Other [countries] don't behave that way—they just get on the ground, and start to push and probe, and work something out.

Canberra's hands-off policy towards industry puzzles Japanese officials. Yasukuni Enoki, the second-in-charge at Tokyo's embassy in Canberra in 1993, said he would often debate the need for Australia to have an industry policy with his friends in the Canberra bureaucracy. Industry policy in Japan is a dynamic combination of factors—of selective intervention, targeted protection and close co-ordination between business and government. But when Enoki raised the issue of industry policy with Australians, he always got a one-dimensional reply. The

Australians simply said that they did not want a return to protectionism. 'The set notion that industrial policy equals protectionism seems to be firmly ingrained', he remarked. The other mystery of the management of the Australian economy for Enoki was how bureaucrats in a business-free Canberra did their jobs anyway. 'In the eyes of one who has worked for years within the tightly inter-connected circles of Marunouchi, Kasumigaseki and Nagatacho [the adjacent business, bureaucratic and political centres respectively in central Tokyo], it still completely amazes me how bureaucrats can be located in Canberra and still manage to absorb the latest economic information,' he said.[24] The ultimate irony is that the intimate political relationship which Australia now boasts about enjoying with Japan is founded on a pattern of trade and business ties that have ossified. Australia's market share in Japan has continued to decline in line with the falling value, and worth, of its commodities. Australia has not been able to make up the slack with other exports.

It comes as little surprise, then, that despite sustained attempts by Australia to promote itself as a sophisticated exporter of high-tech goods and services, Japanese perceptions are dominated by images of a vast utopian lotus-land filled with exotic and cute animals, transplanted white people and boundless natural resources. Paul Keating's visit to Japan in early 1995 was covered extensively and effusively by the travelling Canberra press gallery as a testament to the deep friendship between the two countries. This was the same visit during which Prime Minister Murayama cloyingly called the two countries 'best mates'. The country's leading business daily, the *Nihon Keizai Shimbun*, however, reported not a single word of Keating's round of engagements one day, but found space to record the sad death of a koala in Nagoya. Tokyo's Ambassador to Canberra made a similar point, perhaps unconsciously, in a lengthy dialogue published in 1994 about Australia's value to Japan. Notions of the 'clever country' did not feature. How to live a nice life did. 'We should learn from Australians about taking it easy in life', said the Ambassador, Kazutoshi Hasegawa. 'Yes', replied his interlocutor, the head of a think-tank, Yoshio Nirazawa. 'From the Japanese perspective, Australians may seem a little too relaxed, but that is because the Japanese work too hard, and we Japanese must learn to change our lifestyles and aim to become a lifestyle superpower ourselves. In this respect, Australia will be an excellent teacher.'25 Such stereotypes can be jarring when paraded in the wrong places. At a seminar at the Australian Embassy in Tokyo in 1993 to promote bilateral academic links, Japan's Nobel Prize-winning scientist, Leo Esaki of Tsukuba University, joked about seeing dogs lazily sleeping under trees during a summer visit down under. 'They are just like the people', he quipped. Nobody laughed.

Australia is one of a small number of countries approved for lengthy discussion in school textbooks by the Education Ministry because of its close relations with Japan, but that hasn't always helped students get an accurate picture of the country. To start with, Australia's pristine image has not been disturbed by any tales of the bitterness of war. The official school textbooks used since 1956 to teach primary and junior high school students display maps which show that Australia was left untouched by the conflict. Nor do they reveal that the commander of the Allied force, General Douglas MacArthur, used Australia as a base to launch his counter-attack against Japan. The overall impression created by the books was that Australia remained isolated and untouched. After the omissions were reported in 1995 in the Australian media, the Education Ministry agreed to change the maps to fit reality.26 Just one textbook out of the many which came out later that year included a single small arrow to honour Australia's role in the war.

As late as 1993, the same textbooks still concentrated their writings on the White Australia Policy and depicted it as the foundation of a 'small, rich and white society'. One major textbook said 'most of the population was British' and that the low population was a result of the White Australia Policy. Another described a country which kept out Asians so that 'the whites' could huddle in cities along the coast. When Masami Sekine of Keio University, a rare bird in Japanese academia as a specialist on Australia, decided he wanted to put a question about Australia into university entrance exams, he combed through 24 history books and found a single mention of the country—and that was about the racist immigration policy. Reluctantly he put the question in, until horrified Australian diplomats discovered what he had done and demanded that he take it out. In an address to one of the ministry's textbook inspection committees, Sekine said he had tried to stress that Australia was a modern industrialised country, and not just a farm and a quarry. 'But many Japanese businessmen understand that Australia is an industrialised country, because of all the industrial disputes', he joked. 'They don't understand [that Australia is industrialised]. I want to expand that image.'

The Japanese translation of the White Australia Policy—*hakugoshugi*—is instantly recognised by most Japanese as a description of past, and in some ill-informed circles, present, racist immigration policy. 'We know the White Australia Policy does not exist any more—that's been well accepted in Japan', an Education Ministry official told me. 'But it used to be the key word when teachers were explaining Australia to their students, and was also used in tests, and it takes a while to change that perception gap.' In 1993, after pressure from the Australian government, the Education Ministry in Tokyo agreed to teach Japanese children about Australia's new immigration policies, as well as its old ones. Many race-conscious Japanese, it should be noted, are deeply suspicious of multiculturalism, and bluntly sympathetic to controls on migration. Kazuo Nukuzawa, the Keidanren managing director, told me that he understood the philosophy underlying the White Australia

Policy. 'The Australians do not have an Asian way of life. Yours is a British way of life—there's no disadvantage in that. If that is comfortable, you should keep it', he said.

> The White Australia Policy—there's nothing wrong with it. Why not? The Germans have this sort of policy. In most countries, blood is an important element [of citizenship]. I don't think people should disregard what they feel. If Australia wants to maintain some of its cultural heritage, I think it should adopt an allocation of immigration per year. It should come gradually. Otherwise people react against it. Don't count too much on the rationality of human beings.

WHITE TRASH

Even as 'best mates walking side by side', Australians cannot be what they are not to the Japanese. More troubling might be what they are, or have become. If Singapore's paramount leader, Lee Kwan Yew, ever set foot in Tokyo's nightclub district of Roppongi just as the sun was going down and the bars were filling with customers, he might think his prediction of 20-odd years ago—that Australians would become the 'poor white trash' of Asia—had come true. Scores of broad-vowelled young Australian women marshal the corners in this club district's heartland, hawking flyers promoting the delights of girlie bars where they work as hostesses. Like itinerant workers from developing countries throughout Asia, young Australians flock to Japan to earn incomes that dwarf anything they could expect to pocket at home. For women, the parallels with their Asian sisters don't end there. Hundreds of Australian women, like two who I got to know well—we'll call them Lisa and Jackie—come to toil in the *mizu shobai*, the water trade, as the bar and entertainment industry is known.

Lisa and Jackie were a couple of average 22-year-old girls

from the suburbs of Perth. Just out of university, their first overseas adventure was not the backpacking trails of Asia, or a campervan tour of England and Europe. Like hundreds of Australians in recent years, they'd been lured by tales of the hostess trade in Japan and the fortunes to be earned there. They came to Japan with the same game plan that brought thousands of other foreigners to this expat boom town. They were going to fleece the natives and leave, wealthy and untouched. Lisa wanted the money so she could travel on to England, and Jackie to pursue her dream of enrolling in an arts course in Italy. 'You meet people who come back with heaps of money, and basically, that's why you do it', Lisa says. 'I would never do this in Australia because it wouldn't be accepted. It only works because it is Japan.' Five to six nights a week they sit with businessmen, at the Casanova Club, a hostess club in Roppongi, chatting, dancing and pouring drinks, from nine at night to three in the morning. They get paid the equivalent of about $40 an hour, plus $25 when a customer nominates them to sit with him, and $30 every time they are invited to dinner by a customer. The one that gets the most invitations to dinner in a month, or 20 nominations, gets bonuses worth hundreds of dollars. The pair of them both earn about $1500 a week—Jackie even more because she teaches English during the day.

Bar hostesses in Japan are the inheritors of the *geisha* tradition, but also distant from it. The pure *geisha* (literally 'person with art') sing songs, play traditional instruments and dance. They can be as young as eighteen and as old as 80. They are companions to their customers, which may sometimes mean they form relationships with them. The *geisha* form the elite of the water trade, a business that the Japanese say is like the flow of liquid from a tap. Sometimes the business comes in a rush, other times it just trickles, but it always flows. Some rungs below the *geisha* establishments are the high-class hostess bars. It's in these soft, ego-enhancing sanctuaries that executives leave behind the pressures of corporate life. Surrounded by attractive women who maintain a steady flow of drinks and flattery, the men feel comfortable, reassured. They can relax, and maybe even clinch a business deal. All the better, when there's so much competition between the bars, if the hostesses are white. Asian women, who are brought into Japan by gangsters to work in bars, are assumed to be prostitutes. Western women are mostly treated differently. For the Japanese businessmen who frequent hostess bars, being waited on by white women is both exotic and symbolic of Japan's enhanced standing in the world. Many of these women are Australian, because they can automatically get working-holiday visas to enter Japan, something that isn't available to young Americans. Under a scheme set up in 1980, six-month working-holiday visas are available to anyone 28 years and under.

At the Casanova Club, the hostesses sling themselves over the posh boudoir-like velvet couches with the customers, attentively pouring drinks and making conversation. The ceiling is low and the walls are decorated with hundreds of tiny sparkling mirrors. Men in tuxedos weave their way past the shiny steel replicas of tropical palm trees scattered around the room. Surveying the scene is the formidable club owner, the *Mama-san*. The guests are a mixture of foreign and Japanese businessmen. On the night I visited, Jackie was dancing with a Japanese man to music played by the club's resident Filipino band, while Lisa was sitting with a group of Swiss bankers. 'The Japanese men are just disgusting', Jackie tells me later. 'They do believe we find them attractive. It's a fantasy—that's what's really gross . . . There are two guys who come in. They're really young, and the first time they meet a girl, they always say to her, "You smell". And they think it's an hilarious joke.'

There are the usual dirty jokes about penis sizes ('Japanese men are smaller, but harder'), and the curious questions about the colour of the girls' pubic hair. But their brutishness often regresses to boyishness. 'I'm a child. I'm a child!' one will often say, cuddling up to Lisa. But the Japanese mostly grasp one point of protocol that the Western businessmen don't—that the hostess bar is not a whorehouse.

So many young women from Australia and other countries began exploiting the working-holiday visa to work in hostess bars that in 1994 Japanese police began to deport women. In a number of cases, parents had had no idea what their daughters were doing until they picked up the paper and read that police were about to put the girls on the next plane home. The working-holiday visas were intended to promote 'cultural exchange and international friendship', which apparently didn't cover an inebriated businessman fondling a young woman's knee in a nightclub. 'Anybody with a visa in this category should not be working in industries which affect public morals', said a police spokesman.

Of course, thousands of young Australians entered Japan on the visas to do more mundane jobs, such as working in hotels, and waiting on tables in restaurants. Nigel Langford-Smith, a manager at the International Training Centre, which helped Australians come to Japan to work in hotels, said that Japanese employees saved money by employing Australians. 'I would sum it up like this—basically, Australians are cheap labour'. He maintained that even if they are hired for all the wrong reasons—as token, white-skinned foreigners—they still benefited from the experience. Another breed of Australians who flocked to Japan were the highly educated products of the recent surge in Japanese language study in Australia. Many of them fitted the Canberra-scripted brief for Australia's push into Asia—they spoke Japanese, had studied business and were bright and enthusiastic. But scores of these young people had been unable to get jobs using their skills in Australia, or in Japan with Australian companies. Australia's investment in their education was thus recouped by Japanese and foreign companies. In Japan, and indeed in all of Asia, Australians are generally considered to be adaptable and hard-working. It is an enduring irony that Australians have excellent reputations as workers everywhere except Australia.

The greater the number of white Western women who flooded into Japan, the racier the clubs became. The popular 'One-Eyed Jack's' in Roppongi was famous for its young white women strippers. Just down the road was Seventh Heaven, where Western girls began offering in 1995 what the proprietor called a 'couch job'. The male customer sat down with his arms hung over the back of the couch, while the topless girl sat playfully in his lap, and thrust her breasts in his face. After putting her breasts away, and declaring the session over, one Australian hostess explained to the customer the origins of the couch job.[27] 'It's kinda like the *geisha* thing', she said. Our hostess was clearly confused, but then, so are a lot of traditional female roles in Japan these days.

CHAPTER 8

BAD GIRLS AND MUMMIES' BOYS

'Sure, women are becoming sexually assertive, but it's liberation within the bedroom rather than within the workplace.'

Chizuko Ueno, Tokyo University lecturer

'These men can't fall in love with girls from the time they are students through to university, because their hearts are filled with their mothers. There's a huge imbalance between their highly developed brains, and their immature personalities.'

Dr Yasushi Narabayashi, therapist

A few years ago Keiko Fukuzawa visited the offices of one of Japan's biggest companies, Mitsubishi Corporation, to ask a senior manager about his policies on hiring women. Like most Japanese of his vintage, the Mitsubishi man didn't feel obliged to pretend that women were to be treated as equals to men. 'He said that women should be like shock absorbers between the men—they were there to soften the atmosphere, like office flowers', she says. 'And if you work as an office flower [he went

221

on], then you will have the chance to get married with a big [Mitsubishi] businessman!'. But in his lecture on the lot of Japanese women, the Mitsubishi man was only telling half the story. By day, the women might be demure 'office flowers', but for the rest of the time they were enjoying a larger disposable income, more freedom and, these days, probably even a wilder sex life than any of their male *sarariman* bosses could have ever contemplated. And if the young woman did marry that 'big Mitsubishi businessman', she would have his money to spend as well.

The 'office flowers', or as the Japanese themselves call these women, OLs—short for the borrowed English words 'office ladies'—are best known, and most exploited, as a consumer phenomenon. They have made fortunes for French luxury goods makers, and added a few percentage points to the value of the Australian, Hawaiian and European economies through tourism every year since the late 1980s, to name just two sectors that felt their influence. But more than that, the OL, through her transformation in recent years, is an icon for the times. Through observing OLs, you can get a picture of both the enduring and extraordinary power and strength of Japanese women, but also of their often abject acceptance of a secondary social status and domestic servility. The two things—social empowerment and political impoverishment—go hand in hand. Equally, the OLs' counterpart at work, the male *sarariman*, provides the paradigm for the new pressures facing middle-class men at work and at home. Not all young women are OLs, and not all OLs are young women. Equally, not all young men become *sararimen*. But tracing the fortunes of the two groups is the best starting point for anyone wanting to understand the new battle of the sexes transforming the Japanese workplace and home in the 1990s.

First, let us look at OLs, and their empowerment, Japanese-style. At a time when millions of young Japanese are flush with cash for the first time in the country's history, young women are not only deciding how to spend their own money—they are making up the minds of their boyfriends and husbands as well. 'The main reason why women are decisive is because men are so exhausted from their work. They work so hard they don't have the energy to decide anything, so they leave it to the women,' Fukuzawa, a commentator on women's affairs told me. 'Men think they are too important to make these trivial decisions', said a second commentator, who worked for the OL Research Institute in Tokyo, a body devoted solely to tracking the buying habits of the young and cashed-up 'office flowers'. 'They make a decision about a loan for a big house—they don't care about the rest. As long as the women are happy, the men are happy.'

Japanese husbands have traditionally handed over their pay packets to their wives, who controlled household finances as well as doing the cooking, cleaning and child-rearing, and providing a soft and warm environment for husbands to come home to. That made Japanese wives, in the words of one writer, a cross between 'the Minister of Finance and Florence Nightingale'. But the explosion of wealth in the late 1980s amongst Japanese young people—the first generation to grow up with loads of money and with no experience of wartime deprivation to restrain them from spending it—was something new and powerful.

The average OL works at a big company, wears the corporate uniform and performs menial tasks like serving tea and photocopying. She smiles sweetly, talks in a voice which somehow manages to be both soft and high-pitched at the same time, using especially polite Japanese, and in the past, as often as not, has married one of the men she sits next to at work. Most, but not all, OLs are blushing, squeaky-clean office flowers. Popular comics, like one called *Cactus OL*, celebrate the prickliness and stubborn refusal of some to do what they are told by their male bosses. The 'Cactus OL' is a subset of a breed dubbed by weekly magazines as 'cactus women'. Like a potted cactus which needs little care or water and stays alive in sterile soil, these harsh women reputedly spend their lives lounging around their apartments, and don't bathe.¹ In another comic, *Feeling Metaphysical*, the OLs revenge themselves on their bosses by putting filthy water into their coffee, or laxatives into traditional Valentine's Day chocolates.² Japan's leading feminist lawyer, Mizuho Fukushima, says these comics are true to life. Until the launching of Japan's first sexual harassment action in 1992, such stunts were often the only serious weapons in an OL's armoury against a nasty boss. 'The only way a female worker could have shown her "resistance" to harassment before was to serve a cup of green tea made with dirty water', the lawyer said. 'But now there are quite a few situations in which she can clearly say to the offender that his action is sexual harassment.'³

In Japan, unlike most Western countries, sexual harassment is not an offence proscribed by law. Tellingly, the word itself—*sekuhara*—was borrowed, and then shortened, from its original English to render the concept into Japanese. Harassment is part of life in Japanese offices. Ninety per cent of women in two separate surveys—one of municipal workers in Kumamoto in southern Japan in 1993, and another of university students in three prefectures in 1995—said they had been harassed by male bosses and colleagues.⁴ After the courts found a number of cases proved as a breach of working conditions in the early 1990s, the Labour Ministry officially defined sexual harassment—which in Japan is as good as having an actual law.

The stereotypical reality of an OL's office life is a mixture of servile cooing and subversive revenge. Outside of work, however, a fantasy world flourished, and it went well beyond the standard OL pursuit of overseas travel, French and Italian food and Louis Vuitton bags. The OLs' tastes, fads and fashions spawned their own massive, exotic subculture in the early 1990s. The peak was the *bodicon*—short for English words 'body conscious'—dance craze in 1993. Thousands of young women, chafing at traditional role-playing by day, swapped their bland company uniforms for G-strings and a few deftly-positioned feathers and furs to dance en masse on strobe-lit stages in discos. The *bodicon* uniform extended to the thin 'T-back', and the even racier 'O-back' panty style. The same *sararimen* to whom the women served tea during the day gathered at the foot of the dancing stages to ogle them by night. The men's sole concession to fashion was a touch of hair gel—otherwise, they wore their standard office suit and tie. By midnight, the show was over. The women slipped out of their G-strings and T-backs in time to catch the last train safely home, and were at work the next morning in their prim uniforms, coyly serving cups of green tea to their male bosses.

At the high point of the craze, 50 000 young women in *bodicon* gear held a mass dance party in the cavernous baseball arena, the Tokyo Dome. A furious debate ensued over whether *bodicon* was an example of emancipated, daring self-expression—sexually empowering in the way that Madonna's exhibitionism is, even though there was virtually no direct sexual traffic involved. Or, in the words of one writer, 'a lascivious beauty contest reflecting primal competition amongst women'. Whether it was one or the other, or both, these were women who lived with their parents, paid not a cent in rent, and had the equivalent of more than $2000 a month to spend on whatever they wanted. Naturally, businesses encouraged their exuberant lifestyles. 'OLs have got it made!' said one advertisement for the Takano Yuri Beauty Clinic. 'Get the work done and forget overtime! Sneak about behind the bosses' back and run off to aerobics, karaoke or an aesthetic salon! Isn't it great to be a woman! Come on, OLs—let's go for it!'[5]

Aside from the sorts of products that are popular with women around the world, like long-lasting lipstick and body-hair removers, Japanese OLs are showered with products that are either made solely for them, or that they have claimed as their own. These have in common a single thing—cleanliness. 'Bacteria-free' pens that you can leave lying around, safe in the knowledge that they won't pick up any germs, are one popular new product. The pens are 'specially' treated to retard the growth of bacteria, not only on the bodies of the pens themselves, but also in their ink.[6] 'The pen is mightier than the bacterium', runs the advertisement. The success of the anti-bacterial pen spawned a new breed of anti-germ products and devices, like paper, bicycle handles and even tambourines for people who want to make clean Latin music.[7] A cosmetic called 'Virgin Cream' which is applied to nipples to change their colour from brown to pink, apparently to make them more virginal, has been very successful. The company which makes it sold half a million 65-gram containers of the cream, at $150 each, after its release in 1993. Another hot item are panties that dissolve in boiling water to save women the embarrassment of strangers seeing their discarded undies in the clear plastic garbage bags now mandatory in Tokyo. (City authorities ordered residents to use see-through bags to allow them to check that people were following rules about separating different types of rubbish.) 'For those women who tend to spill their coffee or tea, an extra bit of caution is advised', quipped the *Nikkei Weekly* in its new products column.

Young women, fearful that they might leave a 'bad smell' behind after going to the toilet, snapped up thousands of pills made to eliminate the odour of faeces in the lower parts of the intestines. The company which made the pill, named 'Etiquette View', from a mixture of green tea and vegetable extract, had originally designed it for hospital patients and elderly people confined to bed. Schoolchildren who were being bullied for leaving a smell behind in the toilet also latched onto the pill to get their peers off their backs.[8] Cleanliness is also the reason why many young women insist on having their own personal microphone kept for them under the counter at karaoke bars, lest they use another that is infected.

It's not easy to find a single reason for this obsession with cleanliness. Some speculate it has been brought on by a change in diet. A British author, Sir Edwin Arnold, wrote after coming to Japan in 1907, that 'Though the Japanese wear little underlinen, a Japanese crowd is the sweetest and least objectionable in the world. The natural odour of the people is not unlike the lemon geranium'. Lately, however, the Japanese have started eating more meats and spices, and less fish and rice, and their floral fragrance may have suffered as a result. Japan's so-called shame culture, in which appearances and outward behaviour are all important, is undoubtedly a factor. There may also be a clue in the Japanese word *kirei*, which means simultaneously 'beautiful' and 'clean'. It is probably some of all these things, and a lot of fashion, dating back from the urban craze a few years back for young women to take a 'morning shower', instead of the traditional Japanese bath at night. The OLs also think their cleanliness distinguishes them from their much-loathed middle-aged male bosses. 'This notion that these middle-aged *oyaji* ('old dads') are somehow unsanitary has deeply permeated OL culture', says critic Kazuyuki Obata.

Sometimes, this obsession to be squeaky-clean has caused severe problems, and spawned profitable solutions. Many young women were so concerned about projecting a pure and clean image that they would flush the toilet continuously from the moment they entered the cubicle in order to drown out the sound of their urinating. 'This is Japanese women's psychology—it's a kind of shame to be heard by someone going to the toilet. Making the noise itself is a kind of disgrace', says Fukuzawa. But this wasted so much water that Toto, the Tokyo Toilet company, came up with the ingenious *Otohime* ('Sound Princess'), a machine which is attached to the wall of the cubicle and simulates the sound of a toilet flushing when pressed.

Women simply activated it the moment they entered the cubicle. Everyone was happy, especially Toto, which now sells about 3000 units of the machine a month.

In the mid- to late 1980s, the Australian Tourism Commission was smart enough to spot the emerging money power of Japanese women, and ploughed all of its limited advertising budget into attracting them down under. The campaign started with a single poster, hung on Tokyo's busiest train line in the middle of winter, of a young woman on a white sandy beach, and gained momentum rapidly from that point over many years. 'I knew if I got the girls, I'd get the boys', said Mr Mike Hambley, then head of the commission's office in Tokyo. 'There was no point in going for the young men—they were too terrified to leave their desks, because they thought that when they returned to the office, somebody would have taken them away.' Since then, the number of Japanese tourists coming to Australia has increased almost tenfold. Mostly, it's because the women want to go there—either as young independent travellers, on their honeymoons, or with their husbands. Australia became the OLs' favourite country—a free and friendly land with loads of cute animals. One of the OL bibles, the weekly magazine *Hanako* ('Flower Child'), has had on every cover since it was founded in the late 1980s a colourful painting by Australian illustrator/artist, Ken Done, who owes a substantial part of his considerable fortune to his popularity amongst young Japanese women.

Young Japanese women also make and break the fortunes of many mainstream movies. Bill Ireton, the managing director for Warner Bros in Japan, says he pitches marketing for the studio's films at young women, who watch about ten to twelve foreign movies a year, compared to the national average of one, and always choose which one to see on a 'hot date'. 'If you have a hard-core action movie, you do well, but you don't go into the stratosphere without the women. The key is emphasising the love interest', he says. At the movies, the 'love interest' is usually your classic boy-meets-girl stuff. But outside the cinema, young women are very practical when consuming romantic stories. The most popular of another recent OL marketing success—'ladies comics'—concentrate on gay romances between men, dreamily transporting their readers far away from their conformist everyday lives. One gay comic, *A Male Sleeping Beauty*, about a Japanese doctor who goes to New York and has a lengthy homosexual affair, sold 200 000 copies in 1994. 'One reason is that girls look at their marriage prospects, and it doesn't look attractive', said one commentator. 'Men are very serious, even threatening. Even wimpy men are threats. That's why almost anything homosexual can get an all-female audience. More people have discovered these days that they can make money out of it.'[9]

So with all this raw power at their fingertips, why aren't Japanese women even more demanding, and insistent that they be treated on a par with men, rather than slipping into luxurious but subservient roles? In a distinctive Japanese way, they are.

FEMINISM, JAPANESE-STYLE

Feminism is a funny thing in Japan. The Japanese borrow many words from English, but not always the concepts they describe. One such word is *feministo*, but in Japanese this is used to describe not (woman) feminists, but men who like women. Feminism in Japan does not exist as a political movement, as it does in the West. Politicians court the women's vote, but as housewives, not working women or overtly politicised feminists. If feminists had been organised in Japan, many of the laws and institutions which fundamentally and openly discriminate against women in Japan could never have survived. This discrimination starts at the very top, with the first article of the

Imperial Household Law, which says that only a male heir can ascend the Imperial Throne. At the time of writing, this could pose a problem for the crusty bureaucracy which runs the palace, the Imperial Household Agency, as the last eight children born to the extended royal circle have all been girls. The agency says the principle of male succession is ancient and inviolable, and insists that the eight empresses who reigned centuries ago were an exception. The unstated reason for the rule against women is age-old prejudices against pregnancies and menstruation, which are considered to conflict with official duties, and defile the pure chrysanthemum throne.

Another government rule dictated, until a successful court challenge in 1995, that married women cannot use their maiden name. Lawyer Fukushima had gotten around this requirement by not reporting her own wedding to the local municipal office, and so she was considered only a common-law wife. In the meantime, she kept her name, until the court victory.[10] Other old habits of Japanese families are also dying hard. Officially, the traditional social system under which the eldest, or the 'first', son had right of primogeniture—in other words, would inherit the family estate and business—ended with the American occupation, and all children can now legally press their claims. But the practice of granting the first son special rights continues within many families, particularly in rural areas. The *koseki*—the government's all-important official family register—still lists children according to whether they are the first or second son or daughter, and so on. In one related area, there has been progress of sorts. In 1993, the Tokyo High Court ruled that the children whose mothers were concubines could press claims for part of their father's inheritance. It is still common for prominent men to have children with their mistresses, known colloquially as 'flowers in the shadow'.

Another benchmark issue for Western feminists is contraception. Japanese women cannot buy the Pill.[11] After years of official deliberations, and pressure from some women's groups and from large pharmaceutical companies hoping to market the Pill, the Health Ministry had been expected to lift the ban in 1992. However, the ministry changed its mind at the last minute on two grounds—because the Pill's potential side-effects were too dangerous, and also 'from the viewpoint of public hygiene'—a code for the spread of the AIDS virus. On one level, the ministry's decision made some sense. The ban on the Pill has made the condom the contraceptive of choice in Japan, and has substantially stemmed the spread of the virus. However, women's groups claimed that the stated reasons were a smokescreen concealing the ministry's real agenda—a desire to protect the lucrative abortion business of (mainly male) doctors. The head of the Japan Society of Obstetrics and Gynaecology, Dr Yoshinori Kuwabara, denied this, rather patronisingly, at the time of the ministry's decision. 'Japanese women, unlike women from the West, have very little desire for the Pill', he said. 'Their attitudes to sex and contraception are quite different. Generally, they are very passive about contraception, leaving it up to the man.'[12] A number of women's groups shrieked in protest at the decision, but it passed largely uncontested. After six years and nearly $130 million worth of trials, the Health Ministry announced in September 1995 that it would reconsider the ban in April 1996.

Japan has an equal opportunity law, passed in 1986, but it has so far delivered few benefits to women in the workplace. The law only 'recommends' that employers treat men and women equally when hiring and promoting, and there are virtually no enforcement provisions. The law also allows for institutionalised discrimination by permitting women to be divided into two classes of employees—*ippanshoku*, or general workers, like OLs, and *sogoshoku*, or career-track workers, who can compete with men for promotions. In 1995, nearly ten years after the law was brought in, a Labour Ministry survey found that one in five major companies still maintained different hiring quotas for men and women. One reason commonly given was that women could not do overtime and late-night work—presumably because they should have been occupied with other duties at home.[13]

When a group of women at Sumitomo Metal Industries, who complained they had been systematically underpaid compared to their male colleagues, tested the equal opportunity law for the first time in 1995, Japan's tame courts characteristically declined to adopt a firm position. Instead, the judges 'advised' the company to be more flexible in promoting people, regardless of sex. The Sumitomo complaint was typical of that of women who had been in the workforce for over a decade or so. Although they had the same qualifications and skills as men, they had been hired to do office work and barred from entry to the managerial career track and their salaries were about half those of men who'd worked at Sumitomo for a comparable period. Six women at another trading company, Kanematsu, had a partial victory in a similar action, when a Tokyo city government mediator ruled that the company had discriminated against them on grounds of their sex in May 1995. The action was led by a 28-year veteran of the company, Fumiko Mori, 58, who complained she was getting the same pay as a 26-year-old man. Mori described pay day as 'a ridiculous and indignant experience' for all women working at trading companies.[14]

Judged by the lofty goals of the United Nations, which urges nations to have 30 per cent of leadership positions filled by women, Japan is not doing well. Only 7 per cent of parliamentarians are women, and less than 1 per cent of senior bureaucrats. But if you look beyond these traditional structures, large and small changes are taking place. Women *are* becoming more demanding, and selfish. They are marrying later, having fewer children, and going to university in greater numbers. The birth rate in Japan in 1993 dropped to 1.46 children per woman, one of the lowest in the industrialised world, down from 2.13 in

1970. It edged up slightly in 1994 to 1.50. The average marrying age in 1994 was 26.1 years old, compared with 23.8 in 1955. Japanese women who aren't married by the age of 25 have been rudely reviled by men as 'Christmas cakes'. The seasonal sweets are said to be stale and useless after December 25, and so are women if they are left on the shelf. Now, more and more women are confident enough to ignore the barbs and remain single, rather than marry the stereotypical male who does little besides bring in some money and loaf around the house. The percentage of single women in their thirties doubled between 1975 and 1990, mimicking the trend in Western countries.

Two cornerstone feminist and family issues in the West—maternity leave and child care—get scant attention in national politics. But while national politicians ignore these issues, they are being taken up by numerous women's centres being established at the local level. At one centre I visited on the outskirts of Tokyo, a municipal bureaucrat, Mr Toshiro Ashida, described how local women had demanded, and got last year, their own million-dollar centre solely for 'women's problems'. 'Men have to understand that women are not there just to make the tea', he says, just as the (woman) secretary pops a steaming cup of Japanese green tea before us. This small irony goes over Mr Ashida's head, but that's only because he is too busy enthusiastically extolling the centre's work, and telling me how his job has transformed his relationship with his wife and his role around the house. (He does more housework now.) 'This is a place where women can come for help, and men can come to get a better understanding of women's issues', he says proudly.

The centre handles all manner of issues to give women what its brochures call 'a brilliant life'—ranging from networking with Asian women all the way to advice about tax. It provides counselling for women, and child care—all pioneering services for Japan that no politician will ever be able to take away. The centre even deals with the one-time taboo issue of domestic violence. Just under one in five women who responded to one of the first national surveys on domestic violence in 1995 said they had been beaten up at home, and few had any idea about where they could take refuge. The National Police Agency listed 69 women as having been murdered by their husbands in 1993—8 per cent of all murders. Husband-and-wife cases accounted for less than 1 per cent of ordinary assaults, suggesting that many battered wives do not bother reporting their violent husbands.[15] There are still scant figures on domestic violence, but it is a breakthrough for the issue to be canvassed at all.

In the past, when wife-beating has been discussed in public in Japan, it has often been in terms of men reminding women who's boss. Three decades ago, Japanese Prime Minister Eisaku Sato was severely criticised overseas when he mentioned to foreign journalists—in apparent obliviousness of the reaction it would provoke—that he occasionally hit his wife 'to show her where a woman's place was'. At home in Japan, there was a deal of sympathy for Sato, who was portrayed as a victim of foreign pettiness.[16] Another Prime Minister, Kakuei Tanaka, advised his prospective son-in-law before his marriage to his assertive, outspoken daughter, Makiko, to 'beat her up once in a while to retain your prestige as a man'. There were perversely mitigating circumstances on this occasion. The formidable Makiko, who rose rapidly in national politics to become a cabinet minister in 1994, was brought up by her father to be his son, after his first son died. Later, Makiko would profess not to consider herself a woman at all.

The two most common words for wife in Japanese—*kanai*, which literally means 'inside-the-house', and *okusan*, which is 'Mrs Inside'—give you a fair indication of what men expect of their women. But for some Japanese commentators, grafting Western feminist notions onto Japanese womanhood misses the point. Prominent academic Sumiko Iwao is a strong proponent of the view that Japan is being dynamically altered by powerful women, including the ones who choose to stay at home as housewives. 'Contrary to the image of subjugation outsiders seem to associate with Japanese women, the latter often believe it is they who draw the boundaries within which their husbands move, not the other way around', she says. This kind of relationship between the sexes is described by the phrase *dansei joi, josei yui*—'men superior, women dominant'. A former cabinet minister, Ms Manoe Kubota, has similar ideas about women's liberation. She says women should do it through their purchasing power. This is the 'only area' where Japanese women can wield the same power as men, she says, 'especially because housewives are the ones who hold the purse strings and make major decisions in running the household'.

Iwao doesn't see a contradiction between the two notions of women being liberated both by performing their roles at home and by escaping them. While men continue to be chained to their companies, she maintains that women are increasingly set free by the development of home conveniences, and can put their spare energy into work and cultural activities. But Iwao is far too forgiving. Not only does she ignore the fact that most women still work in sexually segregated jobs, she is also way behind the times. The newer role models for young women are light years away from the traditional 'liberated' wives touted by Iwao, and nor are they the cutesy, giggling archetypes promoted so assiduously by the Japanese media during the 1970s and 1980s. The new role models for young women are more the 'bad girl' types like Ai Iijima, who quit school at thirteen, became a hard-core porn movie star, and in her early twenties re-made herself as an author and TV personality. 'I'm probably the first idol that parents see and say to their kids "Don't become like that". Usually, idols are clean and likeable, and beautiful enough to be special', she said. 'With me, they think, "Hey, they're letting anybody into show business these days"'.[17]

Another young women's hero is Keiko Kono, a bright TV reporter who married the country's number one sumo wrestler, Takanohana, in mid-1995. Kono showed a singular streak of independence as a university-educated woman by hitching herself to a sumo wrestler, who still falls a bit into the freaky and feudal category in Japan—the union was more newsworthy because she was 30 and he was 22, but it was only the most prominent of a number of high-profile unions between older women and 'toy boy' men much commented on in the Japanese media. 'It's a kind of symbol of women's power that many of them are able to pull younger men', says commentator Fukuzawa. Kono has been admired as a tough cookie from way back. Weekly magazines reported how she was asked at her first job interview, as not a few women have been, whether she was a virgin. She stared down the crusty executive from Fuji Television, and replied, 'I am not'. Kono and her ilk are light years away from the old, idealised Japanese wife, the so-called *Yamato Nadeshiko*. *Yamato* means Japan, and *Nadeshiko* is a pink, sweet-smelling plant with a slender, but surprisingly strong stalk. The *Yamato Nadeshiko* wife, as described to me by two young male office workers one night as they bemoaned the fact she no longer existed, 'never eats before you, never goes to sleep before you, and never gets up after you'.

But just as feminism, Japanese-style, was getting up a head of steam, it ran headlong into Japan's prolonged economic downturn, and guess what? It was the women who lost their positions first, and got the new jobs last. Keiko Fukuzawa returned to Mitsubishi in 1995, about a decade after her previous visit, to talk again to the man in charge of personnel management about women. This time, she didn't hear a single word about scented office flowers or prospective husbands. 'We don't need any clerical workers. We want women who are going to earn us more, not take up space', she was told. That was great news, except for one thing—Mitsubishi and many other big companies are still giving just about all these prize jobs to men. Desperate to cut staff, but unable to sack anyone outright, such companies find 'clerical staff'—for which, read, women—easy targets. A host of big companies like Mitsubishi, Mitsui and Nissan simply stopped hiring OLs in the mid-1990s, and set an example for smaller ones to follow. This may spare women the drudgery of being office flowers, but they have been left with precious few alternative jobs to pursue instead. Female graduate job-hunters entered an 'ice age' in 1994 and 1995, with only about 70 per cent getting jobs, compared to 89 per cent of men. A survey in 1995 by the leading employment agency, Recruit, found that there were 133 jobs for every 100 male graduates, but only 45 for every 100 women.[18] Many women were particularly angry that patently less competent men were hired over them merely because they had attended prestigious universities. 'The recession has really pushed to the surface all those discriminations that were not so obvious before: your gender; your school; your university major and how well you are connected', said Sakata Takaaki of Waseda University.[19]

The simultaneous rise of career women and OL culture is too vast, powerful and rich a trend to be wiped out by a mere economic recession. Fashionable and expensive brand-name products continue to sell well, and young women still lead the country in taking overseas holidays. 'Life is riskier now', admits the former employee of the OL Research Institute, 'but every flower still needs a little watering'. All the same, the end of the Japanese economic miracle does mean that the glory days are over. Like the rest of the country, OLs and young women generally struggle to find their way in the new world that confronts Japanese values, lifestyles and work at every turn. The impact of this has not been all bad. With entrepreneurial zest, young women have been snapping up retirement schemes originally offered by many companies to thin their thick ranks of male middle managers. There is also a mini-boom in women starting their own businesses. Kyomi Saito, a former investment banker with an American firm, and now a business consultant, has begun touring Japan lecturing local women's collectives about how to run their own companies. 'There are so many good women who are frustrated that they can't get a good position in an organisation. They are highly motivated and energetic', she says. But she says that for every self-starting entrepreneur there are just as many women who remain willing to accept their lot in life, and not push themselves forward. 'They have to change their attitude', she says.

In a survey about feminism in early 1995 in *Spa!* magazine, 81 per cent of women said they were discriminated against, but 47 per cent also said, with characteristic Japanese resignation, that there was nothing that could be done about it. Such results reinforce the view that for all the thousands of successful, independent women in Japan, the bulk are either willing, resigned or happy for things to stay just as they are. Take Mitsubishi Corporation. The company hired twelve women to join the firm's career track in 1995, which is better than no one at all, albeit not many compared to the 140 men the corporation took on at the same time. But the male personnel manager pleaded innocent to charges of sexism. 'The answer is simple', he says. 'Ten times more men applied.'

In one sense, you can hardly blame them, because there's one thing that Japanese women know they don't want to be, and that's Japanese men. Except, it seems, in one sphere of human activity—sex.

YELLOW CABS

When young Japanese women go to the beach in Hawaii, Thailand and Bali for their holidays, they are often armed with more than their towels and tanning lotions. These days, many of them carry a warning thrust into their hands by Japanese expatriates on their arrival at the airport. 'There are many playboys and bad guys in the world', reads one message distributed in Hawaii. 'Even if you have been approached by these men, please do not follow them. They would give you a drink with drugs, and later on, rape you and rob you of money. Many of them have various diseases, including AIDS.'[20] The expatriates who hand out these messages are not the only Japanese who think that AIDS is something that they can only catch overseas. When he was Prime Minister, Kiichi Miyazawa singled out the virus for special mention in a commentary on the decline of American civilisation. But what was really remarkable about these messages was that they were not handed out to Japanese men, who are notorious for their sex tours overseas, but to young Japanese women.

If you walk half a mile from the temples and old wooden streets of the Asakusa district of northern Tokyo, you'll come to an area known as Yoshiwara. These days, it is a fairly tawdry sight—a few streets lined with neon-lit 'soapland' brothels, and eager, thin-moustached spruikers of the kind you find in any red-light district in the world. But for centuries, before Japan banned prostitution to bring its public morals ostensibly into line with the Christian West, Yoshiwara was home to the 'glittering world of the Japanese courtesan'. The district thrived as an officially designated pleasure quarter, where men could enjoy freedoms forbidden elsewhere. Author Nicholas Bornoff writes that Yoshiwara was more than just a 'haunt of harlotry', it was also a cultural microcosm, with fancy shops, kabuki theatre and a centre for literature and the visual arts.[21] The famous *ukiyo*, the woodblock prints celebrating 'the floating world', flourished in this quarter. But Yoshiwara today has only one thing in common with the district of yesteryear—and that is prostitution. It is a living symbol of the fact that Japanese men have long been used to getting their way with women. Sex, says Bornoff, 'is the one area in which Japan's dichotomy between archaic values and post-industrial society is most apparent'.

The 'soaplands' of Yoshiwara—which are a sort of cross between a bathhouse and a brothel—are themselves even a little passe in the 1990s. The most fashionable new places for sexual play are a myriad of so-called 'image clubs' which cater to almost every possible male fantasy.[22] Men who want to 'sexually harass' female colleagues can do so in a room that is equipped with fax and copy machines to look like an ordinary office. Another room in the same establishment, Five Doors, in the Shibuya area in Tokyo, has a car for people who enjoy car sex. *AERA* magazine tracked down image clubs which allowed customers to sneak into a make-believe woman's apartment at night, and one which catered for men who wanted to abuse pregnant women. One of the most popular image club boudoirs is decorated to replicate the inside of a train carriage. Inside, a female passenger waits to be groped, and to grope back.

The practice of men groping women on trains—known as *chikan*—is rampant in Japan. In one survey of high-school girls in Osaka in 1994, 75 per cent said they had been molested on trains, but only 2 per cent had reported the incidents to police. Rail companies were initially reluctant to support a campaign by citizens' groups to put posters up in trains and stations warning molesters to desist. 'Since we have male passengers, too much emphasis on molestation would hurt their feelings', an official of the Osaka Transportation Bureau told the media.[23] Even worse, the same women who were groped on trains, and were squeezed out by the tightening job market caused by the recession, found themselves in these image clubs earning their living. The sex industry, or in this case the foreplay industry, has always been a fallback for women who needed money to live and couldn't earn it elsewhere.

But parallel to this booming sex industry, something else was happening. To the surprise and horror of many men, Japanese women had begun to aggressively seek out sex themselves, at home and abroad. In some respects, young Japanese women appear just like their counterparts in the West. Spurred on by a popular magazine culture bursting with stories about sex, young women started to do it earlier, and with more partners. Many thrill-seeking schoolgirls even took it up to earn pocket money after class. A survey conducted by the National Parents and Teachers Association in June 1994 found that an astounding one in three teenage girls had flirted with telephone sex clubs. Men pay to enter these clubs, where they wait for calls to chat to women, and often arrange dates. Most telephone clubs are cutely disguised fronts for prostitution. Police cracked down on them in 1994 after two different groups of teenage girls beat up and robbed their bewildered male customers. One pair of 15-year-olds, who stunned their paying customer by spraying teargas in his face before robbing him, said they had just wanted money 'to have a good time'. Other schoolgirls cashed in by selling their uniforms, and used panties, to the popular so-called 'blue sailor' shops catering to one of the most perversely prurient interests of Japanese men.

The abiding image of self-sacrificing and passive Japanese womanhood took another pounding with the popularity of strip clubs featuring muscular foreign men, first in Tokyo in 1993 and then all over the country. The highlight of the evening's entertainment came at the end—when the women stuffed money into crevices of the skin-tight jockettes worn by the male strippers as they paraded their wares through the audience at the end of the show. The men said they were showered with gifts by women after each show, and ceaselessly propositioned. 'These women look so prim when they come in', said one of the strippers.

They sit with their little handkerchiefs spread out on their laps, and they have this sort of embarrassed expression. I couldn't believe, at first, how many came up afterwards and blurted out, 'Take me home with you'. Most of them don't speak much English, so they can't really chat you up, but that doesn't stop them. One night, I got so sick of being propositioned that when the sixth girl asked me, I said, 'OK, let's go back to my place—now!'. So we did. It was all right. She still comes to the show. But that was it for me.[24]

The most brazen and shocking (for mainstream men) display of women's sexual power, and one chronicled and condemned in lascivious detail by the media, was the 'Yellow Cab' phenomenon. The phrase 'Yellow Cab' is the nasty nickname given to apparently promiscuous young Japanese women who go overseas in search of sex with foreign men. Like taxis, the women are meant to be 'easy to get into, and out of'. They were also the target of the concerned citizens handing out warning pamphlets at airports. The 'yellow' part of the nickname sounds like a pointed Asian addition to the expression, but it is probably a result of the phrase's origins—in New York, where there are in fact yellow cabs. Nobody has claimed credit for making the phrase up, but the phenomenon was popularised, and sensationalised, by author Shoko Ieda in her 1992 book, *Yellow Cab*. Ieda interviewed eleven women living in New York, mostly aspiring actresses or singers, some of whom were heroin addicts. From this small survey, she drew some startling conclusions—that 70 per cent of Japanese women in New York were drug users, that the area in the East Village frequented by Japanese women was referred to as a 'Japanese Harem', and that there was a 'cult of black men living parasitically off the earnings of Japanese women'. Her second book was a variation on the theme; it was about 'resort lovers'—OLs who sought out mainly black men on trips to Hawaii. In both works, the women are unsophisticated and gullible, and the black men are portrayed as 'emotionally primitive, relatively uneducated and sexually insatiable'—a gross irony, as Ieda herself is married to a black American.[25]

The media ignored a subsequent book which exposed Ieda's research in New York as fraudulent, and launched themselves into an investigative frenzy on the basis of her flimsy evidence, displaying greater enthusiasm and vigour for chasing the story than for the country's endless political scandals. A TV station produced a documentary on the miserable lives of Japanese women in New York, and also hired a beach-bum type to pick up OLs on holidays in Hawaii. The low point came when a television documentary purported to show women being picked up and taken into hotel rooms in Hawaii, shot thrillingly at a distance through a long lens. It was later revealed that the producers of the documentary had, in fact, staged the pick-ups from beginning to end. What the media did not realise at the time was that Ieda had got the story partly right, but the location all wrong. Japanese women were going on sex tours overseas, but not to New York, and only occasionally to Hawaii. Their favoured targets were the smooth, brown-skinned boys of Thailand and Bali.

A male host interviewed in a gay bar favoured by Japanese women in Bangkok described to one reporter how Japanese women were not a 'little bit shy'. 'They act like millionairesses when they are here. They give us anything—money, clothes and all sorts of pleasures', he said. Another complimented the Japanese women for their 'good etiquette in bed', and said how they would come to his bar en masse, and take five or six boys back to their hotel at a time.[26] This anecdotal evidence was confirmed by a study funded by the Japanese Foundation for AIDS Prevention about 'risk behaviour of Japanese female tourists' on the resort island of Phuket. The report said that Japanese women quickly developed a 'false sense of control' once on holidays. About 80 per cent of the Thai beachboys interviewed in the survey said they had sex with Japanese women who they met on the beach every day. 'All beachboys find making advances with female tourists part of their work and fun. Compared to all women tourists of other nationalities, beachboys reported that almost 70 per cent of their tourist lovers were Japanese', the report said.[27] Worst of all, condoms were rarely used.

While providing some excitement for the racier sections of the Japanese media, the 'yellow cab' story tugged at the insecurity of Japanese men about their newly sexually liberated women. One of the nation's leading *manga* (comic book) artists, Yoshinori Kobayashi, savagely sent up scared Japanese men in his best-selling series, *'Goman-izumu'* ('A Declaration of Arrogance'), a brazen, inflammatory and witty strip, which tackled all of Japan's touchy taboo topics. The Japanese read *manga* like Westerners consume books and watch videos. Nearly half of Japan's publications are *manga*, and more than a third of their readers are adults. Kobayashi was scathing about both sides in his strip, 'How the Japanese Penis is Superior to the Foreigners' ', but he particularly targeted the paranoia of Japanese men about Japanese women sleeping with 'white and black men'. 'Japanese men behave like they have no guts or spirit', he told me. 'They're childish and close-minded. I want to stimulate them—to tell them that if they keep going in the same direction, Japanese women will keep going abroad to chase foreigners.'

These OL 'sex tours' were tiny, of course, compared to the organised busloads of men on company trips who had flooded into first of all Korea and Taiwan to hire women, and then later to Thailand, guidebooks and all.[28] But it spoke volumes for the changing times that even a few young women would do something similar. In some respects, they exhibited a bold, contrarian streak in seeking out sex on their own terms. But the women were also crudely copycatting the worst habits of Japanese men, and not simply in buying sex overseas. They fell into the classic

Japanese pattern of situational behaviour—fulfilling their duties as meek, self-sacrificing OLs by day, so they could pursue their fantasies on holidays and weekends. The two worlds did not impinge on each other. Thus the sexual revolution of Japanese women took place in a political vacuum. 'Sure, women are becoming sexually assertive, but it's liberation within the bedroom rather than within the workplace', said Chizuko Ueno, of Tokyo University.[29]

Some of the same contradictions are found in Japanese pornography, and their female stars, known as AV (Adult Video) actresses.[30] In the debate on this issue in the West, one school of feminists contend that pornography is potentially empowering for women. One proponent of this view, the American author of *Talk Dirty to Me*, Sallie Tisdale, wrote that pornography didn't necessarily symbolise a man wielding power over women, but 'virility, endurance and lust' in general. Because women often initiate sex, they are no longer mere victims of male lust, but released to express and pursue their own sexual urges. But Sallie Tisdale had obviously never been to Japan, or watched much of its porn. The stars of Japanese porn movies are nearly always women—the male studs barely rate a credit—but they are far from the forceful types that Tisdale describes.[31] The two lines used most by AV actresses are *yamate* (stop it), and *itai* (it hurts), and in acting them out, the women appear more ensnared and impaired than empowered. Passive resistance, rather than aggressive assertiveness, is their coy trademark, and for that reason AV actresses are more or less interchangeable, and disposable. The 'bad girl' role model for young women, Ai Iijima, is one of the few AV stars who's had enough smarts to make the transition to the mainstream media. In video shops, the shelf stacked with all her old films is now often labelled—'Ai Iijima, 21—retired'.[32]

With a flexibility, or if you like, an amorality, second to none, the Japanese will rapidly commodify a woman's sex industry if there's a buck to be made out of it. Already Tokyo has spawned bars with male hosts for women which are mirror images of the hostess bars for men. And if male hosts are not to your taste, there are also bars with women dressed as men to serve drinks and chat to their exclusively female customers. Politicised or not, Japanese women are changing, in and outside the bedroom. An old Japanese proverb goes: 'Women are not entitled to a will of their own, for they must obey their parents in childhood, their husbands when they marry and their sons in their old age'.

Most parents and husbands wouldn't recognise that woman any more. The mother's relationship with her son, however, is something else again.

THE MOTHER COMPLEX

At the start of an interview with the leading film-maker, Juzo Itami—the director of satiric successes like *The Funeral*, and *Tampopo*—a colleague visiting Japan for the first time breezily pitched a gentle question to get conversation going. Tell us about the 'soul of Japan', he said. Itami's eyes widened, and he took a deep breath. More than half an hour later, he was still talking about what he said was the single thread running through the soul of his country's 'most curious culture'—mothers, and their power over their sons. 'There is a complete lack of a father figure in Japan', he said. 'For people coming from a culture where there is a definite definition of the father, this must seem strange and astounding. But the father figure is a cultural invention nurtured and perfected by the West. In Japan, it is the mother who is important.' Doodling on a piece of paper in front of him, Itami expounded on his mini-treatise on Japanese society. He drew a circle to symbolise the child in the comfort of the mother's womb, and then added a set of concentric circles to display the relationships that are built surrounding it. The circle at the centre contains the mother and child. Then comes the family, classmates, the company and finally, the family of all Japanese. 'The sole principle of the cocoon [which the mother provides for the child] is the pleasure principle—that's all that counts,' he says. 'If the baby could stay in the cocoon for the rest of its life, it would be happy, but in reality, they have to go out.'

But not too far out, if the more dominant modern-day mothers get their way. The phenomenon of the *maza-con*— Japanised English for the Freudian concept of the 'mother complex'—is not new in Japan. Nor does it by any means apply to all relationships between mothers and their sons. But if a raft of reports, popular dramas and specialists are to be believed, more men are suffering from it than ever, leaving many young women to deal with grown boys who still behave like babies. In a country where husbands are consumed with their work, and all of the after-hours obligations that company jobs entail, bored wives focus their love and attention intensely onto their children—in particular, their sons. Sometimes, this attention goes beyond cleaning their rooms, washing their clothes and urging them to study. The most extreme cases involve *kiyoiku-mamas*, or 'education mothers', who place their children under intense academic pressure in cram schools and the like. When the economy slowed sharply in the early 1990s, seminars and books training mothers to secure jobs for their children surged in popularity. Some universities were forced to set aside special rooms at exam time to accommodate mothers accompanying their sons, who were sitting the all-important entrance tests. In the mid-1980s, the Japanese media created a great fuss over a number of *kiyoiku-mamas* who anonymously confessed to having sex with their sons, to rid them of distractions from their studies. 'Some stopped short at masturbation and fellatio, others went the whole way', writes Nicholas Bornoff. When these sons become adults, their work also takes precedence over everything else, as their study did previously, leaving a yearning, psychologists say, for the precious and gentle indulgences of the mothers.

In the most benign form of *maza-con*, the wife takes the place of the mother. One weekly magazine for men, *Popeye*, detailed 46 *maza-con* techniques that men could use to attract, and turn on, the nurturing instinct in young Japanese women. To show their 'eagerness, frankness and childishness', the magazine advised young men to wear clothes that didn't match, wrinkled shirts, or to helplessly fumble over the office copying machine.[33] In the worst cases of *maza-con*, the mother maintains a grip on her son even after he marries. The results can be excruciating. Dr Yasushi Narabayashi, who runs a marriage counselling clinic in Tokyo, says that 60 per cent of his patients suffer from what he calls the 'no-touch syndrome'. They won't hug, kiss or have any physical contact with their wives, for fear that it will lead to sex. As a result, their marriages remain unconsummated.[34] Narabayashi calls this the 'I love Mummy' syndrome. 'They can't fall in love with girls from the time they are students through to university, because their hearts are filled with their mothers', he said. 'They go to cram school and study hard just so they can please their mothers, and many of them go on to top universities. There's a huge imbalance between their highly developed brains, and their immature personalities.'

The *maza-con* story is not retold here because it offers foreigners a chance to giggle cheaply at the 'funny Japanese'. It is also of major interest in Japan. One of the most popular dramas in Japanese television history—it attracted a third of the viewing audience when it was screened in September 1992—chronicled an archetypal *maza-con* tragedy. In the drama, 'I Have Been in Love With You for a Long Time', Fuyuhiko, a banker and graduate of the elite Tokyo University, marries Miwa, in a wedding arranged by his mother, Etsuko. The strait-laced, nerdish Fuyuhiko devotes all his free time to his personal computer and his butterfly collection, and seeks his mother's approval at every turn. Miwa first realises that all is not as it should be when she returns home just after the wedding to find Etsuko, unannounced, in the kitchen. Etsuko lectures her like a primary-school teacher—on how to clean, on what sort of food Fuyuhiko likes and doesn't. 'I have written down the *miso* I use at home', she tells her. On another day, Etsuko arrives on the doorstep and barges in, without asking, after the door is opened, carrying a bag full of classical music CDs. 'Please study these', she says. Miwa has to ditch her hobbies of tennis and movies, because her mother-in-law tells her classical music is a more suitable hobby to discuss at company functions. Etsuko also says it is good for babies, something which was academic at that point, because Fuyuhiko had not yet been able to have sex with his wife.

Miwa leaves Fuyuhiko, but comes back after he sends her a video apologising for his behaviour. In his darkened office one night, he reads a how-to manual for sex, as one would study a book on mathematics, before his one fumbling sexual encounter with Miwa. But things don't improve. He loses his job and all his confidence, and Miwa leaves him again, after enduring another tirade from Etsuko. In the drama's sharpest scene, Fuyuhiko finally chastises his mother for never letting him make a decision about his life. 'Look carefully!' an upset Etsuko replies. 'I have bought you everything you wanted. The computer, and this butterfly specimen. I even chose your wife. I won't allow you to throw something I've given you', she says, as Fuyuhiko throws away the glass container with the butterfly. He cuts himself in the process, and resists Etsuko when she tries to kiss and suck his bleeding little finger. In the struggle that follows Fuyuhiko stabs his mother, but even then she doesn't waver. 'You shouldn't have called the police,' she tells a visitor in hospital. 'It could be damaging for Fuyuhiko's career.' In the final pathetic scene, Fuyuhiko confesses to Miwa that he has, in fact, been in love with her since he was a little boy. 'I was confused between people and materials', he says. 'Maybe, I dealt with you like an object. I loved you, but I didn't know how to love you.'

Much has been written in recent years about *karoshi*—'death from overwork'—after a number of people died as a result of the gruelling demands of their jobs. Much less has been written about another stress-related condition treated by Japanese doctors in recent years, and the role of mothers in curing it. The condition, 'fugue', is a state of psychological amnesia brought on by excessive pressure. In one case reported by the *Asahi Shimbun*, a 38-year-old middle manager, stressed out by problems at work, fled, and didn't contact his office or work for three days. Finally, the psychiatrist who treated him said, he went to his mother's home and ate a meal that she had prepared. He sighed with relief, and pronounced, 'Now, I'm saved'.

Such mothers' miracles were in increasing demand in the 1990s. As the lot of Japanese white males—the *sarariman* class—reached a crisis, men needed all the help they could get.

WHITE-COLLAR WOES

As the Japanese economy ground slowly to a halt in the early 1990s, labour lawyer Yoshio Mizuguchi began to receive calls from middle-aged men who were being pushed out of jobs that they had thought they had for life. One mid-level manager at a home electronics company arrived at the office one day to discover that his desk had been moved into the basement, and that he had no work to do. A computer software company sent a group of technicians to work in a rural subsidiary cutting down trees, the corporate equivalent of the punishment meted out to politically incorrect Chinese made to work as peasants during the Cultural Revolution. Twenty 50-something managers from a supermarket chain found themselves dispatched to do heavy lifting work in a factory.[35] Others suffered verbal harassment, like a manager in his forties whose boss would tell him every day, 'If you quit, we can hire two new people'. The majority of these people, said Mizuguchi, were all 'above 45 years old, and held managerial positions at big corporations'.[36]

Just as men could once rely on their women and their wives, and boys on their mothers, the archetypal *sarariman* could also expect to be looked after by his company. To be sure, the stereotypical image of a Japanese company, with diligent workers and harmonious consensus-style management toiling together for the common good, has always been a myth. In this idealised world of Japanese corporate culture, the age-old sacred treasures of the traditional Chinese and Japanese family (*ie*), village (*mura*) and province (*kuni*) have all been recreated and homogenised in the modern industrial enterprise, with both men and women assigned their roles.[37] Thus the most distinctive features of Japanese capitalism, like lifetime employment, the seniority wage system and enterprise unionism, were deliber-ately formulated as the natural offspring of Japan's unique culture, and its 'all in the family' economic system.

That's the official story. But there is a darker, and more accurate picture of the inner working of Japanese companies, and one unvarnished by culture, to be found in the 'economic novels' which proliferate in Japan. This distinct and popular genre of semi-fiction, the kind of art you'd expect to find in a country in which all life centres on work, reveals a corporate culture which is anything but harmonious. Aside from the odd inspirational tale of business triumphs, office romance and tech-nological invention, the books portray a world of boardroom backstabbing, intense pressures and emotional revolts by staff. The authors of these books, such as Ikko Shimizu, invariably have worked inside companies or their trade unions, and employ researchers to ensure that their works are true to life. Many stories are in fact thinly veiled fictional accounts of recent real-life scandals and boardroom brawls, and all of them chronicle a tough and unforgiving business culture. In one of Shimizu's books, *Silver Sanctuary*, the lights abruptly dim at a bank's end-of-year party, and a branch manager is dragged away and pushed roughly down the stairs by a group of thugs. Mr Shimizu depicts the incident as 'a sinister rebellion by the underdogs against the institution which forced them into a uniformity in which one must not stand out, [nor] be praised or berated; one must not be in the news; one must strive in every possible way not to commit either vice or virtue'.

Harmony—*wa* in Japanese—doesn't rule in Japan, and it never has. The relentless official stress on harmony, and all the arrangements to enforce it, spring from the fact that there is so little *wa* and so much entrenched, institutionalised rivalry both between companies and ministries and within them. Likewise, the unique cultural qualities of Japanese capitalism, as academics such as Chalmers Johnson and Ronald Dore have shown, are all the products of twentieth century Japanese politics, not its immutable culture and Confucian values. Lifetime employment, where it exists, for example, grew out of companies' fears of left-wing unions, Japanese workers' worries about their jobs being lost to Taiwanese and Korean labourers in the 1920s, and an attempt by the militarists to stabilise the industrial workforce in the 1930s.

But be they the offspring of politics or culture, or a misty mixture of both, Japanese companies, and their employment, pay and union systems, have evolved into something distinctly different from the more explicitly Darwinian ways of the West. Typically, new recruits have been hired as much as members of a team as they are for their occupational skills. Unlike the pragmatic and cold-hearted Anglo-Saxons, prominent novelist Ayako Sato says the Japanese see efficiency as 'the natural outcome of working with the same set of colleagues over the years, and fostering an environment conducive to smooth human relations'.[38] The first pillar for 'smooth human relations' is lifetime employment, the totemic, sacred cow of the Japanese social contract. Although it has only strictly applied to male workers at medium-scale to large companies, the ethic set an example for smaller enterprises, and acted as an important symbol for the familial benevolence of the system at large. The second pillar is seniority pay. The two practices were founded on the tacit understanding that male employees would stay at the company for their working lives, and rise through the ranks at a predictable pace. The employment system has built-in flexibilities to ease the impact of its rigidities, the most important being the way workers are paid. About two-thirds of salaries come in the form of weekly wages, about 10 per cent in overtime and the rest in biannual bonuses which are directly linked to the health of enterprises. With the co-operation of in-house-trained unions, wages are thus easily reduced during down times. The payoff is that jobs are preserved. In many ways, this is a sensible and rational policy. Japan avoids the serious social and dislocation costs that occur when people lose their jobs and homes, and is better prepared to handle the pressures of an economic recovery when it arrives.

More than in other business cultures, the social rituals surrounding work in Japan, especially the consumption of alcohol, have always reinforced male business bonding. One of the first things that strikes many foreigners when they first visit Japan, particularly those who arrive with preconceived views about the polite and retiring Japanese, is the scores of boisterous, and mainly male, drunks roaming the streets late at night. They are playing out the Japanese tradition of fellow workers drinking 'until all hearts melt as one'. In Japan, unlike other countries, drinking is still considered a badge of male merit. When the austere Yasushi Mieno was appointed head of the central Bank of Japan in 1989, the bank's PR officials proudly announced that he was a consummate drinker. Unlike his predecessor, who imbibed only whisky, wine and brandy, Mieno 'drank everything', his PR man said. The chairman of NEC, Tadahiro Sekimoto, says good drinkers are important to gather 'wet information', the kind you get through direct, personal contact, as opposed to day-to-day 'dry information'. The chairman of Cosmo Oil, also a renowned boozer, earned himself the nickname *Hakken-san* (Mr Eight Places), because he never went home before drinking at eight places after formal dinners.[39]

Drinking traditions have weakened somewhat in recent years, along with *sarariman* culture generally, but they have not disappeared altogether. Japanese managers engage in such rituals because they know that their success depends at least as much on relationships as technical achievements. 'He realises that loyalty, dependability and easy access to other top managers is critically important to the advancement both of his career and status, and that of his company's interests', says Terry Young, who manages a large Japanese company, General Sekiyu, in Tokyo. 'He therefore spends a significant amount of his time on what are vital but essentially social activities. He is, in fact, a corporate politician rather than a businessman in the Western sense.'[40] Businessmen who do break the mould now by disregarding the officially approved consultative processes are berated by the media for instituting a 'one-man' rule over their companies. The Japanese borrow the English words to denounce what they consider to be autocratic, 'unJapanese' behaviour.

The flipside of the company's loyalty to male employees is the employee's submission to the company's will. During the latest recession, overtime pay has been eliminated, but not overtime. Workers have been coerced to put in hours of 'service'—in other words, free—overtime instead. Middle managers have meekly accepted transfers to subsidiary companies, and the large cuts in pay that often go with such moves. Very few employees have taken the full complement of ten days annual holiday, even during the present economic slowdown. With some fanfare, the Labour Ministry announced in 1994 that just under 80 per cent of companies it had surveyed would permit their workers to have three consecutive days off during Japan's sweltering summer. Only a quarter said they would allow their workers to take more than ten days straight. The official reason for their generosity—and these gestures were considered to be generous—was the desire to cut the working week, in line with government policy to build Japan into a 'lifestyle superpower', and create 'international harmony' by being less economically aggressive. The real reason, however, was that companies wanted to shut down their factories because they weren't able to sell what they were producing. The average Japanese worker, who is, on paper, the best paid worker in the world, took 7.5 straight days vacation in 1994, a single day more than in 1990.

The forced resignations of the kind described to the labour lawyer, Mizuguchi, were portrayed in some quarters as a fundamental breach of the time-honoured understanding between Japanese companies and their workforces. 'Forced resignations are not merely cruel, they are essentially a violation of the social contract which has kept these employees at their jobs for so many years', says *Tokyo Business Today*.[41] In truth, Japanese companies have long used these intimidatory tactics to cut staff during difficult times. The small enterprises at the bottom of the *keiretsu* corporate families—the shock-absorbers of the Japanese economy—have never provided guarantees of a job for life. Such companies have always been the first to be squeezed, and have shed labour in all of the upheavals of the past two decades—during the oil shocks of the 1970s, the initial surge of the yen in the mid-1980s and in the present post-bubble era.

Many commentators and journalists have been reporting the imminent demise of lifetime employment since the bubble burst, exactly as they did during Japan's other downturns years and decades ago. It is certainly true that many chief executives, desperate to cut costs, are intensely debating the worth of the system. But at the time of writing, no major Japanese company has bitten the bullet and sacked large numbers of workers, as happened during the recent recessions in Europe, the United States and Australia. The Japanese word for being fired—*kubi kiri*—means literally 'to be chopped off at the neck', and it is not an acceptable way of doing business. The electronics company, Pioneer, gave 35 middle managers 'the shoulder tap' in 1993—the more polite Japanese way of indicating to someone that their services are no longer required. But when the executives protested, and the media indignantly took up their cause, the company quickly retreated, and its top executives took a 10 per cent pay cut instead.

One foreign company, Kodak, on the orders of head office in the United States, laid off two-thirds of its staff in 1993 at a newly opened research centre in Yokohama, and withdrew job offers to eight graduates. As a result, Kodak will always struggle to hire good graduates in Japan. 'Kodak has told their current and prospective employers that they are not trustworthy as employers. They should cut costs further, because they have no future in Japan', was the harsh assessment of one Japanese banker.[42] Often companies want to sack people, but have no idea how to do it. A senior editor at Japan's major business daily, the *Nihon Keizai Shimbun*, invited a foreign journalist employed on the paper's English-language edition to dinner when he wanted to sack him. The foreigner, misunderstanding the gesture, thought he was being promoted, and was stunned when halfway through the main course was told he was being fired. Why hadn't they simply sacked him, the editor was asked later. Why had they asked him out to a cosy dinner to deliver the bad news? 'We didn't know what to do', he replied, 'because in this department, we have never sacked anyone before'.

The middle managers protected by lifetime employment

have become a kind of labour aristocracy, shielded by virtue of the symbolic positions their jobs occupy. But without machine-gunning their employees, and abruptly dumping the system's principles, Japanese companies managed to cut their workforces by 3–5 per cent annually in the early 1990s. Companies have closed their front doors and sharply cut the hiring of new graduates, and quietly opened their back doors, through which they have shunted out as many surplus staff as they can. Instead of just mercilessly hounding middle-aged managers out of jobs, many companies have offered workers sugar-coated packages for early retirement. Honda's 'new life support plan' offers anyone 45 years and over a years salary and training for other jobs. By 1994, 42.5 per cent of companies with 50 employees or more were offering early retirement packages, and 38.5 per cent had asked executives to take mandatory retirement.

While leaving it untouched in name, companies are chipping away at the foundations of lifetime employment by putting workers on annual contracts. One reason for the popularity of contracts was that they fashionably mirrored the independent way professional baseball players are employed. Merit pay is also being introduced for the first time in a concerted fashion to cultivate and reward specialists. While preserving the *tatemae* of seniority pay, Nippon Steel introduced a 'Fellow' system to allow them to pay top researchers as much as executives, without giving them the title. A Sony spokesman was blunt about his company's long-term plans. 'Fixed pay is nothing more than a kind of parental indulgence that is peculiar to Japanese society', he said.[43]

All the ingredients of the management of the Japanese economic miracle—the employment and pay system, consensus-building and bottom-up decision making, the division of labour between men and women, and cosy relations with *keiretsu* suppliers—are under challenge as never before. But so far, they have been chipped, but not cracked.

It is fashionable these days to tag attributes once lauded as Japan's great strengths as fatal weaknesses that ought to be dumped in the name of efficiency. But look at things another way and the situation does not look nearly so desperate. Few countries would have kept their social fabric so nearly intact as Japan under the stresses of the last five years let alone the past fifty. When Nissan announced in 1993 it would be closing its Zama plant near Tokyo, the first car-making plant closure since the war, for example, it was mourned as the passing of a golden era, and the dawn of a new and frighteningly insecure world. Long touted as a shining showpiece of Japanese manufacturing prowess, the Zama plant, with its workers and robots labouring harmoniously side by side, had been shown off to numerous foreign dignitaries, including Margaret Thatcher and Deng Xiaoping. Nissan closed the plant at a time when it was suffering mounting losses and declining sales. Its American competitors claimed that the company's position was so perilous that it was lucky to be open for business at all. 'If Nissan were in this country, it would not even exist. They would have closed the doors long ago', said the chairman of Chrysler Corporation, Robert Eaton.[44] Yet Nissan promised when announcing the closure that no one would lose their jobs, and two years later, when the plant shut its doors on schedule, and the robots shifted to a new state-of-the-art factory on the southern island of Kyushu, the company kept to its word. Nissan found jobs for its Zama workers at its other plants and offices around Japan. The same staged and planned approach is even applied in dinosaur industries like coal-mining. Japan had just three major coal mines operating in 1995, compared to 306 in 1963, when MITI launched the first of eight programs to close mines and subsidise the communities they supported. Nissan's preference for losing workers through natural attrition, rather than sacking them, and the slow wind-down of the coal industry, are good examples of the truly socialist nature of aspects of the Japanese system. Economic organisations in Japan often appear motivated by what Westerners would consider to be non-economic reasons, such as preserving the symbolic sanctity of the lifetime employment system, or keeping a community intact. Nissan, and other listed companies, also have a flexibility not available to their Western competitors, because their stable network of shareholders do not hound them for dividends.

The broader benefits from these arrangements are obvious. Japan's economy is being rapidly restructured—its manufacturing assembly plants are sprinting offshore, and growth is shifting towards service and information-based industries. In a few short years, the economic landscape will look vastly different, but the managed mine closures have ensured that mining communities have not turned into battlefields as they did in England in the early 1980s, when Margaret Thatcher shut down pits. Nissan's employment practices also mean that places like Zama will never end up looking like the wastelands of downtown Detroit.

It is not surprising, then, that amidst all the fin-de-siècle angst that has possessed so many Japanese, there were many prominent and powerful people who were keener to play up the country's good points. Nationalism had always been a dirty word in postwar Japan, but a new generation of leaders emerged in the 1990s with a nicer new version to sell to their people, and the world.

CHAPTER 9

A NICER NEW NATIONALISM

'It's easy for the Japanese to become fanatical as a group. Aggressiveness is incorporated into the Japanese blood with peculiar characteristics.'

Hiroshi Abe, veteran of the Thai–Burma railway
and convicted war criminal

'Unless material wealth can successfully be turned into a sense of national identity and mental well-being, the Japanese will find themselves in a perpetual catch-up syndrome, always in a state of restlessness and mental hunger.'

Eisuke Sakakibara, bureaucrat

It was, at least to an outsider, an innocent enough gesture. As the sombre Germanic strains of Japan's *kimigayo* national anthem echoed across the field, and the Rising Sun flag was hoisted on a pole posted high above the stadium, Kazuyoshi ('Kazu') Miura lightly placed his right hand over his heart. Closing his eyes, the soccer star seemed momentarily overwhelmed with the emotion of leading his nation in front of his countrymen. Miura was the captain of Japan's soccer team, and the country's most popular player in its most fashionable sport. The national soccer competition, the J. League, had quickly swamped Japan's well established number one sport of baseball when it was launched in 1993. Unlike the stodgy, short-back-and-sides baseball players, who travelled between matches in tight, conservative suits and ties, the soccer players were wild, youthful and uninhibited. They had long hair and glamorous girlfriends, and teams peppered with imported players from sexy, samba-dancing countries like Brazil and Argentina. Miura performed a brazen, knee trembling dance in front of spectators every time he scored a goal. But he became just as popular with young fans for his public displays of patriotism when captaining his country against the world.[1]

In any other nation, such a basic display of love of one's country would be predictable and unremarkable. Indeed, it would only draw comment if players representing their nation *didn't* salute the flag and sing their national anthem before matches. But not in Japan, where patriotism and national symbols, especially the anthem and the flag, are weighted down by grim associations with militarism and the destruction of war. For decades, left-wing politicians refused to recognise both the flag and the anthem, and teachers campaigned against their use in schools. As a result, many students had no idea what the old Japanese words of the anthem meant. In one survey of schools, a student said that he thought the line referring to the Emperor's longevity—'until the moss begins to grow'—had something to do with hair care. 'I don't understand how moss turns into mousse', he remarked.[2]

One of Kazu's teammates on the national squad and in the J. League, Tsuyoshi Kitazawa, said his captain had started putting his hand over his heart after seeing players from other nations do the same before matches. 'Kazu and I talked about doing it a few years ago, and we started doing it too. Of course, it would be better if the Rising Sun patch were on our chests instead of our sleeves,' he said. The copycatting artificiality of Kazu's actions didn't worry the fans. The hand over the heart transcended politics, and thrilled the J. League's followers, most of whom were born decades after the war ended. They thought he was 'cool', and thousands of spectators soon turned stadiums into a sea of white and red flags during national games. Miura's gesture leapt over decades of political dogma in a single bound. The media hailed the uncomplicated new patriotism of youth, and very quickly, waving the flag and getting misty-eyed at the anthem became natural—at least at sporting events. 'We're not taking sides in the controversy about the flag and the anthem', cautioned Kitazawa. 'We just want people to understand how proud we feel about representing Japan. In that sense, our gesture is a good influence on kids.'

Muira's pop patriotism coincided with a much more significant change of heart on Japan's national symbols. Out of a mixture of political fatigue and pragmatism, the most prominent, and long-standing, opponents of the flag and the anthem—from the then Socialist Prime Minister down—fundamentally shifted their position at around the same time. Tomiichi Murayama stunned his party, and the nation, by announcing in July 1994 that he would 'respect the feelings' of people who supported the two national symbols. In doing so, he upended half a century of dogged opposition to two symbols that left-wingers considered indelibly stained by war. His party, a touch grumpily, supported his switch a week later. Even the Japan Teachers' Union, for years an unyielding enemy of the conservative Education Ministry and many tenets of the Japanese system, finally dropped objections to both symbols from its charter in 1993.

To be sure, youthful indifference to the ugly history of the two symbols might have been the product of a politics-free education rather than genuine patriotism. But the soccer players and their fans weren't the only ones who thought Japan had something to be proud about, and weren't ashamed to say so. In the early 1990s, a new breed of bureaucrats, politicians, academics and writers came to the fore to articulate pride and confidence both in their nation's ancient traditions, and in its modern achievements. Rather than shelter sullenly behind Japan's growing mounds of wealth, cowering at criticism from a hostile world, they were assertive, and less tangled up by feelings of guilt about the war. These new nationalists wanted to do more than reactively defend Japanese values and policies against foreign critics. In the economic field, they wanted to export them as well. They bridled at the constant criticism of Japan by the West, particularly the United States, and most of all, rejected the notion that Western values had universal application. They also were confident, articulate and sure enough of their ground to engage Japan's critics aggressively in debate, ironically using adversarial skills they had learned while studying in the West. 'You people try to analyse a situation thinking there should be something universal in it—that is not necessarily true', said senior Finance Ministry official Eisuke Sakakibara, one of the most prominent new nationalists in the bureaucracy. 'If there is one characteristic of the Japanese system, it is pluralism. Or strategic pluralism. We are very pragmatic, and to your mind very untransparent. And sometimes shrewd.'[3]

The *Economist* dubbed the emerging patriotic trend 'Japan's Nice New Nationalism'.[4] 'Nice' is not a word usually associated with nationalism in Japan, especially as all the trappings of the nasty old kind are still on constant display in Japan today. Businessmen and bureaucrats are often arrogant and haughty in boasting of their successes against foreign competitors. Every few months or so, a politician can be counted on to pronounce on Japan's superiority as a unique, pure-blooded race, and insult foreigners at the same time. Patriots still deny Japan did any wrong in the war, and anybody who says otherwise can expect violent retribution from the rightists who roam the streets at will in sound trucks, roaring out vile, ear-splitting messages. Numerous nationalist pressure groups also maintain a constant campaign to undermine the secular reforms of the American occupation, and return Japan to prewar values of a divine Emperor, presiding over the native state religion of Shintoism.

Another stream of Japan's elite, particularly those who lived through the war, see these outbursts as proof that a violent, uncontrollable impulse still lurks deep in the collective Japanese psyche. They also maintain that the country's political system has no mechanism for controlling these energies, no matter which direction they are headed in. Long-time conservative strongman, and former LDP deputy Prime Minister, Masaru Gotoda, who turned 81 in 1995, is the chief proponent of this view, and has done everything in his power for years to block any overseas role for the Japanese military. 'Once derailed from the right path, Japan could be led in the wrong direction, without anyone being able to stop it,' he warned.[5] Gotoda's spooky view of an emotionally immature, out-of-control Japan matches that held by many foreigners, particularly Asians, who also considered the war not some temporary excess but the result of something deeply ingrained in the Japanese personality.

The new, younger nationalists disagreed. While the ultra-rightists may violently enforce the taboos surrounding the Imperial family, equally, the new nationalists point out, they are a crude embarrassment to the man in whose name they purport to speak, Emperor Akihito. The Japanese people are strongly xenophobic, but they are also better travelled and able to speak their minds more freely than at any time in their history. Old-style nationalists are often still enamoured with military adventurism, but the Japanese people shrink from it, as a child does from thunder and lightning. So while modern Japanese nationalism may not be entirely nice, it is certainly nicer than anything that went before it. The new nationalists both trust the Japanese people, and the values of the society which has nurtured them. Politicians like Ichiro Ozawa maintain that the propagation of phobias about the old nationalism had prevented Japan from ever gaining true political independence. He has made it his life's work to wean Japan off its infantile reliance on the United States for security and make the country not just a paid-up member of the family of nations, but a grown-up member as well.

The roots of the unresolved schisms over nationalism lie as much in the structure of postwar politics as they do in culture and history, an issue we will return to later. But the nationalist ethos is nonetheless rich in mythology and, as you might expect, intensely Japanese.

WARE WARE NIHONJIN . . . (WE JAPANESE . . .)

There is a joke about the Japanese that goes something like this. Three people—an Italian, an Englishman and a Japanese— are all sent to Africa to observe a newly discovered colony of elephants, and then write a book about their experience. The Italian returns with a book called 'The Sex Life of Elephants in Africa'. The Englishman is next to complete his tome, called 'The Discovery and Civilising of the African Elephant', which, of course, he thinks only a Briton could have done. The Japanese visitor takes the longest because he has written two books. The first one is straight and studious, with extensive footnotes— 'A Study of the African Elephant'. His second book is called 'How the African Elephant Sees the Japanese—a Study in the Elephant–Japan Perception Gap'. The target of this joke is the self-obsession that possesses the Japanese. *Da Capo* magazine originally printed a version of it as part of a special 25-page feature comparing Japan to other countries in everything from the price of fruit to economic output and the consumption of pornography.[6] In Japan itself, the art of 'talking about the Japanese'—known as *nihonjinron*—is a thriving industry in itself.

Australian scholar Peter Dale, in his book *The Myth of Japanese Uniqueness*, says it is difficult for outsiders to grasp the dimensions of the *nihonjinron* industry in Japan. Dale said it would be as if the whole of English letters over the last 100 years had been singularly preoccupied with a study of 'Englishness'.

> Imagine, then, dozens, if not hundreds of works pouring from the presses of Oxford and Cambridge, in which the Hare Professor of Moral Philosophy discussed the uniqueness of English ethical tradition, or Wittgensteinians examined at length hundreds of terms in the Oxford English Language Dictionary to derive concepts of Englishness in such terms as 'fair play', 'good form', 'gentleman', 'guvnor', etc., or wrote books on the influence of bad weather on parliamentary institutions and democracy, of cricket on the outlook of English people, on matriarchy as a constant element underlying British traditions from the times of Boadicia through to Mrs Thatcher; treating everything under the English sun as consequences of some peculiar mentality unchanged since one's ancestors first donned woad, and did battle with Caesar. Imagine this as something that filtered down through newspaper and regional media to everyday life, and you have something of the picture which has taken place in Japan, where almost any discussion, from the formally academic, to the colloquial marketplace exchange, can reflect the ideology of nationhood.[7]

Dale isn't exaggerating one bit. The English obsession with Englishness is not unlike *nihonjinron*, except that the Japanese version, characteristically, is more extreme and insular. Living in Japan, you quickly lose count of the number of sentences you hear which begin with the words—'*Ware ware nihonjin* . . .', or 'We Japanese . . .'. Not a day passes that the media don't feature at least one discussion or media column about qualities which are peculiar to Japan and the Japanese. A popular book published in 1994, simply called *Nihonjinron*, featured the writings of 100 different specialists in the field. Their opinions of what made the Japanese special were divided into four categories—climate and nature, history, psychology, and statistical measures. The *nihonjinron* mindset is so pervasive that it often spills into the political arena, with embarrassing consequences for Japan's leaders. As a senior cabinet minister, Tsutomu Hata fended off pressure for imports of foreign beer by saying that Japanese intestines were too long to digest it. Similarly, European skis were barred from Japan initially because the bureaucrat in charge of the matter said they would not slide on Japan's 'unique snow'. Both statements sparked an uproar overseas, and the Japanese government was forced to back down to ensure harmonious relations with the outside world.

An entertaining exercise in the popular politics of *nihonjinron* is the annual agitation by Japan's Fisheries Agency to rally support for lifting the international ban on whaling. On the eve of the 1993 International Whaling Commission's meeting in Kyoto, the Japanese government organised for foreign journalists to visit Ayukawa, a traditional whaling town on the beautiful far north coast of Japan's main island. These days, Ayukawa is like a theme park for so-called traditional whaling values. From the model of a whale which sits in the town schoolyard for the kids to play on, to the four-feet long and leathery whale penises scattered like sentinels through the town, the mammal is inescapable. The local and central governments put up A$20 million to build a flashy, state-of-the-art museum full of preserved whale foetuses of varying ages, interactive games for children and old harpoons and model ships. Whale meat is a delicacy in most of Japan, albeit of little interest to most young people, who prefer American fast food. But in Ayukawa, you can buy whale as cheaply as meat. The town conveys a single message—that whales are part of the community's, and Japan's, vital essence.

We are not talking about nurturing just eating habits here, but 'food culture', a phrase mouthed by every villager one met.

The most eloquent plea for the mammals came at the end of a long question-and-answer session in the local town hall late one evening, when a villager, Yuichi Kimura, stood up and demanded to be heard. 'I am 63, and when I was born I grew up on my mother's milk, who ate whale meat as her daily food. Please,' he said, turning to the foreign interlopers, 'we just want to resume our traditional food culture again'. After hours of sharp, accusatory lectures from the locals, and some visiting Norwegian whalers, about their right to catch, kill and eat the mammals; about the animal-rightists and the eco-terrorists who were destroying their livelihood; and the evils of the International Whaling Commission (IWC) which was conspiring to help them, it came down to this: Yuichi Kimura's mother's milk. It was the most emotive metaphor in a day and a night which positively lactated with them. The Norwegians, who were even more aggressive in their support of whaling than the Japanese, were puzzled by all the talk about culture. 'I don't really know what they mean by "food culture" ', confessed Steinar Bastesen of the North-Norwegian Small-whaler Association, shaking his head after the meeting. 'This is a hunt like any other hunt.'

The Japanese obsession with blood and blood types is another sub-genre of *nihonjinron*. Job applicants are required to state their blood type on most employment forms, and chiefs of some of the largest companies in the land, including the past president of Nippon Steel, openly admit that it influences their choice of employees. Most Japanese are either A-type (precise, fastidious and hyped-up) or O-type (relaxed, easy-going and adaptable). Knowing someone's blood type can be as crucial as awareness of their family background, and it often plays an important role in matchmaking. Superstitious notions about blood types are superficially not very different to the popularity of astrology, except that the idea of blood runs so thickly through the whole issue of Japanese identity. Casually flicking through the TV channels one day, I stumbled across a talk show about the life of the famous Japan scholar and one-time US Ambassador to Japan, Edwin Reischauer. The show replayed an incident where Reischauer was knifed by an insane 19-year-old youth behind the US Embassy in Tokyo in March 1964, and rushed to hospital where he received an emergency blood transfusion. The host recoiled in wonderment. 'You mean they pumped Japanese blood right into him?' Indeed they had, and the talk show guests speculated as to whether this was why Reischauer, considered to be the most sympathetic of Japan scholars, had truly been able to 'understand' the Japanese. They appeared to have forgotten that the blood given to Reischauer had been contaminated, and gave him a liver problem that made him ill, on and off, for the rest of his life. But like a true stoic Japanese, Reischauer never complained.

Even though the essence of truly being able to understand Japan is being Japanese, the opinions of foreigners are particularly valued by those in the *nihonjinron* industry. This is not for their insight, but because they serve to confirm everything the Japanese tell themselves—that their race is special and different. If foreigners deliver another message, they are not nearly as popular. Long-time Tokyo resident, American writer Elizabeth Kiritani, recounted the dilemma of an American PhD student researching a topic related to Japanese culture. His American university refused to accept his thesis unless it contained some new idea or insight. His Japanese supervisors, however, considered that as a foreigner he had no right to come up with any new theories about Japanese culture. He was expected to simply cite the theories of established Japanese professors.[8] But if this basic rule is observed, as any canny foreigner coming to Japan quickly realises, there are small fortunes to be made in telling the Japanese about themselves. Many foreigners do in fact make a living as professional *gaijin* on the lecture circuit, and on television chat shows.

Conversely, there are also small fortunes to be made in bringing the world to Japan, as I discovered one day when I met Dr Muneto Yoshioka, his wife Fumiko and daughter Nozomi, 6, on a quick trip to 'Europe'. The Yoshiokas, who live in Osaka, the capital of western Japan, had set aside just four days to go to Holland on vacation, but they did it with ease. They saw most of the beautiful buildings there were to see, ate loads of Dutch food, shopped for souvenirs, and still had a couple of days to spare. The Yoshiokas, in fact, never even left Japan. Just outside the city of Nagasaki is a place where all the highlights of Amsterdam, The Hague and Rotterdam are collected into one single town, complete with working canals, whirling windmills, and tulips. Named after one of Queen Beatrix of The Netherlands' official residences in The Hague, 'Huis ten Bosch' is a precisely rendered old Dutch city, complete with painstaking reproductions of both the inside and outside of famous buildings. The Yoshiokas, who were visiting for the second time, love it. 'Here, all the monuments are in the one place', said Fumiko, as we rode the bus into the city. 'There's entertainment. It's clean. There's no litter, and because everyone speaks Japanese, it's a lot easier.' And one other thing too. 'There are fewer foreigners than if you go overseas.'

The millions of Japanese who have visited Huis ten Bosch since it opened three years ago—about as many who have gone to Holland itself—are either happy to escape foreigners as well, or simply get a kick out of being in a foreign fantasy land while they're in Japan. If they get bored with Holland, there are many other foreign lands they can experience without having to leave Japanese soil. In Wakayama, in west Japan, developers have built 'Porto Europe', where locals can experience the 'authentic atmosphere' of eighteenth-century Spanish, Italian and French port cities. Spread across 690 000 square metres on the island of Shikoku in Takamatsu is Reoma World, which has an Oriental village with parts of Bhutan, Thailand and Nepal. Nearby is a New Zealand village, where visitors can watch a sheepdog demonstration—'by a real New Zealander!', assured a spokeswoman—and buy jerseys of the national All Black rugby team, and souvenirs of coffee cups covered with kiwis. At Tobu World Square north of Tokyo, developers have expertly built in miniature 102 famous Japanese and foreign landmarks, like the Colosseum, Big Ben and St Marco's Plaza in Venice, and put them into one large theme park. The genius of this concept is that the shrunken buildings, unlike the real things, can be completely fitted into a single camera frame for photos, with the happy visitor in the foreground.

But for sheer scale and audacity, none of these places can match Huis ten Bosch. Built with 30–40 million bricks imported by the tankerload from Holland, Huis ten Bosch has replicas of some of the country's most famous town halls, castles and hotels, and one of the most impressive porcelain collections in the world. In some cases, the city has even improved on the original. The Palais Huis ten Bosch in Japan features a French Baroque garden which was planned for the original in The Netherlands, but never built. The director of the project, Tatuaki Nagashima, told me that Dutch people were 'amused' when they first arrived in the town. 'They feel very funny, because they can see famous buildings in Holland from all different sorts of cities sitting side by side. The next thing they say is that it is very beautiful and clean. There's no litter. No shit!' he says, with a hearty chuckle. The curiosity value for the Dutch is understandable. But how does one explain Japan's enduring fascination with this elaborate and opulent foreign kitsch? In an essay on Tokyo Disneyland, anthropologist Mary Ann Brannan wrote how the American owners had originally wanted to include sideshows like Samurai Land in the Tokyo version. Their Japanese partners were horrified by the idea, and rejected it. They wanted Japanese visitors to feel as if they were taking a completely foreign vacation. Brannan says the aim is to keep 'the exotic exotic', and at the same time, much like *nihonjinron*, reinforce the Japanese sense of difference from the outside world.

Nihonjinron has always required an upmarket, spiritual lustre, something which is furnished by prominent academics like Takeshi Umehara, the founder of the International Research Centre for Japanese Studies in Kyoto. The scholarly high priest of politically orthodox *nihonjinron*, Umehara says that Japanese values are the product of a fusion of two different religious traditions—the native Shinto religion and Buddhism—with a dose of the Confucian ethics of loyalty and filial piety thrown in for good measure. In Japan, the saying goes, one is 'born Shinto, and dies Buddhist'. Shinto—literally 'the way of the gods'—has no doctrine, scripture or set of moral codes. It is a religion of rituals and festivals which celebrate beginnings—from fertility to birth, and adulthood to a new job. For almost every important rite of passage, the Japanese visit shrines to pay homage to the gods—to usher in the new year, to mark children's birthdays and later the coming of age, and to pass all-important exams. Shinto emphasises the purity of renewal and life, rather than the pollution of death. Scandal-stained politicians put themselves through a Shinto-style purification ritual—first by humbly resigning, and then spending a period in the political wilderness—to cleanse themselves of their past sins. Everyday Shinto rituals are also aimed at coaxing and cultivating the capricious, but essentially benevolent, natural forces that swirl around the Japanese archipelago. So just as farmers celebrated each new season and harvest with Shinto services and festivals, so now large industrial companies also invoke the gods to inspire production. Most big enterprises have in-house altars for their patron *kami*. There is no shortage of choices for them—Shinto gods, or *kami*, are innumerable, and can take any form anywhere. What is important in these rituals is not any ethical code, or form of judgement, but the correct performance. 'The reward for the right ritual at the right time is to be found in a favourable response of the *kami* to whom it is addressed', writes anthropologist Thomas Crump.[9]

Buddhism, by contrast, has extensive texts and writings preaching a tradition of individual enlightenment and consolation in the face of death. Japanese funerals are usually Buddhist. The important thing about both religions is that they are practical and user-friendly, and provide an emotional reassurance to a people concerned about their identity as Japanese.[10] Umehara says they have also allowed Japan, uniquely among industrialised countries, to modernise 'without losing its soul'. The cycles of life, death and rebirth of Shinto, and the emphasis on harmony between human beings and nature, has inbred in Japan a sense of community responsibility and tamed egotism. Umehara calls this 'mutualism'. Sakakibara, the Finance Ministry bureaucrat, uses a word which is similarly clumsy when translated into English—'peoplism'—to distinguish Japan's inclusive capitalism from the dog-eat-dog Western version. Umehara is not modest about where this unique Oriental blend leaves Japan. He says the collapse of Marxism is simply the opening act to a much larger event—the fall of Western liberalism. The new principles of the post-modern world will come not from the West, but from Asia, especially Japan. 'With the scales pulled from its eyes by the dead end of modern philosophy, the West is just arriving at the realisation of these truths lodged deep in the recesses of Japanese civilisation', he says.[11]

For anyone who has spent any time in Japan, the oft-repeated notion that the Japanese have a special and harmonious relationship with nature is an extremely bad joke. Catch the *shinkansen* (bullet train) from Tokyo to Osaka, and you pass little besides wall-to-wall housing and industry. The classic view of Japan's national symbol of harmony and perfect form, Mount

Fuji, on your right about 90 minutes out of Tokyo, is blurred by belching smoke from the chimneys of one of Japan's worst polluters, the Daishowa paper company. I remember looking out of an aeroplane window the first time I flew over Japan and being stunned at the way so many mountains and valleys had been strip-mined, until I realised that the gouged landscapes were golf-course developments, one of the worst environmental scourges in Japan. Greenies, who rightly attack Japanese companies for their vandalous logging and wasteful consumption of the pristine tropical forests in South-east Asia and Papua New Guinea, are also usually possessed by a notion that the same companies behave differently at home. They don't. They act in the same destructive and profit-driven way—moving whole mountains in the service of single construction projects. The only difference is that in Japan the compensation costs for shifting or injuring residents is much higher.

While praising harmony with nature, Umehara's Shinto also perversely lays the philosophical basis for this frenzy of destruction. The Imperial Ise Shrine on the island of Shikoku is rebuilt once every 20 years, a renovation which symbolically represents the Japanese belief in renewable cycles. 'If God's power is not made new every 20 years, its spiritual power will wither,' says Umehara. The same principle, broadly applied, clears a path for the 'renewal' and remoulding of all sorts of natural sites, and the destruction of buildings which would be classified for their heritage value in any other country. To sustain the belief that the Japanese have a special relationship with nature these days requires an act of faith, because it is so much at odds with contemporary urban culture, and construction industry politics.

The real problem with Shinto, however, is not necessarily what Umehara says it is now, but what it became under nationalistic and militarist governments. Japan's new rulers in the Meiji Restoration elevated Shinto from a 'folk' religion of lusty harvest festivals and ancestor worship into a state creed embodying a newly formulated ideology of 'Japaneseness'. The Emperor was deified as the divine representation of all ancestors, and honoured as 'the supreme power, the head of state and chief God of the ancient animist shrine religion of Shinto'.[12] He became the father to a nation of gods, and the shrine at which the militarist rulers prayed as they suppressed dissent, banned rival religions and brutally invaded Asia. Umehara, to give him his due, publicly spurns the ultra-nationalist Shinto philosophies in favour of the kinder, gentler version he espouses himself. But like the flag and the national anthem, Shinto's xenophobic core values endure in many quarters as a symbol of the nasty old nationalism. Feisty anti-Emperor groups are on a constant look-out for any breach of the postwar constitution's strict separation between religion and the state, and mount legal challenges when they spot any government monies being paid towards the cost of Imperial rituals.

The traditionalists find the objections of anti-Emperor activists particularly galling. Because if anything makes Japan special, and distinguishes it from all other nations, it is the unbroken rule of their divine Emperor, a direct descendant of the Sun Goddess, Amaterasu Omikami.

UPSTAIRS, DOWNSTAIRS

A light tap on the *shoji* screen signalled the start of the only close encounter I ever had with the Imperial family, on the eve of an official visit to the United States in mid-1994. We rose as one does when a priest approaches the altar to begin mass, and the screen door slid back to allow the Emperor Akihito and Empress Michiko to enter the room in the heart of the Imperial Palace. He was diminutive and dapper in a double-breasted suit. She followed a few paces behind, pale and withdrawn by comparison, following a recent illness. After an apology from

Japanese journalists for 'bothering' the Imperial couple, the press conference began. There were no tapes and translators— the former perhaps for fear that unauthorised recordings of the Emperor could circulate out of control, and the latter because the Imperial Household Agency insisted that it alone should fashion and release later translations of the couple's pronouncements. The questions were prepared and printed more than a week prior to the press conference, and asked according to unalterable rules. The Japanese journalists went first with five questions. The foreigners, only privileged to attend on this occasion because the subject was a foreign visit, finished by asking the last two.

The public business of the Japanese Imperial family remains tightly scripted and controlled. But behind the scenes the story is different. Two games were being played out behind the moat and thick walls surrounding the Imperial Palace in the heart of Tokyo during the final decade of the twentienth century. The first was an attempt by a slightly more worldly and liberal Emperor and Crown Prince to nudge the Chrysanthemum Throne gently into the next century. The second was a nasty counter-movement spearheaded by conservatives, with the support of some former and serving chamberlains, to take the institution back, and restore its mystical and religious traditions. Caught in the middle were the Imperial family's two commoners, Empress Michiko and the Crown Prince's bride, a Harvard-trained diplomat, Masako Owada. Prowling around the edges, and—uncharacteristically—sorting through the dirty laundry of the world's longest surviving monarchy, were sections of the Japanese media.

The Japanese use two calendars to measure the years— a Western-style one for convenience, and their own official calendar, in which the count restarts with each new Emperor. Hirohito was the Showa Emperor, and his era goes by the same name. *Showa* means 'shining peace'. The years from 1926 to

1989 are thus known as Showa 1 to Showa 64. Like many supposedly immutable conventions surrounding the institution, this age-old practice was only revived in the middle of last century, with the reinstatement of the Emperor at the sacred heart of the Japanese system. Japan's new rulers moved the Emperor from centuries of seclusion and irrelevance in the ancient capital of Kyoto, and re-installed him in the palace in the centre of Tokyo. Through the new education system, the rulers ensured that he had both a religious aura and sufficient street credibility to sustain the office. The Emperor became the divine father of the new Japanese nation, and the Meiji oligarchs were then able to rule the country in his name.

The Meiji Emperor was succeeded by his grandson, Crown Prince Ito, known posthumously as the Taisho Emperor. Ito was never going to be the best advertisement for the institution. He was, as one scholar wrote, vain, sadistic and promiscuous, and interested in becoming Emperor solely because it gave him more chances to dress up in a military uniform and ape his idol, Kaiser Wilhelm II of Germany. He was also mad.[13] At one opening of parliament, instead of giving the keynote address, the Emperor rolled his speech into the shape of a telescope and peered through it at the startled MPs. The Taisho Emperor died in his early forties in 1926, and was succeeded by his son, who reigned for 67 years, a dramatic period spanning Japan's military build-up, its utter defeat and postwar resurgence as a global economic power. Hirohito ascended the throne as a living god, and most Japanese people had never heard his voice until he broadcast the nation's surrender in 1945. He went overseas just twice—to Great Britain in the 1920s and to the United States in the early 1980s—and had little say in how he lived his life. In an interview in 1974, he recalled how his own marriage had been arranged in 1925. 'One day, the chamberlain for the Impe-rial family came to me and told me the Emperor had decided

I was going to get married', he said. And that was that. He met his wife some time later.

Akihito—the Heisei ('clarity and harmony') Emperor—is different. It is certainly true, as critics of the Japanese monarchy will point out, that in all the rituals that count, Akihito has not budged from the traditional ways. His own enthronement climaxed in the *daijosai* ('Great Food Festival') in which the Emperor is transformed from an ordinary man into a supernatural being. The Crown Prince's wedding ceremony was conducted in the presence of the Imperial family's—and thus the Japanese nation's—mythical ancestress, the Sun Goddess. Both ceremonies were mostly secret rituals, intended to shroud the court with the mystique and power of ancient Japanese gods and values. Monarchists—and anti-republicans—will note. This is just how a traditional monarchy should be. The Emperor bears the accumulated charisma of his nation's history. He lives behind a wall in the centre of the capital, and the less seen of him the better. Without the mystery, he would be powerless. The benefits of his office are intangible, and all the greater because of it. The Emperor is useful because of his very uselessness.[14]

But for all the deliberate ambiguity of his enthronement ceremony, Akihito has never been deified. He was the first Emperor in history to marry both a woman of his own choice (even if their initial meeting was arranged), and a commoner. Both Akihito and Michiko had Christian teachers when they were growing up—another first. Akihito has also had a lot to live down. His father avoided being tried as a war criminal after he agreed to renounce his divinity, and preside over the American occupation of the country. The Imperial family is by no means a liberal institution, but Akihito has managed to take his image subtly beyond the ancient trappings and historical baggage. He has projected himself as a moderate, relatively liberal figure, and clearly identified himself with the pacifist postwar constitution. He has also assumed a low-key, but important, diplomatic role under the direction of the Foreign Ministry, with pioneering visits to China and South-east Asia. The trip to China, in particular, was made in the face of violent objections from conservatives. A few trite, symbolic gestures for a media-conscious age, like having his car stop for the first time at a red light, have played well with the public. Akihito was de-mystifying the institution, very gently, and only at the margins, but even that was enough to strike horror into the hearts of many people who still considered it sacred. Because of that very sacredness, the conservatives didn't dare target Akihito. Instead, they attacked his wife.

The press campaign engineered by conservatives started after Michiko refused to answer an unscripted question at a press conference before an official visit to Europe. She was asked how she felt 'as a graduate of a Catholic university' to be visiting the Pope in the company of the Emperor, the Hereditary High Priest of Japan's indigenous Shinto religion. Michiko's Catholic education, along with her commoner status, had long been a sore point for traditionalists and a taboo topic in the press. 'The Honourable Michiko Loses Her Cool at Question' screamed a headline. The article reported that she had resorted to 'haughty language' in refusing to answer, and triggered an unprecedented series of catty and critical attacks in the up-market weekly, *Bungei Shunju*. Michiko was painted as a domineering and insensitive harridan, willing to trample over time-honoured traditions and the memory of her husband's father, Hirohito. One story upbraided her for demanding bowls of instant noodles and peeled apples at 2 am. In another, she was portrayed as prodding the Emperor into breaking the rules as well. 'The Imperial couple are very fussy', the article said. 'They invite their friends around, they sit up chatting late at night and are far too self-indulgent. The Empress is hysterical.'

The series of stories left a clear trail back to the black hands behind the anti-Michiko campaign—former court officials loyal to the Japan of the Showa Emperor. One reportedly wept at the news that Michiko had ordered some of the late Showa Emperor's favourite trees to be cut down to clear the way for the construction of a new palace. Michiko was apparently so stunned by the stories that she collapsed, and then literally lost her voice. For four to five months, she didn't utter a single word in public, and if we are to believe the agency, in private either. She didn't speak again in public until the press conference before the US visit. This was not the first time she had suffered in the palace. It was an open secret that she had had a nervous breakdown in the early days of her marriage under bullying from her mother-in-law—the archetypal harridan of Japanese society. Michiko's wretched lot may have also been a factor in the extreme reluctance of the second commoner to marry into the family—Masako Owada, who tied the knot with the heir to the throne, Crown Prince Naruhito, in 1993. By the beginning of the 1990s, Naruhito's failure to find a bride had made him a sitting target for mocking weekly magazines. When one magazine published twelve different pictures of Naruhito with twelve different hairstyles to try and make him look attractive, the Imperial House Agency put its foot down. The Japanese media agreed to observe a 'voluntary' blackout on any discussions about the wedding. So obedient were the media bosses on this occasion that frustrated members of the journalists' club attached to the Agency, who knew of the eventual engagement to Owada but couldn't report it, leaked the news to the *Washington Post*. Only after the American newspaper had published the story did the Japanese press tell their readers who their next Emperor planned to marry.

Even more interesting was the pitched battle fought by Naruhito to persuade Owada to marry him. Naruhito proposed to Owada twice, but each time was politely but firmly rebuffed. While the court chamberlains provided him with some cover by persuading the press to stop pursuing the story, Naruhito continued his campaign. Through go-betweens and a flurry of late-night phone calls to her home, Naruhito refused to take no for an answer. No one can know the pressure Owada was under to accept the Crown Prince's proposal. How could a woman like her, an elite career diplomat, for whom ambition was duty, keep saying no to the future Emperor of Japan, particularly with the knowledge that her father, the bureaucrat who then headed Japan's Foreign Ministry, would have felt compelled to resign unless she accepted. One important part of his job would have become impossible—the regular briefings of the Emperor on affairs of state.

Naruhito's winning words to his bride-to-be were his promise to her to 'always do everything to protect you'. The assumption was that he would protect her from the rigid and authoritarian Imperial court in a way that his father had failed to do for his mother. (The mother-in-law was not expected to be a problem.) The courtiers, however, scenting an overdose of foreign influence in her character, made it clear the institution might need to be protected from her. 'Hey, she's cute—that was my first reaction when I saw her', said Minoru Hamao, one former court chamberlain, who had also attacked Michiko. But he added that the moment she began speaking at the joint press conference with Naruhito to announce their engagement, his impression changed. 'When she said—' "[Naruhito] has a good personality"—it was like a teacher talking about a student, or a mother to a child. She was so rude and talkative. For every three words he says, she should say one.' One magazine calculated that Naruhito had spoken for 9 minutes and 5 seconds, whereas the uppity Owada had talked for 9 minutes and 13 seconds. 'I even saw her walking into the palace ahead of him once. After all, she is Americanised—it's as if she's full of this "Ladies First" attitude', said Hamao.

Owada was a smart choice for a royal family which had worked hard to rehabilitate itself, along with the whole country, in the eyes of the world. Intelligent, attractive, with a degree from Harvard University and four foreign languages (English, French, German and Russian), she could only enhance the diligent but unexciting Prince, and perhaps even the institution. No one was quite sure whether she was marrying down, or up. She was turning her back on a promising career, but in its place she might have found one even more influential. Amongst ordinary Japanese, the wedding excited a respectful interest but no wild enthusiasm, in contrast to Akihito's wedding three decades before. A survey by the advertising agency, Dentsu, found only 10 per cent of people questioned were genuinely thrilled by the union, and less than 5 per cent of teenagers. But very few people, apart from groups steadfastly opposed to the Emperor system, seriously questioned the Imperial family's legitimacy, or its importance in defining Japan and what it was to be Japanese. The soap opera over Naruhito's search for a bride was contained, and did not turn into the kind of salacious vaudeville act that has undermined the British royals. In some respects, it even slightly humanised an institution that inevitably struggles to articulate its relevance in a multi-media age.

The main argument used in defence of Hirohito after the war was that he was powerless to stop the militarists. The catch-phrase was that he was trapped like a 'bird in a cage', and unable to influence events from confinement in the Palace. It is way beyond the scope of this book to pronounce on Hirohito's guilt or innocence, but whatever the case, the Imperial cage is a very different place these days. Inside it are two better-travelled and educated men, and two wives who have been lured in from outside. It is well-nigh impossible to see any of them being co-opted or coerced into a folly like the one triggered by the nasty old nationalists of yesteryear.

The Imperial family is important for other reasons. Despite its re-positioning, it remains a powerful conservative force. It is also convenient for the powerful bureaucrats, who have a higher allegiance of loyalty to the Emperor, over the heads of Japan's dirty politicians, and they govern their patches accordingly. The Emperor is the head of state, but, like Hirohito after the war, responsible for none of its actions. It suits the bureaucrats who run Japan to leave it that way.

Owada, who was a bureaucrat herself until recently, would understand this perfectly. The ultra-nationalists, who noisily claim to embody the pure essence of Japan's imperial spirit, aren't so sure any more.

THE RIGHT WING

A friend visiting Tokyo, a city in which most streets maddeningly have no names, and houses are numbered in the order they are built, inevitably got lost one day. While meandering around, she noticed that the only other beings who appeared to be wandering aimlessly, along streets and around corners, were the people driving the ultra-nationalist sound trucks that are an everyday sight in most of the big cities all over Japan. Concluding that they had lost their way as well, she joked that their irksome squawkings must be in protest against the lack of street markings. In over five years in Japan, I think this was the only joke I ever heard about the ultra-right, and their sound trucks. People rarely joke about these creatures, as they are considered to represent the dark and scary underbelly of Japanese hyper-nationalism. With just a flick of the culturally programmed switch dwelling inside all of the Japanese race, these same drivers and their cohorts would have *sararimen* swapping their dour suits for soldiers' uniforms for another military excursion into Asia. Or so the glib theory goes. But if you listen to what they actually say, you get a very different slant on what motivates these extreme patriots.

From the fearsome visages, and the sinister markings on the

sides of their dark armoured trucks—like the (communist) red streak that spreads north of Hokkaido to cover the Russian-held Kurile Islands claimed by Tokyo—you'd expect that these right-wing groups were pretty concerned about Japanese politics and foreign policy. Maybe this was true when they performed outside the Russian embassy, once one of their favourite locations, but it is not the case in the central business district. For a few months, from the vantage point of my newspaper's office in Otemachi, Tokyo's business and banking centre, I attempted to track their ear-splitting announcements as they prowled, growled and scowled their way past the building. Like anyone with a bit of information to sell, they had done their research, and tightly targeted their messages.

The day usually started outside the Tokyo office of one of Japan's and the world's largest financial institution, the Sanwa Bank. Positioned in front of the main entrance, the gravel-voiced men in the trucks opened their broadcast in a tone of mock gentility, with the sound turned down low. 'Could you please pass on our regards to head office in Osaka. We can't afford to pay the cost of petrol to get there, so we've come here,' they said. This was probably not at all reassuring to the bank employees inside, especially as they would then crank up the sound to heavy-metal levels to continue their broadside. 'We have been asked to investigate a crime committed by Tokyo Dome [Tokyo's main baseball stadium]. As the main shareholders, you should fully investigate this criminal act. For the time being, we will put aside the issue of your relations with Sagawa Kyubin [the scandal-stained trucking company] so you can act immediately.' And then softer again with a nice Japanese touch, the broadcast concluded, 'Sorry to cause you trouble, but this is a serious act involving a large amount of money'.

The next favourite target was the nearby tax office, where their noisy bile was directed at Daisaku Ikeda, the head of the powerful and secretive Buddhist sect, Soka Gakkai, for his allegedly favoured treatment by the tax department. Then the truck proceeded to the Immigration Bureau, to abuse its officials for taking backhanders in return for granting foreigners work permits. What you quickly notice is that all these messages have one thing in common. They have nothing to do with politics, protecting the Japanese spirit or buttressing the monarchy, and everything to do with blackmail and making a living. Ultra-nationalists in Japan have always been mixed up with *yakuza* gangsters, and the *sokaiya* group, which specialise in extorting money from large companies by threatening to disrupt their normally docile annual general meetings. This is why most corporate annual general meetings are held on the same day under heavy police guard in Japan—to spread the *sokaiya* thin. But these days, the distinction between gangsters and patriots is more blurred than ever before.

The ultra-rightists earn their living through blackmail. But their true political power lies in their ability to wrap themselves in the flag of patriotism and curtail debate by intimidating their opponents. The National Police Agency estimated in June 1995 that Japan had about 1000 different extreme right-wing groups, with a total membership of about 100 000. Group members regularly attack and harass any public figures, or media organisations, which criticise the Emperor. The Mayor of Nagasaki was shot outside his office in 1990 after he suggested that Hirohito should take some responsibility for the war. The parents of the magazine editor who published the articles critical of Empress Michiko were shot at outside their home in late 1993, rather perversely, as the reports had been planted by Hirohito loyalists. The powerful *Asahi* media group, renowned for its pacifist editorial stance and lukewarm support for the emperor system, is a regular and favourite target.

In one of the spookiest incidents, a right-wing leader, Shusuke Nomura, committed suicide in the middle of a meeting with the president of the *Asahi* newspaper group in the company's executive suite. Nomura had come to the newspaper office to receive an official apology for a cartoon in one of the group's magazines which had mildly lampooned his political party. The cartoonist had altered the characters of Nomura's 'Party of the Wind' to transform it into 'Party of Lice'. Hardly worthy of an apology, except that a refusal to do so would have left the *Asahi* vulnerable to further violent confrontations. Nomura's parting words before he fired two pistols into his abdomen in front of the horrified executives were, 'Nomura and the *Asahi* will die together!'. About a year later, two of his supporters returned to the *Asahi* office and held a number of senior executives hostage at gunpoint to 'avenge' Nomura's death.

The showy patriotism of the ultra-nationalists has another advantage—it wins them a large degree of unstated political and police protection. The Tokyo city government passed a law limiting the decibel level of public broadcasts in 1993, ostensibly to control the right-wing sound trucks, but it is almost never enforced by police. If you telephone to complain about a noisy broadcast outside your own building, the police will tell you that they can do nothing unless they are on the spot with sound monitors—which, of course, they're not. Left-wing organisations cannot get away with similarly brazen behaviour. Before the summit of Asia–Pacific leaders in Osaka in November 1995, local police distributed leaflets throughout the city containing hysterical warnings of threats from leftists. 'Radical factions equal left-wing extremist groups,' the leaflet said. 'These criminal gangs, using violence, are plotting a communist revolution and are trying to destroy our peaceful, democratic society.'[15] The police target was the *Chukaku-ha* ('Middle Core Faction'), a group associated with protests in the 1970s against the construction of Tokyo's Narita Airport. By the 1990s, the *Chukaku-ha* was a marginal, ineffectual bunch of radicals, well under the control of police, and no threat to anybody. The right wing is far more pervasive and violent, but is not targeted by police at all.

The ability of ultra-nationalists to exploit opportunities for blackmail extends beyond companies and private individuals. As we saw in an earlier chapter, the country's then two most powerful politicians, Noboru Takeshita and Shin Kanemaru, relied on a *yakuza* leader to silence a small, obscure right-wing group broadcasting from their sound truck details of political corruption in the lead-up to the election of a new Prime Minister in 1987. Ultra-nationalist groups have their roots dug deep into the soil of Japanese politics, and they are by no means just an alienated fringe. But like anti-communist groups throughout the world, the end of the Cold War bewildered the hard right in Japan by depriving it of easy enemies. The decline of the left and its functionaries in the teachers' union and the like has deprived it of another simple target. The ultra-nationalists are also an embarrassment to the country's sophisticated bureaucrats. But most worrying for them, their ugly trucks and pathological sloganeering are a big turn-off for Japan's affluent, largely politically neutered youth. Young Japanese are diligent and hard-working, but they are not pumped up with the sort of intense indoctrination of self-sacrifice and suicide that their fathers and grandfathers took into battle.

Take Wataru Tsurumi, the successful 29-year-old author of a morbid 1993 bestseller, *The Complete Manual of Suicide*. The book's densely packed pages contain a cold and clinical account of different ways to take your own life. The surest, cleanest and least painful methods of suicide are all laid out in detail, plus some tips on how to ensure your body still looks good when it is found. Helpful diagrams tell you everything from how to tie the rope, to the best time to jump in front of a train and the way to ensure someone collects on the life insurance. But completely absent is what many Westerners would expect to find in a Japanese book on suicide. There is not a single mention of Japanese traditions on the topic. Not a word about honour, and the methods that have been used to express it over the centuries—like *hara-kiri* ('belly-slitting').

Every Japanese school child is raised with the famous 'Tale of the 47 Ronin', who revenged the death of their lord before dying an honourable warrior's death by committing ritual suicide. But even this story does not get a mention in the book. 'I don't think this sort of tradition has been continued amongst young people in Japan', Tsurumi told me. 'The Japanese way of suicide these days is just like the European way.' Sitting in a coffee shop in Tokyo's outer suburbs, Tsurumi was the very model of the cultish modern young author—polite, world-worn, and still a little listless in the late morning. 'I am not recommending that people commit suicide', he said. 'But I'm saying suicide is not a bad thing, and people can live life more positively if they know it is there as an alternative.'

Tsurumi's view of suicide as a positive alternative to the tedium and stress of everyday life in Japan is miles away from that of his forebears. Japan's most famous postwar author, Yukio Mishima, for example, believed in his country's traditions of glorious, violent death. On a military parade ground in Tokyo in 1970, he slit his belly open in ritual *hara-kiri*, and his companion then sliced his head off with a samurai sword in line with the author's orders. Inside and outside Japan, Mishima's actions resonate with symbolism. Like the suicide attacks of the wartime kamikaze pilots, his act was seen as a product of an ethic incomprehensible to rational, Christian Westerners. But it was almost a parody of the real thing. The French author, Maurice Pinguet, wrote that Mishima 'determined to die as a tourist would imagine a real Japanese ought to do it'.[16] For many Japanese these days, Mishima's bloody exhortations and Nomura's noisy send-off are a big yawn. 'For our generation, I think his way of suicide is trivial, even irrelevant, even for people who like his books', said Tsurumi. 'It has no great meaning or importance. I know this is all part of our history, but our generation has not carried this sort of thing on.'

Young people may not be thrilled by belly-slitting and other Japanese traditions, but the presence of bellicose right-wingers has a broader significance nonetheless. Their activities not only check open political debate, they also cast a shadow over a large slice of the national psyche, and provide a constant reminder of the brutal, self-defeating military adventurism of the 1930s and 1940s.

NICE NATIONALISTS AND THE BUSHIDO GENE

It is striking when talking to ordinary Japanese how many of them do not trust either their country, or its institutions, to have a military like any other country. Like the politician Masaharu Gotoda, the Japanese do not even trust themselves as individuals to be part of a professional army. 'Oh, no, no, Mr McGregor. You cannot allow the Japanese to do that,' one senior bureaucrat told me over lunch when I suggested that Japan could have an army like any other. The bureaucrat shook his head ruefully as if to indicate that I just didn't understand what would be unleashed. One commentator said the Japanese were treated as if they possessed a 'Bushido' gene, which could be switched on and off, allowing them to be used by unscrupulous leaders to commit acts of unspeakable viciousness. ('Bushido' literally means 'the way of the warrior', and was often cited by Western analysts during the war to explain the apparent fanaticism of Japanese soldiers). When the Thai–Burma railway veteran, Hiroshi Abe, talks about why the Japanese behaved as they did in the war, his views echo the wartime propaganda pumped out at the time by the Allies. 'It's easy for the Japanese to become fanatical as a group', he said. 'Aggressiveness is incorporated into the Japanese blood with peculiar characteristics.' Even in the late 1980s, nearly 50 years after the conflict, a senior American commander in the Pacific described the US forces based in Japan as being 'the cork in the bottle' to protect the region against resurgent Japanese militarism. The issue was characteristically considered in terms of cultural and racial programming. Ultimately, of course, it was purely political.

The debate about Japan's security and military policy begins, and often ends, with Article Nine of the constitution, suggested by Japanese left-wingers and agreed to by General MacArthur's occupation. In Article Nine, the 'Japanese people' renounce war as a sovereign right of the nation, and accept the country will never maintain 'land, sea or air forces'. This section has since been liberally reinterpreted to allow Japan to have first a civilian disaster corps, and later its Self-Defence Forces. The interpretation was extended again in the early 1990s to allow Japanese troops to join the United Nations' peace-keeping mission in Cambodia—the first Japanese army unit to serve overseas in almost half a century. But the rationale behind Article Nine—that Japan's cruel aggression in the Pacific War required its military to be straitjacketed—still survives strongly today for two reasons.

The first reason is that many Japanese believe it is necessary. Politicians like Kiichi Miyazawa and Gotoda, who lived through the war, maintain a profoundly melancholy and pessimistic view of the Japanese people. In an interview given on the 50th anniversary of the end of the conflict, Gotoda warned that the Japanese were still dangerous if they were pointed in the wrong direction. 'As individuals, the Japanese people are very weak and lacking identity. The Japanese would move towards one direction as a people, but when it fails, there is nothing left except misery', he said. 'This nature has not changed to date, despite the great nation-building achievement after the war.'[17]

Gotoda is no liberal pussycat. As chief of the National Police Agency in the 1970s, he was a notorious super-hawk who methodically crushed the Red Army terrorist group and radical students. As Justice Minister in the 1990s, he reactivated use of the death penalty. Appropriately, Gotoda gave his interview on the perils of militarism to the *Asahi Shimbun*, the left-leaning daily which crusades relentlessly against any expansion of Japan's international military role. Many Japan-wise foreigners also think that the Japanese could be easily led into hysterical military excesses once the military gained control. Singaporean patriarch Lee Kwan Yew said that allowing Japan to have an international military role would be like giving an alcoholic 'liqueur-flavoured chocolates'. Tokyo-based Australian academic, Dr Greg Clark, regularly warns that the West would be wise to remember that Japan is not 'an ordinary nation'. 'The moment the Japanese begin to think of themselves as a world military power, their psyche will start to unravel again', he said. 'As happened in the thirties, the soldiers will seek zealously to prove themselves, even if it means disobeying orders. Nationalists in Japan will play on emotional sympathies. The Japanese war machine will gradually slip out of control again.'[18]

If you step back for a moment and examine these statements, which are made by all sorts of people with bland regularity, they are extraordinary and extreme, more applicable to a warlike tribe than one of the most sophisticated countries on the globe. But these sentiments have informed Japanese policy for decades. Gotoda thwarted an attempt by the then hawkish Prime Minister Yasuhiro Nakasone to extend Japan's defence role during the Persian Gulf crisis of 1987. The US Navy, and then the British, French, Italian, Belgian and Dutch, all chipped in to escort Kuwaiti tankers past the threat of Iranian mines. Nakasone thought that Japan, the greatest beneficiary of free-flowing Gulf oil, should do the same, but Gotoda, then Chief Cabinet Secretary, said he would refuse to sign the cabinet order. To Foreign Ministry officials who came to lobby him on the issue, he yelled, 'Try it if you can. I will smash it. Get out of here!' And smash it he did. Nakasone backed down.[19]

The second reason Article Nine has survived and prospered in Japan has been the inability of the political system to withstand a searching debate on the issue and establish structures which inspire confidence that the military can be contained. The structured conflict of postwar politics, which shunted security issues to one side to allow everyone to concentrate on the economy, ensured that debate over Article Nine never really got started until the end of the Cold War. At the heart of Japan's inability to have a full-blooded debate about defence is concern that a weak central government could not control the army today, as it couldn't contain the militarist bully boys in the 1930s. Just as, say, the Finance and Agricultural ministries resist accountability and control, so might a resurgent military. 'Where would a less shackled military come to rest in the postwar constellation of forces?' asks Karel van Wolferen.

> Would it lodge itself under MITI? Would the Keidanren have leverage over it? Would it become subservient to the police? Or would the Budget Bureau of the Finance Ministry keep the military under permanent control? The Japanese military cannot possibly be under the effective command of an institution, a group, or a person constituting a civilian centre of political accountability. For at this time, there is no such entity.[20]

These concerns gave Gotoda and his ilk the upper hand on this issue for decades. But the two security crises in the 1990s—the Gulf War of 1991, and the North Korean nuclear threat—swung the issue his opponents' way. Japan's humiliation during the Gulf War, when it resentfully shelled out cash to help the war effort after months of in-fighting over whether to commit flesh and blood to the conflict, presented Ozawa with the opening he had been looking for. Ozawa, to his credit, supported not only a more activist role for the military but also the construction of a political system in which elected leaders would be held accountable for the military's actions. With the support of the Foreign Ministry, Ozawa and the LDP government pushed through a bill allowing Japanese troops to join the UN forces in Cambodia. The troops went there carrying only light arms, and ready to pull out at the slightest sign of fighting, but their presence marked a milestone in Japanese domestic politics nonetheless.

The North Korean crisis was solved before it could have any immediate impact on Japan's security policies, but it also allowed Ozawa, and like-minded people, to underline the absurd and dangerous position that Japan's one-country pacifism put it in. A former senior Foreign Ministry official, Hisahiko Okazaki, pointed out that the US Navy could go to the aid of a Japanese naval boat if it was attacked on the high seas, but a Japanese ship could not help a US one because of the constitutional restrictions. 'Would the US Congress keep silent if Japan, with its 700 fighter planes, including 170 F-15s and state-of-the-art submarine technology, remained idle while American youths shed blood on the Korean Peninsula?' he asked.[21] Okazaki said despairingly that '99.9 per cent' of the Japanese people had no idea that this was the case. But in the not-too-distant future they are bound to find out. Because if Japan does not alter the environment in which its military operates, Washington is likely to force reform on it.

After a number of years of threats to link trade outcomes directly to security policies, the Pentagon in February 1995 issued a report reaffirming America's commitment to maintaining all of its 100 000 troops in East Asia. The report seemed to be only a temporary corrective to rising isolationism in the United States, however. Critics of America's continued military presence support a troop withdrawal not just because they consider Japan has enjoyed a free ride at America's expense for the past half-century. They also think that the American military's presence continues to warp Japanese domestic politics and stymie debate. The most scathing and provocative critique was issued by historians Chalmers Johnson and E.B. Keehn, in an article in *Foreign Affairs* magazine. 'The Department of Defence, in effect, has declared that nothing essential has changed in East Asia, and that US policy should be to freeze relations in the Pacific indefinitely,' they wrote.

> To many East Asians, such a policy shows that Americans do not comprehend how hollow their superpower pretensions are, and that Japan and China have a few years to consolidate their ascendancy before telling the Americans that they are no longer even marginally useful . . . The US should recognise that its outdated security policy does not encourage a healthier liberal democracy in Japan, but instead strengthens reactionary, narrow-minded political leadership.[22]

When people think about nationalism, and by extension militarism, in Japan, they usually conjure up visions of ultra-rightists in sound trucks and the like. If the American troops did leave, this crowd would be there to send them off. Shinto priests would, no doubt, offer to sanctify the occasion with a ceremonial blessing. Japanese nationalists have long considered the continued American 'occupation' an affront to national dignity. Johnson and Keehn's article, however, was aimed more at the 'new nationalists' in Japan than at the old ghosts. In many respects, the threat to remove American troops is an attempt to call the bluff of this breed. The new nationalists may be assertive about Japan's economic independence, but they have failed, or simply do not want, to mount a similar argument about political sovereignty. The military issue is too sensitive. So would the new nationalists happily banish American troops from Japanese soil too? Instinctually and emotionally, the answer is yes; but practically, no.

Eisuke Sakakibara of the Finance Ministry, a symbol of 'new

nationalism' in the 1990s, wrote books defending Japan's economic policies, organised study groups of like-minded people
from fields as diverse as philosophy, history and business, and
enjoyed tough, Western-style debates with any foreigner willing
to take him on about the merits of the Japanese system. After
a period during which he was sidelined in the ministry, he was
promoted back onto the fast track, and into a senior position in
mid-1995. Sakakibara took every opportunity to spread his message, at home and abroad. Unlike most Japanese bureaucrats,
he allowed himself to be liberally quoted on the record when
speaking to foreign reporters. Sakakibara is a combative and
upfront personality, but so fraught was the term 'nationalist' in
Japan that even he backed away from using the word to describe
himself. He preferred to call himself a 'relativist'. Yes, Japan was
different, he said, but that was because it was Japan, and not
the West. 'I'm talking about cultural pluralism', he told me
during an interview.

> I don't want to be lectured. This kind of lecture has been going
> on and on in the foreign analysis of the Japanese economy and
> society. My reaction is go back to your own country, and stop
> preaching to other countries like a missionary. I don't give those
> kind of lectures to other countries. When I go to Vietnam, I might
> share my experiences, but never lecture. I would never say
> Vietnamese society is abnormal.[23]

With a touch of hyperbole, Japan-watcher David Hale,
of Kemper Financial Services in the United States, said the
appointment of nationalist bureaucrats like Sakakibara to senior
positions 'would probably go down in the history books as a
watershed moment'.[24] Other appointments to top positions in
the bureaucracy at the same time were interpreted in a similar
vein. Kazuo Ogura, the Foreign Ministry official who had
advocated closer ties with Asia and Australia as a bulwark against
US dominance in the region, returned from a short stint as

Ambassador to Vietnam to a job which positioned him to one day head the ministry. Ryutaro Hashimoto also rewarded MITI officials who supported his tough and openly nationalistic stance in trade negotiations with Washington. This new generation of leaders were thoroughly internationalised, but also Japanese to the core. Their Western sensibilities (and, in many cases, training) were offset by their hostility to the endemic conviction of Americans in particular of the universal validity of US values and the need for them to be accepted by everyone else. But their focus was in the area where Japanese values had succeeded most spectacularly—on the economy.

Sakakibara could sound like a classic revisionist—of the kind crudely labelled a 'Japan-basher' by the Foreign Ministry's propagandists—when describing the Japanese economy. In a discussion with former US trade negotiator, Glen Fukushima, titled 'Is the Japanese Market Peculiar?', Sakakibara readily conceded many obvious points that professional Japan-boosters are programmed to deny. He admitted that the *keiretsu* corporate families were a barrier to foreign businesses; that Japanese companies were virtually impervious to hostile foreign takeovers because of the interlocking shareholdings; that the bureaucrats monopolise information to maintain power, and so on. But that didn't mean, he maintained, that the Japanese system was wrong, or not working.

'When people characterise something as peculiar or not peculiar, there is a standard somewhere for such an argument', he said.[25] 'I cannot necessarily accept that such a standard lies in American capitalism.' Sakakibara correctly points out that Japan looks a lot less odd when compared to European countries, than it does when it is held against the singular, and presumed universal, American standard. He quotes a survey of executives in six countries who were asked whether they were motivated by 'rules or friendship'. In the US, Germany and Britain, 94, 92 and 83 per cent respectively gave priority to rules.

By comparison, only 61 per cent in Japan, 51 in Italy and 50 in France put rules first. 'This proves', he said, 'that France and Italy are even more particularistic than Japan'.[26]

As a self-confessed 'relativist', Sakakibara baulked at identifying Japan too strongly with Asia. But the intellectual self-confidence of officials like him brought the Japanese establishment out of its shell, and they glowed with pride at Japan's influence on the region's economic policymaking. Rather than adhering to the American line about the primacy of free markets in economic development, these officials openly propagated the importance of government intervention and 'priority industries'. MITI presented two reports to Russia in 1991, one outlining the ministry's history, and the other describing Russia's predicament, but neither was adopted by the authorities in Moscow. In Asia, the story was different. South Korea, and to a lesser extent Taiwan, copied large sections of Japan's economic model. The latest pupil is China. MITI officials chose the Chinese language for the first foreign translation of its seventeen-volume in-house history. They planned to publish only a slim, one-volume summary in English. When Beijing's economic czar, Zhu Rongji, visited Japan in February 1994, he spent little time in his lengthy ten-day visit talking to politicians, preferring to visit state-of-the-art factories and the like to see if the Japanese model could be applied to Chinese socialism.

Sakakibara's study group included the *nihonjinron* philosopher, Takeshi Umehara. His theories of Japan's unique blend of Shinto, Buddhism and Confucianism converge with the new nationalist emphasis on the importance of history and culture in framing government policies. 'The problem with some of the Western neo-classical economists is that they argue that these systems can be analysed without looking at culture and history— that's the basic problem with that framework,' said Sakakibara. 'We could never be Americans, just as you could never be Japanese,' he told another reporter.[27] Another member of the study group was Mitsuhiro Mizutani, an historian from Tokyo Metropolitan University. He contended that Japan was able to successfully copy and catch up to the West because it had always managed to combine 'strict social rules with healthy flexibility'.[28] Many other countries had also tried Western-style industrialisation, but only Japan had developed so impressively. Japan, after all, had modernised not so it could Westernise, but to make traditional Japan viable in the industrial world.

This dovetailed nicely with the positions of Sakakibara and other bureaucrats, then struggling to stave off pressure for deregulation. Regulations fitted naturally with the warm and wet web of human relations that bound Japan's homogeneous, monocultural society. Deregulation, by contrast, was being forced on Japan by culturally insensitive Westerners, and threatened to break down the relationships that kept the society together. It was no coincidence that Sakakibara's nationalist bandwagon hit town at precisely the time that Japan's political and economic system was at its weakest and most vulnerable in 50 years. In a sense, this timing gave the game away. For some of this disparate group, the call to nationalism and immutable cultural values was nothing more than a ploy in their battle to preserve the postwar system as it was. But Japan's new nationalists represented more than just a sterile defence of an economic model past its use-by date. They wanted to build a new rationale and purpose for Japan to replace the single-minded pursuit of economic growth that had prevailed since the war.

To date, they have only been partially successful.

Sakakibara, for example, was persuasive and sure-footed when discussing the intermingling of culture and economics. But once he strayed beyond these areas, he could be dangerously bombastic, and politically naive. During a private dinner at the home of a US diplomat in Tokyo, Sakakibara was reported to have suggested that Japan could forge an alliance with China if Washington maintained a 'coercive attitude' towards Tokyo.[29]

Sakakibara denied making the comments, but few who knew him doubted that they were completely in character for the abrasive official. No doubt, sometime in the future, Japan may be able to forge a pact with China, but any suggestion that such a move could be used to bargain with the US now is absurd, for a number of reasons. For Japan to make such a momentous and historic shift away from the US would take years of consensus building with both the public and policymakers in Japan, none of which has taken place. China, too, harbours a deep level of distrust towards Japan that won't be easily changed. Japan was stunned when Jiang Zemin, during the first visit of a Chinese president to Seoul in November 1995, openly rebuked Tokyo's attitude to the war in a joint statement with his South Korean counterpart, Kim Young Sam. Sakakibara is right that many Japanese—and Koreans—are increasingly questioning the presence of US troops on their soil. This is a debate that will continue. But equally, in Japan at least, politicians and the public have shown no stomach for building institutions which would equip them to shoulder the military burden on their own.

The Japanese are intense human beings. They are comfortable with extremes and contradictions, exhilarated by both the most delicate aesthetics, and the bloodiest violence. They also do nothing by halves—be it copying Western industrialisation, waging war and then rebuilding the economy, cramming for examinations, perfecting a manufacturing system or even trawling the Pacific Ocean for fish with mile-long drift nets. When they had a speculative economic boom, they really had a boom, and outstripped anything the world had witnessed for over a century. The crash that followed was similarly dramatic. In transforming their country into a secular, consumer society, the Japanese have managed to outdo other industrialised nations in the range and breadth of marginally differentiated products available to buy. Japan is a bit like the little girl with the curl in the middle of her forehead: when she's good, she's very very good, but when she's bad, she's horrid.

It is well to remember this when puzzling over the course that Japan will take next. It seems strange to worry about a military threat from Japan on the eve of the twenty-first century, especially when casting an eye across the sea at the rise of an assertive China. It seems even stranger when you walk around flash Tokyo youth meccas like Shibuya, and try to imagine the teenagers that flock there swapping their American jeans for army uniforms. Somehow, it doesn't fit. The old saying about the Japanese is they will go in any direction they are aimed. These teenagers could be aimed at a karaoke box, or at a holiday in Hawaii—but as aggressors into Asia?

But concentrating solely on military threats misses the point. It is Japan's excessive way of relating to the world—be it manifested in military overkill, or economic over-production— while at the same time retreating from it, that is the problem. For all the flinty modernity of twenty-first century Japan, the country is still riddled with the old nationalistic values of racial superiority and purity, self-sacrifice and self-abnegation. The fashion victims of Shibuya quickly dispense with their baseball caps and baggy jeans when they enter the workforce, and become loyal corporate *sararimen*. So do young people all over the world, you could argue, when they become adult members of the workforce. True enough, except that in Japan, the trans-formation is more complete and thorough. Japan's enduring xenophobia, combined with its intense and insecure competitive streak, is what makes so many Japanese and foreigners alike nervous about nationalist revivals. As the *Economist* wrote, many nationalists mix 'reasonable desires [for political independence, and preservation of their own culture] with unreasonable emo-tions—nostalgia for the martial values of old Japan, instinctive suspicion of foreigners. A Shinto revival would not be like a religious revival elsewhere. Shintoism is exclusively Japanese, and its mythology fosters racial consciousness'.[30] The inability of the country's political system to confront this reality is also the reason why the new nationalists have been so successful in promoting the Japanese economic model, but such failures in engaging political and military issues.

Japan cannot forever trade off economic strength for political weakness—and the reverse is true, of course, for the United States and Europe. Nor can Japan swing between the two poles for time immemorial. Politicians like Ozawa are right when they say Japan can only deal squarely with the United States, and the world, when it is truly independent. A master-and-servant relationship can never be a true alliance. Sakakibara puts Japan's dilemma in more spiritual terms. 'Unless material wealth can successfully be turned into a sense of national identity and mental well-being', he says, 'the Japanese will find themselves in a perpetual catch-up syndrome, always in a state of restlessness and mental hunger'.[31]

But do such qualities—its insularity and xenophobia; its impulsive and unchecked adventurism; its inability to free its politics from the taboos of history—make Japan a genuinely hostile power? A glance at the other side of the postwar ledger is not nearly so alarming. Since its defeat in the war, Japan has remained resolutely Japanese, but anchored itself in the West. Japan's adversarial trade policies have given it great trade surpluses and economic wealth, but also benefited consumers around the world by presenting them with better and cheaper products. Japan has pursued policies to capture Asian economies, but in the process has helped build the region's nations to a point where they will not be beholden to anyone, including Japan. For many Japanese who have lived through the best and the worst of Japan's action-packed recent history, the positive achievements of the postwar years far outweigh the negatives. A person like novelist Shiba Ryotaro, who survived the Great Depression and the Pacific War, does not think Japan's future looks so grim at all. Ryotaro recounted in a newspaper article in 1994 how he had complimented a young mother one day on her beautiful baby.[32] Playing the wise old fortune-teller, as he put it, he smiled and said the baby looked as though it would never go hungry. But the mother turned on him sharply.

'What kind of thing is that to say to a newborn baby? You're supposed to say he looks intelligent or is sure to have a brilliant career. You don't tell parents their child will never be hard up for a meal. Anyone can get something to eat!'

Ryotaro, chastened, tried again. 'OK. How about this—he'll never want for a shirt on his back.'

'Who does?' came the sharp reply.

Clearly, there was a communication problem. What Ryotaro had meant to convey was that the child would always be spared real adversity. 'In the Edo period (1600–1868), lots of people had only one outfit. On laundry day, they wrapped themselves in a mosquito net until their clothes dried', he wrote, after his baking at the hands of the ambitious mother. 'During the depression, writer Fumiko Hayashi, who was 25 at the time, sold all her clothes and spent a whole summer in her bathing suit, according to her biographer. The current business slump has caused a lot of distress, but nobody is living in a bikini.'

Ryotaro had more than just a crotchety old timer's 'you-never-had-it-so-good' message to deliver here. Sure, times were tough, but he wanted to remind people that Japan had achieved something it could be proud of—without sliding into fascism, as it had in the past. 'One important difference in our favour now is that we are not being pulled apart by ideology', he said. 'Spared the dogma of communism, we have to think for ourselves. If we have the guts to do that, future generations will remember the spirit of today's Japan as a blessing without disguise.'

NOTES

1 THE MISTS OF CONCEALMENT

1 The Myth of Japanese Uniqueness Reconsidered, Yushi Itoh, Victoria University of Wellington, Graham Squires, Newcastle University, Australia.
2 'Closed Markets Hurting the Domestic Economy', *Nikkei Weekly*, 20 February 1995.
3 Kurt Singer, *Mirror, Sword and Jewel—The Geometry of Japanese Life*, Croom Helm, London, 1973.
4 'Skilful in the Art of the Sincere Lie,' *Asahi Evening News*, 3 February 1995.
5 See Chalmers Johnson, *Japan—Who Governs? The Rise of the Development State*, W. W. Norton & Company, New York, 1995 p. 218.
6 Some might contend that Japan's longest-serving postwar Prime Minister, Shigeru Yoshida, fits the Reagan/Thatcher mould. Yoshida's relatively autocratic style of governing earned him the nickname of 'One Man', which was none too flattering in consensus-oriented Japan, but his power and policies ultimately

depended on the assent of the Americans. Equally, Kakuei Tanaka had a lasting influence on Japanese politics, but mostly from behind the scenes. See Chapter four.

7 Eamonn Fingleton, *Blindside—Why Japan is Still on Track to Overtake the US by the Year 2000*, Houghton Mifflin, New York, 1995.

8 Karel van Wolferen and R. Taggart Murphy, *International Herald Tribune*, 23 February 1994.

9 Joseph Grew, *Ten Years in Japan*, Hammond, Hammond and Company, London, 1944, p. 137.

2 BEYOND THE BUBBLE

1 Author's interview, *Australian*, 23 January 1993.

2 See Christopher Wood, *The Bubble Economy*, Sidgwick & Jackson, London, 1992.

3 *Far Eastern Economic Review*, 19 November 1992.

4 Author's interview, *Australian*, 27 March 1993.

5 *Australian Financial Review*, quoted in *Tokyo Journal*, May 1995.

6 Fingleton, op. cit., pp. 324, 326.

7 'Strong Yen Distorting GDP', *Daily Yomiuri*, 26 April 1995. The Yomiuri's business editor, Jin Nakamura, using an exchange rate of Y79/US$1.00, reached on April 10, calculated the real Gross Domestic Product (adjusted for inflation) of both countries at US$5.34 trillion.

8 Transport Minister Shizuka Kamei, well-known for his nationalist views, made this remark at a private debating club. They were reported in the Japanese media on 28 April 1995.

9 Tokyo Meteorological Agency.

10 *International Herald Tribune*, 23 January 1995.

11 It wasn't until months later—after brazenly boasting about their relief work, and showing it off to foreign reporters, including yours truly—that the gang was caught embezzling money it had collected for quake victims.

12 *Shukan Hoseki*, 9 February 1995.

13 *Daily Yomiuri*, 31 January 1995.

14 *Sankei Shimbun*, 28 March 1995.
15 'The Other Poison in Japan's Air', *Washington Post*, reprinted in *Daily Yomiuri*, 15 March 1995.
16 'The Liquefaction', *Business Intelligence*, April 1995.
17 *Tokyo Business Today*, February 1994.
18 See Fingleton, op. cit., pp. 68–75, for a comprehensive list. Also the JETRO report, *Nihon Kogyo Shimbun*, 3 March 1995 and *Tokyo Business Today*, August 1995.
19 *Japan Times*, 14 July 1995.
20 *Sankei Shimbun*, 25 April 1995.
21 See Chapter eight for a more comprehensive discussion of this.
22 Ronald Dore, *Flexible Rigidities*, The Athdowne Press, London, 1986.
23 *Australian*, 4 July 1994.
24 See the *Independent*, 2 May 1994.
25 Quoted in the *Economist*, 9 July 1994.

3 ASIA'S SIREN SONG

1 Gavan McCormack, Groping for Asia: The Dilemmas of National Identity, Australian National University, 26 May 1994.
2 Seizaburo Sato, quoted in Robert M. Orr, Jr., *The Emergence of Japan's Foreign Aid Power*, Columbia University Press, 1990, p. 4.
3 Ian Buruma, quoted in the *Australian*, 4 April 1993.
4 The form and the structure of the systems were borrowed. Whether they function like the Western systems they were copied from, or in a peculiarly Japanese fashion, is a question to be considered separately.
5 *Asahi Evening News*, 18 December 1994.
6 *Nikkei Weekly*, quoted in the *Australian*, 5 May 1995.
7 *Economist*, loc. cit.
8 Author's interview, 3 March 1995.
9 *Australian*, 21 January 1994.
10 'Asia Hangs in the Balance', *Japan Times*, 8 June 1995.

11 'Asia', for the purposes of these figures, and this chapter, includes all countries east of Burma.

12 *Far Eastern Economic Review*, 9 June 1994.

13 *Sekai Ohrai*, January 1991.

14 *Asian Wall Street Journal*, 21 August 1990.

15 *Financial Times*, quoted in the *Australian*, 26 December 1992.

16 *Asahi Shimbun*, quoted in the *Australian*, 12 November 1994.

17 Paper given at United Nations forum, 11–15 May 1992, Chitose, Hokkaido.

18 Kyodo News Service, 16 February 1993.

19 *Chuo Koron*, reprinted in *Japan Echo*, Autumn 1993.

20 *Los Angeles Times*, 1 August 1995.

21 *Gaiko Forum*, February 1994.

22 Speech to Kyushu Asian Summit, 21 October 1994.

23 *Nikkei Weekly*, 12 December 1994.

24 *Australian*, 15 February 1992.

25 *Nikkei Weekly*, 25 April 1992.

26 Jung Bock Lee, *The Political Character of the Japanese Press*, Seoul National University Press, Seoul 1985.

27 NHK denies it has any 'three-T' policy. See *Tokyo Journal*, May 1994.

28 China turned the tap of war guilt off when it suited it. In August, 1995, when it was worried about strains in its relations with Tokyo, Beijing refused permission for a number of individual Chinese suing Tokyo to travel to Japan, or publicise their claims at press conferences in China.

29 *Asuterion*, June–July 1994.

30 *Nikkei Business Weekly*, 31 October 1994.

31 Francis Fukuyama and Kongdan Oh, *The US–Japan Security Relationship After the Cold War*, RAND, National Defence Research Institute, 1993.

32 *Australian*, 24 March 1993.

33 *AERA*, 19 December 1994.

34 *Asahi Evening News*, 1 August 1995.

35 *Mainichi Shimbun*, 4 January 1995.

4 MONEY POLITICS

1 *Mainichi Shimbun*, 25 September 1992.

2 *Financial Times*, 2 October 1992.

3 Hideaki Kase, 'Kimochi Feeds Japan's Money Politics', *Asian Wall Street Journal*, 28 October 1992.

4 Chalmers Johnson, 'Tanaka Kakuei and Machine Politics', *Japan— Who Governs?*, op. cit. p. 187.

5 Quoted in 'Curse of the Kingmakers', *Tokyo Journal*, May 1993.

6 Taro Yayama, *Sankei Shimbun*, 1 March 1995.

7 *Kanryo*, Nihon Keizai Shimbun-sha, Tokyo, 1994.

8 Johnson, op. cit.

9 Cited in Gavan McCormack, Japan's Construction State, Australian National University, 1994. Other figures in this section also come from this paper.

10 *Yomiuri Shimbun*, 19 May 1993.

11 *Japan Times*, 1 February 1994.

12 Johnson, op. cit., p. 217.

13 McCormack, Japan's Construction State, op. cit.

14 *Tokyo Journal*, December 1992.

15 Hidenori Itagaki, *Ozawa Ichiro to yu Otoko no Yabo*, quoted in *Tokyo Journal*, op. cit.

16 Tanaka died in December 1993.

17 The wife of Takeshita's half-brother was the sister of Ozawa's wife.

18 Author's interview, *Australian*, 21 June 1993.

19 *Weekend Australian*, 10 October 1992.

20 Seizaburo Sato, 'The Spirit of '55', *Look Japan*, April 1995.

21 In recent years, Japan's billion-dollar foreign aid budget has given MPs a greater interest in diplomacy. Many now compete to head Dietman's Friendship Leagues devoted to building ties with other countries because of the sway it gives them over the aid dollar. See Chapter three.

22 *Sei, Zai, Kan Yuchaku Kaitai eno Mittsu no Kadai* (Three Theses to Break the Adhesion between Politics, Bureaucrats and Business), *Economisto*, 24 August 1993.

23 Eisuke Sakakibara, *Beyond Capitalism*, University Press of America, Maryland, 1993, pp. 10, 63.

24 *Shukan Toyo Keizai*, 17 July 1993.

25 *Asahi Evening News*, 16 October 1992.

26 *Yomiuri Shimbun*, 6 November 1992.

27 *Yomiuri Shimbun*, 29 November 1992. Both Kanemaru and Takeshita denied asking Watanabe to use the *yakuza* to intervene, and said they had no knowledge of it until *after* it had happened. See Takeshita's testimony to parliament on 26 November 1992.

28 *Asahi Shimbun*, 1 March 1993.

29 *Shukan Hoseki*, 5–12 January 1995.

30 See Peter Tasker, 'The End of Japan Inc.', *Asian Wall Street Journal*, 26 June 1993.

31 The party's name in Japanese, *Shakaito*, is translated literally as 'The Socialist Party'. The party maintained its name in Japanese, but in 1991 changed it in English to the Social Democratic Party to burnish its image overseas in the post-Cold War era. For convenience sake, we will stick in this text to the original and literal translation.

32 Takeshita ran as an independent for fear that his involvement in scandals would damage the LDP, but rejoined the party soon after the poll.

33 Quoted in *Tokyo Journal*, May 1993.

34 Sato in *Look Japan*, op. cit.

35 See Sato's speech, Implications of the New Tide in Japanese Politics, Trilateral Conference: Germany–USA–Japan, Berlin, 12 June 1995.

36 Author's interview, 16 March 1995.

37 The word *tarento* is the Japanese rendition of the English word 'talent', and refers broadly to a whole host of entertainers and actors who are known less as performers than as personalities.

5 THE NANNY STATE

1 *Tokyo Business Today*, June 1995.

2 *Kanryo*, op. cit. Ch. 8, Part 8.

3 Ichiro Ozawa, *Blueprint for a New Japan*, Kodansha, Tokyo, 1994.

4 Ozawa, op. cit.

5 Marvin J. Wolf, *The Japanese Conspiracy*, Empire Books, New York, 1983, quoted in Contending Perspectives on the Japanese 'Economic Miracle', Takamichi Mito, Monash University, 1992.

6 Richard Samuels, *The Business of the Japanese State*, Cornell University Press, 1987, quoted in Mito, op. cit.

7 See Peter Tasker, *Tokyo Business Today*, July 1995.

8 *Mainichi Shimbun*, 26 March 1994.

9 Clyde V. Prestowitz Jr, *Trading Places: How America Allowed Japan to Take the Lead*, Charles E. Tuttle, Tokyo, 1988.

10 Sumo wrestlers fight fifteen bouts in each tournament. Whoever loses the least number of bouts wins.

11 *Foresight*, March 1994.

12 *Tokyo Business Today*, April 1995.

13 The then head of the Treasury, John Stone, coined this phrase when attacking advisers of Australian prime minister Malcolm Fraser in the early 1980s. According to the *American Heritage Dictionary*, 'meretricious' means 'pertaining to or resembling a prostitute', or 'lacking sincerity'.

14 *Mainichi Shimbun*, 23 February 1994.

15 *Shukan Asahi*, 29 July 1994.

16 *Newsweek*, 14 March 1995.

17 *Economisto*, 24 August 1993.

18 *Bungei Shunju*, September 1993.

19 *Shukan Toyo-Keizai*, 17 July 1993.

20 *Mainichi Shimbun*, 8 April 1995.

21 *Asahi Evening News*, 5 February 1995.

22 *Mainichi Shimbun*, 14 July 1995.

23 *Asahi Evening News*, 22 April 1992.

24 *Kanryo*, op. cit., Ch. 7, Part 7, for both figures and quote.

25 *Kanryo*, op. cit.

26 Koei Kaga, 'Why Did Bureau Director General Naito Quit?', *Bungei Shunju*, March 1994.

27 The Ozawa-inspired coalition changed its name to *Shinshinto* in 1995.

28 Kaga, op. cit.

29 *Bungei Shunju*, loc. cit..

30 Kaga, op. cit.

31 *Yomiuri Shimbun*, 27 December 1994.

32 *Mainichi Daily News*, 25 April 1995.

33 The Mainichi newspaper recorded some of the local delicacies handed out in 1994. Nara brought its own special persimmon leaf; Toyama its trout sushi; Oita its mandarins and sweet dough crackers; Yamanashi its wine and Akita its rice gruel. A good supply of beer coupons, a nice portable gift, was also on hand.

34 Sakakibara, op. cit., p. 64.

35 Fingleton, op. cit.

36 *Kanryo*, op. cit., Ch. 7, Part 3.

37 Karel van Wolferen, *The Enigma of Japanese Power*, Tuttle Editions, 1993, p. 577.

38 *Tokyo Business Today*, July 1995.

39 *Tokyo Business Today*, April 1995.

40 'Is Deregulation a "Nightmare" or a "Panacea"?', *Shukan Economisto*, 30 August 1994.

41 *Nikkei Weekly*, 1 May 1995.

42 *Kanryo*, op. cit.

43 The rules were eased in US–Japan trade talks, which concluded in May 1995.

44 *Mainichi Shimbun*, 28 September 1993.

45 *Australian*, 17 June 1994.

46 *Voice*, October 1994.

47 *Bungei Shunju*, 31 August 1994.

48 *Bungei Shunju*, January 1994.

49 Speech on 8 March 1995.

50 Author's interview, *Australian*, 29 December 1993.

51 *Asahi Shimbun*, 14 May 1995.

52 *Asahi Shumbun*, 19 November 1994; Law Council of Australia.

53 *Asahi Shimbun*, loc. cit.

54 *Asahi Shimbun*, loc. cit.

6 THE WAGES OF WAR

1 Author's interview, *Australian Magazine*, 28 November 1992.
2 *Japan Times*, 6 August 1992.
3 *Mainichi Shimbun*, 4 May 1994.
4 *Shukan Bunshun*, 26 May 1994.
5 Ian Buruma, *The Wages of Guilt*, Farrar, Straus, Giroux, New York, 1994, p. 119.
6 Dower, *War Without Mercy: Race and Power in the Pacific War*, Pantheon, New York, 1986, p. 6.
7 Author's interview, *Australian Magazine*, 3 July 1993.
8 Author's interview, *Australian Magazine*, 21 May 1994.
9 Kaneda's evidence is summarised in George Hicks, *The Comfort Women*, Allen & Unwin, Sydney, 1995. See also the *Australian*, 10 July 1992.
10 *Shokun*, November 1992.
11 Rikki Kersten, *Australian Financial Review*, 1 January 1995.
12 Gavan McCormack, Remembering and Forgetting: The War, 1945–95, Australian National University, 1995. See also *AERA*, 5 May 1992.
13 *Asahi Shimbun*, 12 September 1994.
14 *Australian*, 26 October 1994.
15 *Los Angeles Times*, 13 November 1994.
16 *Denim*, September 1995.
17 Buruma, op. cit.
18 McCormack, op. cit.
19 Johnson, op. cit. pp. 257–8.
20 *Tokyo Shimbun*, 17 August 1994.
21 See Ishihara comments in Chapter three. By querying the casualties, many politicians manage to muddy debate about the massacre, without flatly denying it happened.
22 *Japan Times*, 29 January 1994.

7 THE ODD COUPLE

1 *Gaiko Forum*, December 1992.

2 Author's interview, *Australian*, 6 November 1993.

3 *Australian*, loc. cit.

4 *Wedge*, May 1993.

5 *Australian*, 29 May 1995.

6 *Australian*, 29 May 1995.

7 *Yomiuri Shimbun*, 1 May 1993.

8 *Australian*, 25 October 1994.

9 *Straits Times*, reprinted in the *Japan Times*, 4 November 1994.

10 Henry P. Frei, *Japan's Southward Advance and Australia, From the 16th Century to World War II*, University of Hawaii Press, Honolulu, 1991, p. 27. Frei's book is the definitive work on this subject, and this section of the book is much indebted to it.

11 Frei, op. cit., p. 40.

12 Frei, op. cit., p. 52.

13 *Bulletin*, no. 387, 2 July 1887.

14 W. Macmahon Ball, *Australia and Japan, Documents and Readings in Australian History*, Thomas Nelson, Melbourne, 1969.

15 Peter Drysdale and Hironobu Kitaoji (eds), *Japan and Australia, Two Societies and Their Interaction*, Australian National University Press, Canberra, 1981.

16 Frei, op.cit., p. 105.

17 Alan Rix, *Coming to Terms, The Politics of Australian Trade with Japan, 1945–57*, Allen & Unwin, Sydney, 1986, p. 21.

18 Speech to the nineteenth Australia–Japan Relations symposium, Canberra, February 1995.

19 *Asahi Shimbun*, 9 June 1995; AERA, 23 January 1995.

20 Author's interview, 1 March 1994.

21 Michael Byrnes, *Australia and the Asia Game*, Allen & Unwin, Sydney, 1994.

22 Author's interview, 4 July 1995.

23 Gavan McCormack, Outsiders in Asia: Australia, Japan and the Dilemmas of History, 8 September 1993, La Trobe University.

24 *Nichigo Press*, January 1993, p. 19.

25 *Sekai Keizai Hyoron*, February 1995.

26 *Australian*, 3 March 1995.

27 See *Tokyo Journal*, July 1995, for account of Roppongi clubs.

8 BAD GIRLS AND MUMMIES' BOYS

1 *Spa!*, 15 June 1994.
2 On Valentine's Day in Japan, women give men chocolate. Men give women chocolate on so-called White Day later in the year. Dividing the holidays doubles the commercial opportunities for chocolate makers.
3 *Nikkei Weekly*, 3 April 1995.
4 *Nikkei Weekly*, 17 May 1993; *Yomiuri Shimbun*, 14 July 1995.
5 *Los Angeles Times*, 15 December 1993.
6 *Dime*, 2 February 1995.
7 *New York Times*, reprinted in *South China Morning Post*, 28 July 1995.
8 *Mainichi Shimbun*, 27 April 1995.
9 *Australian*, 4 March 1995.
10 *Nikkei Weekly*, 3 April 1995.
11 The high-dosage pill is available for certain medical conditions. The ordinary low-dosage one, however, could not be prescribed.
12 *Australian*, 3 March 1992.
13 *Yomiuri Shimbun*, 9 July 1995.
14 *Asahi Shimbun*, 10 May 1995.
15 *Asahi Evening News*, 31 May 1995.
16 *Asahi Evening News*, 7 June 1995.
17 *Tokyo Journal*, April 1995.
18 *Japan Times*, 31 July 1995.
19 Keiko Fukuzawa, 'Women's Hiring Woes', *Japan Quarterly*, April–June, 1995.
20 *Crea* magazine, quoted in the *Australian*, 8 June 1992.
21 Nicholas Bornoff, *Pink Samurai, Love, Marriage and Sex in Contemporary Japan*, Pocket Books, New York, 1991.
22 *Asahi Evening News*, 9 March 1995; *Spa!*, 22 March 1995.
23 *Japan Times*, 2 July 1995.
24 *The Times Magazine*, 3 June 1995.
25 See *Asahi Evening News*, 18 September 1994.
26 *Views*, 11 May 1995.
27 Report issued by the Institute for Population and Social Research, Thailand.

28 Not that the Japanese are the only men to travel to Asia for sex. Western men, perhaps in a less organised fashion, do exactly the same.

29 *The Times Magazine*, loc. cit.

30 Sixteen per cent of all videos stocked in Japanese video rental stores are pornographic.

31 The one exception to this rule was a male star called Choco Bon-Bon, so called because his testicles (*bons-bons* in Japanese porno-speak) 'showed up surprisingly dark, or almost chocolate coloured, on video tape', according to Karl Taro Greenfeld in his book about subcultures, *Speed Tribes*.

32 See Philip Brasor, 'Media Mix', *Japan Times*, 15 June 1995.

33 Associated Press, printed in *Daily Yomiuri*, 9 November 1992.

34 Author's interview. See also the *Times*, 'Men Suffering from "I Love Mum" Syndrome', *Asahi Evening News*, 21 April 1991.

35 *Tokyo Business Today*, April 1994.

36 *Asahi Evening News*, 15 October 1993.

37 Naohiro Amaya, quoted in Chalmers Johnson, *MITI and the Japanese Economic Miracle*, Charles E. Tuttle, Tokyo, 1982, p. 13.

38 *Japan Times*, 13 April 1994.

39 *AERA*, 3 August 1993.

40 Speech to the Sakura Bank Foundation, Tokyo, 19 February 1993.

41 *Tokyo Business Today*, April 1994.

42 *Asian Wall Street Journal*, quoted in the *Australian*, 1 March 1993.

43 *Daily Yomiuri*, 15 June 1995.

44 *Asian Wall Street Journal*, 21 April 1995.

9 A NICER NEW NATIONALISM

1 *Tokyo Shimbun*, 1 August 1994.

2 *Tokyo Shimbun*, loc. cit.

3 Author's interview, 3 March 1995.

4 *Economist*, 14 January 1995.

5 'Eternal Lessons', *Asahi Evening News*, 28 June 1995.

6 *Independent*, 3 May 1993.

7   Peter Dale, *The Myth of Japanese Uniqueness*, Routledge, 1986, Introduction.

8   'Silence is Golden', *Daily Yomiuri*, 29 June 1995.

9   Thomas Crump, *The Death of an Emperor*, Oxford University Press, Oxford and New York, 1991, pp. 18–20.

10 *Japan Times*, 23 March 1993.

11 Takeshi Umehara, 'Ancient Japan shows Postmodernism the Way', *NP Quarterly*, Spring 1992.

12 Tony Barrell and Rick Tanaka, *Higher Than Heaven*, Private Guy International, Sydney, 1995.

13 Crump, op. cit.

14 I am indebted to Pierre Ryckmans for his phrase, used in an essay about the role of universities.

15 *Mainichi Daily News*, 13 May 1995.

16 Quoted in the *Independent*, 28 November 1994.

17 'Eternal Lessons', op. cit.

18 *Australian*, 2 February 1992.

19 *This is Yomiuri*, October 1992.

20 van Wolferen, op. cit.

21 *Daily Yomiuri*, 4 July 1994.

22 *Foreign Affairs*, Vol. 74, no. 4.

23 Author's interview, 3 March 1995.

24 *Newsweek*, 3 July 1995.

25 *Gaiko Forum*, July 1994.

26 *Chuo Koron*, 10 July 1995.

27 *Asian Wall Street Journal*, 9 June 1995.

28 *Economist*, loc. cit.

29 Shukan Bunshun, reported in the *Asian Wall Street Journal*, 21 November 1995. The Finance Ministry asked the magazine to withdraw the issue from sale, but was rebuffed. It also issued a three-page denial of Sakakibara's comments, including that he called Prime Minister Murayama and other political leaders 'idiots'.

30 *Economist*, 12 August 1995.

31 *Beyond Capitalism*, op. cit.

32 *Mainichi Shimbun*, 1 January 1994.

INDEX